T0330556

"In most social systems, there are four categories of participants: the peripherals who dangle by weak affiliations at the edge of a social system; the cliquers who confine themselves to a satellite group in the social system; the brokers who connect across satellite groups seeking access to the inner circle; and what might be termed the *guanxians*, the people who live in the inner circle. The four categories each have their social logic, variably emphasizing access at the periphery, to obligation, and status within the inner circle. Elite inner circles are familiar in the West, but they are a way of life in China such that the country has become a laboratory for studying how *guanxi* networks operate. This book is a productive introduction to the study of *quanxi* networks in Greater China with a focus on entrepreneurship, including works by many of the leading scholars on the subject."

Ronald Burt, University of Chicago

"The Greater China – mainland, Hong Kong and Taiwan – is a fertile ground for the study of social capital because of the cultural and institutional regime rich in social relations and *guanxi*, and in economic exchanges. Yet so far we have not seen a comprehensive treatment of this social-economic terrain. Jenn-hwan Wang and Ray-May Hsung put together a wonderful collection of papers on the intra- and inter-regional social capital and economic activities. It will be a definitive and must-read volume for those interested in social capital and economic sociology."

Nan Lin, Duke University

"Not so long ago, a number of scholars were ready to record the decline of *guanxi* in business and in other spheres of Chinese life. Were they ever wrong! Here is a much needed book that looks at *guanxi* and *guanxi* webs in Greater China. With chapters from some of the best sociologists now working on Chinese society, this book allows us to compare these essential building blocks of Chinese society in three different locations – Mainland China, Taiwan, and Hong Kong – and thereby to see the interplay between historical context and contemporary social structure. A terrific book for all those interested in Chinese society."

Gary Hamilton, University of Washington, Seattle

Rethinking Social Capital and Entrepreneurship in Greater China

Family networks and wider personal social relationships – *guanxi* (關係) – have long been held to be a significant factor for the success of many Chinese family businesses, and *guanxi* is often seen as a special characteristic that shapes the nature of all business in China. This book re-examines this proposition critically, bringing together the very latest research and comparing the situation in different parts of "Greater China" – mainland China, Taiwan, and Hong Kong. It considers entrepreneurship, venture capital, intergenerational succession, disputes, and in particular family businesses in different sectors of the economy. Among the book's many interesting conclusions is the observation that *guanxi* capitalism has evolved in different ways in the different parts of Greater China, with the particular institutional setting having a major impact.

Jenn-Hwan Wang is a Professor in the Graduate Institute of Development Studies at National Chengchi University, Taiwan.

Ray-May Hsung is a Professor of Sociology at National Chengchi University, Taiwan.

Routledge Culture, Society, Business in East Asia Series
Editorial Board:

How and what are we to examine if we wish to understand the commonalities across East Asia without falling into the powerful fictions or homogeneities that dress its many constituencies? By the same measure, can East Asian homogeneities make sense in any way outside the biases of an imagined East-West dichotomy?

For anthropologists familiar with the societies of East Asia, there is a rich diversity of work that can potentially be applied to address these questions within a comparative tradition grounded in the region as opposed the singularizing outward encounter. This requires us to broaden our scope of investigation to include all aspects of intra-regional life, trade, ideology, culture, and governance, while at the same time dedicating ourselves to a complete and holistic understanding of the exchange of identities that describe each community under investigation. An original and wide-ranging analysis will be the result, one that draws on the methods and theory of anthropology as it deepens our understanding of the interconnections, dependencies, and discordances within and among East Asia.

The book series includes three broad strands within and between which to critically examine the various insides and outsides of the region. The first is about the globalization of Japanese popular culture in East Asia, especially in Greater China. The second strand presents comparative studies of major social institutions in Japan and China, such as family, community, and other major concepts in Japanese and Chinese societies. The final strand puts forward cross-cultural studies of business in East Asia.

Rethinking Social Capital and Entrepreneurship in Greater China

Is *guanxi* still important?

Edited by Jenn-Hwan Wang and Ray-May Hsung

Routledge
Taylor & Francis Group

LONDON AND NEW YORK

First published 2016
by Routledge

2 Park Square, Milton Park, Abingdon, Oxfordshire OX14 4RN
711 Third Avenue, New York, NY 10017

Routledge is an imprint of the Taylor & Francis Group, an informa business

First issued in paperback 2017

British Library Cataloguing in Publication Data
A catalogue record for this book is available from the British Library

Library of Congress Cataloging-in-Publication Data
Names: Wang, Jennhwan, 1956– editor. | Hsung, Ray-May, editor.
Title: Rethinking social capital and entrepreneurship in Greater China: is
  guanxi still important? / edited by Jenn-hwan Wang, Ray-May Hsung.
Description: Abingdon, Oxon ; New York, NY : Routledge, 2016. | Series:
  Routledge culture, society, business in east asia series ; 4 | Includes
  bibliographical references and index.
Identifiers: LCCN 2015041388 | ISBN 9781138925892 (hardback) |
  ISBN 9781315683515 (ebook)
Subjects: LCSH: Entrepreneurship—Social aspects—China. |
  Social capital (Sociology)—China. | Social networks—Economic
  aspects—China. | Economic development—Social aspects—China.
Classification: LCC HB615 .R4873 2016 | DDC 338/.040951—dc23
LC record available at http://lccn.loc.gov/2015041388

ISBN: 978-1-138-92589-2 (hbk)
ISBN: 978-1-138-47724-7 (pbk)

Typeset in Times New Roman
by Apex CoVantage, LLC

Contents

Figures

Tables

Contributors

Yanjie Bian is Professor of Sociology at the University of Minnesota. Concurrently, he is the Dean of the School of Humanities and Social Science and the Director of the Institute for Empirical Social Science Research at Xi'an Jiaotong University, China. His research focuses on *guanxi* networks, social capital, and stratification and mobility in China. His recent book is *Social Networks and Status Attainment* (Social Science Academic Press 2012).

Liang-Chih Chen obtained his PhD in City and Regional Planning from University of California at Berkeley. Currently, he is an Associate Professor in the Graduate Institute of Building and Planning of National Taiwan University. He specialized in the studies of industrial clusters, industrial upgrading of newly industrializing counties, and Taiwan's machine tool industry.

Tsung-Yuan Chen is currently Assistant Professor of Institute of Overseas Chinese/College of International Relations at the Huaqiao University of China. His research interests include development issues in East and Southeast Asia, Chinese Ethnic Business, Economic Sociology, and Business History. His articles have been published in the *Taiwanese Journal of Sociology, Development and Change,* and *Malaysian Journal of Chinese Studies.*

Shiuh-shen Chien is Associate Professor of Development Geography at National Taiwan University. His research interests cover development geography, the geography of globalization, transnational studies, and the political economy of urban and regional development, with empirical focuses on the Global South in general and postsocialist China in particular. His articles in print are able to be seen in the *Asian Journal of Political Science*; *Asian Survey*; *China Information, Environment and Planning C*; *Geoforum*; *Global Networks: A Journal of Transnational Affairs*; *Regional Studies*; *Urban Studies*; and more.

Tsai-man C. Ho is Assistant Professor in the Center for General Education of Chung Yuan Christian University, Taiwan. Her research interest includes entrepreneurship and culture, family enterprises, Taiwan studies, and various issues of modernity in Chinese societies. She is the author of a forthcoming chapter on "Deciding Whether to Return to Taiwan: Koo Chen-fu, 1945–1952" (published in the Cornell East Asia Series).

Ray-May Hsung is Professor of Sociology at National Chengchi University. Her research interests include social capital, interorganizational networks in Taiwan's semiconductor industry, and dynamic social network analysis. She has recently published articles on urban policy network, innovation networks, and the decline of participation in voluntary associations in *Research in the Sociology of Work*, the *Taiwanese Journal of Sociology*, and the *Taiwanese Journal of Political Science*. She edited a book with Nan Lin and Ronald Breiger, *Contexts of Social Capital: Social Networks in Markets, Communities, and Families* (Routledge, 2012).

Yu-Ying Lee is an Associate Professor at Yuan Ze University in Taiwan. Her research interests are gender issues and consumer culture. She has published several articles on Taiwanese wedding photography and shopping culture. Currently, she studies collection and auction with particular emphasis on the Greater China art market. Her latest publication is a journal article titled: "Pricing Antiques: Social Embeddedness of Chinese Cultural Relics Auction Markets." Currently, she is undertaking a book project: *Collecting, Knowledge and Power – On Ancient Jade Consumption in Taiwan*.

Yi-Jr Lin obtained his PhD in sociology from Tunghai University in Taiwan. His research interests include social capital, interorganizational networks in Taiwan's semiconductor industry, and dynamic social network analysis. He has recently published articles on social networks, social capital, and innovation in *Research in the Sociology of Work*, the *Journal of Humanities and Social Sciences*, and the *Industry and Management Forum*.

Chiu-wan Liu is a PhD student of SOAS, University of London. Her research interests cover gender study, citizenship, migration, entrepreneurship, and e-commerce. She is currently working on a project entitled "Emerging Female Returnee Entrepreneurs in E-commercialization of Rural China."

Jar-Der Luo is a professor of Sociology at Tsinghua University in Beijing. He earned his PhD degree in Sociology at the State University of New York, Stony Brook. He researches numerous topics in social network studies including social capital, trust, social networks in big data, self-organization processes, and Chinese indigenous management concepts, such as *guanxi*, *guanxi* circles, and favor exchange.

Chen-Ya Wang obtained her Master's Degree of Technology, Innovation and Intellectual Property Management from National Chengchi University in Taiwan. Her main research fields are technology and innovation.

Jenn-Hwan Wang is Chair Professor of the Graduate Institute of Development Studies at the National Chengchi University, Taiwan. His research focuses on innovation and technology in Taiwan, South Korea, and China and Taiwan's economic development as well as China's regional development. His recent book is *The Limits of Fast Follower: Taiwan's Economic Transition and Innovation* (2010), *Border Crossing in Greater China: Production, Community and Identity* (Routledge, 2014).

Wenbin Wang is Associate Professor of sociology department at Jilin University, China. His research focuses on social capital, social networks, and economic sociology in China. His recent book is *Social Capital and Human Capital in Social Change* (2013).

Chao-Tung Wen is Professor of Graduate Institute of Technology, Innovation and Intellectual Property Management, National Chengchi University (NCCU) in Taiwan. He has been Director of Executive Master of Business Administration (EMBA), the Graduate Institute of Technology and Innovation Management, and Center of Creative and Innovation Studies (CCIS) in NCCU, advisor to prize winners in various innovation and start-up competitions. Besides academic journal papers, he is a frequent contributor to business newspaper and magazine columns. He has reviewed more than ninety books. More than ten books about management education and innovation management have been published.

Siu-Lun Wong is currently Emeritus Chair Professor of Sociology and Honorary Professor at the Hong Kong Institute for the Humanities and Social Sciences (including the Centre of Asian Studies) of the University of Hong Kong. His research interests include the study of entrepreneurship, business networks, migration, social indicators, and the development of sociology in China.

Han-yo Wu is interested in issues about economic sociology, China's local economic development, globalization, and local industry. He obtained his PhD in sociology from Tunghai University in Taiwan. He is currently engaged in research areas relevant to business history and Taiwan's pharmaceutical industry.

Lei Zhang is a PhD candidate in the Department of Sociology at the University of Minnesota. His dissertation is a quantitative investigation of how Chinese *guanxi*, an isotopic form of social capital based on social ties of particularism, multiplexity, and mutual obligations, helps Chinese entrepreneurs to obtain business information, maintain contractual relationships, control transaction costs, and secure financial supports, all of which facilitate the business performance of Chinese enterprises. His research areas include quantitative methodology, social networks and social capital, labor markets and entrepreneurship in emerging economies, organizational study, social stratification, and mobility.

Victor Zheng is currently Assistant Director of the Hong Kong Institute of Asia-Pacific Studies and codirector of Centre for Social and Political Development Studies of the institute. His major research interests are (1) Chinese family business, including entrepreneurship, business networks, corporate governance, and business successions; (2) social policy and the social history of Hong Kong and Macao, including migration and ethnicity, institutional set up and transformation, social development, and social indicators.

Acknowledgments

This book originates from a study group for the business history of Taiwanese enterprises at the Center for China Studies, National Chengchi University, Taiwan. The group consists of scholars from various disciplines including sociology, business management, innovation studies, and history. Because *guanxi* network or social capital is so obvious in doing business in Chinese culture, we decide to hold a conference based on the issue and to publish a book as a result of group discussions. We thus invited scholars from Hong Kong and China as well as overseas Chinese scholars to participate, so as to compare the similar and divergent routes in Greater China in order to highlight the theoretical significance of the phenomenon. The conference, called "Globalization, Social Capital and Entrepreneurship in Greater China," was held on March 8–9, 2013, at National Chengchi University, Taiwan. Some chapters in this book were and have been revised from the conference papers, and some were invited again after the conference in order to enrich the book's main theme – "Does *Guanxi* Still Matter"?

As the editors, we are grateful for the financial support from the TOP University Program of National Chengchi University. It was due to this support that we have the resources to engage in intensive meetings and debates regularly. Of course, we also want to thank the authors who devoted their time on numerous weekends to engage in hardworking workshops at the Center for China Studies. If not for their hearty devotion, this book would not have been possible. Also, we are grateful for anonymous reviewers of the manuscript and those conference discussants who provided valuable comments to improve the quality of our chapters, such as Siu-Lun Wong, Chia-Ming Chang, Kuo-Hsing Hsieh, Chyi-In Wu, Tsu-Lung Chou, Shin-Jia Hsu, Chih-Jou Chen, Pei-How Huang, Hsi-Mei Chung, Po-An Lin, Zong-Rong Lee, and Fei-Yu Hsieh. We also want to pay our deep gratitude to Ms. Yi-horng Chiang for her laborious assistance at almost every step in the preparation of this book. We especially want to thank Routledge's Chinese Culture and Society series editor, Professor Dixon Wang, for supporting the publishing of this book and to Ms. Yi-chih Huang, Ms. Eugenia Wang, and Dr. Tsung-yuan Chen, for their editorial assistance of proofreading at the final stage of the whole book.

Jenn Hwan Wang
Ray May Hsung
National Chengchi University, Taiwan
August 2015

1 Introduction

Guanxi matters? Rethinking social capital and entrepreneurship in Greater China

Jenn-Hwan Wang, Tsung-Yuan Chen, and Ray-May Hsung

This book re-examines the role of social capital in the emergence and expansion of private enterprises in the Greater China area, namely, China, Taiwan, and Hong Kong. Here, social capital is defined as "the potential resources embedded in the social relationships and available to individuals or collectives in purposive action" (Nahapiet and Ghoshal 1998; Lin 1999; Adler and Kwon 2002; Payne et al. 2011; Gedajlovic et al. 2013). Entrepreneurship, on the other hand, indicates the creation of new organizations or the revitalization of mature organizations in response to perceived business opportunities (Nahapiet and Ghoshal 1998; Gedajlovic et al. 2013). Although many people use the term "entrepreneurship" to designate the creation of new enterprises or start-ups in business, the term has been extended to social and political entrepreneurial activities in recent years. This book uses the term in this broader sense in order to look into the newly emerging issues that have resulted in the growth of the recently developing entrepreneurial activities in the Greater China area.

Linking the concept of social capital with entrepreneurship has been a burgeoning research area over the last few decades, ranging from business studies to sociology and area studies. This linkage attracts even more scholars' attention in Greater China studies due to the rise of China in the age of globalization, when many privately owned Chinese businesses have made their existence felt in the world's markets. In this area, a *guanxi* network has become a catchword in recent literature (Tsui and Farh 1997; Batjargal and Liu 2004; Carlisle and Flynn 2005; Lee and Anderson 2007; Guo and Miller 2010), highlighting the role of social networks in the emergence of the Chinese private enterprise in the Chinese reform era (Wank 1996; Bian 1997; Guthrie 1998; 2002; Hsu and Saxenian 2000; Lin 2001; Gold et al. 2002; Nee and Opper 2012; Bian and Lei 2014).

Nevertheless, although there is an agreement in the academic world that the meaning of *guanxi* is similar to the concept of social capital and that a *guanxi* web is similar to a social network in the social science literature, there are still issues that need to be clarified, such as the relationship between concepts of *guanxi* and social capital? Is *guanxi* a static and pre-existing relationship or a dynamic and constructed social tie (Yang 1994; Bian 1997; Gold et al. 2002; Guthrie 2002; Nee and Opper 2012)?

In addition, given the fact that the topic of social capital and Chinese entrepreneurship has recently gained considerable attention, few works have endeavored to juxtapose and compare business experiences and their relationships with social capital in different regions of the Chinese society, specifically Taiwan, Hong Kong, and China. Indeed, in the age of globalization, capital and social relations can go beyond physical space and then be extended to other places in a very short period of time. How have those enterprises in the above specified areas developed business models to accommodate the new globalized environment in order to survive and to become prosperous? How have the Chinese entrepreneurs in those areas developed innovative spatial strategies to conquer social and cultural limitations in order to rapidly accumulate their capital (i.e., Yeung 2009, 224–226)? To our knowledge, very little contemporary literature pays attention to these complex time-space issues.

This book is intended to fill the gap, with special attention being given to the most recent developments of the relationship between social capital and entrepreneurship in the Greater China area in the context of globalization. The issue is especially important, not only due to the fact that the rise of China has become an eye-catching phenomenon in the world economy, but also because our studies can highlight the possible routes of Chinese business development in the future, based on rigorous theoretical construction and empirical comparison. More specifically, we now ask the following questions:

1   What is the role of social capital, or more specifically *guanxi*, in facilitating the formation of business in the three Chinese areas at different time periods?
2   Given that Taiwan has had a Japanese colonial experience, Hong Kong has gone through British rule, and China has transformed from a socialist to a capitalist economy during the reform era, do family businesses in these three Chinese areas share similar and different characteristics in their emergence and succession? Does social capital play a similar or different role in these areas? Or, have different kinds of social capital been developed in these three areas?
3   Finally, as Chinese business in the three areas becomes globalized, how are social capital and social networking used to develop spatial strategies in facilitating cross-border transactions? What are the similarities and differences among these three areas in this regard? What are the new relationships being developed among these three areas as their trade and production network relationships have been developed extensively over recent decades?

The chapters in this book are trying to answer the above questions both individually and collectively. Although most of the chapters are based on single-country studies, their theoretical implications can be comparative so that together they can be composed as a whole. In the following sections, we will first discuss the theoretical concept of *guanxi* and its relationship with the concept of social capital. This will be followed by a discussion of social capital and entrepreneurship in the Greater China area in a comparative perspective, which will also discuss the framework of this book, and a brief introduction of the chapters. The final section will be the conclusion.

The concepts of *guanxi* and social capital

The existing literature on entrepreneurship in China has paid quite a lot of attention to the role of *guanxi* and social capital in the formation of private enterprises and their routes of development. But what are the similarities and differences between the concept of *guanxi* and social capital? Do they indicate the same social and cultural contents? In the next section, we will explain that what we perceive as *guanxi* is a form of social capital that has a specific cultural context.

Guanxi *as a form of social capital*

Many have regarded the term "*guanxi*" in the Chinese language as being similar to "relationships" or "connections" in English. Nonetheless, they are very different. In a more rigorous definition in the Chinese cultural context, *guanxi* refers to not only a static relationship in English terms, but also a dynamic "reciprocal obligation and indebtedness" (Yang 1994; Guthrie 1998). Therefore, it consists of a particularistic and vigorous relationship between individuals that involves favors, services, and gift-giving. Most of the time, this relationship is built upon the existing links or ascribed and primordial traits such as kinship, native place, and ethnicity; sometimes this can also be built upon achieved characteristics such as attending the same school, being coworkers, and even having shared experiences (Gold 2002, 6). But most importantly, *guanxi* can be consciously constructed when no prior ties existed. In this situation, when an individual wants to engage in specific economic or political activities, such as finding potential business partners, they may rely on intermediaries to fabricate this specific relationship. In Chinese terms, it is called *la guanxi* (pulling relationship) – manufacturing a closer relationship by middlemen when no prior basis exists. Therefore, *guanxi*, in a rigorous sense, refers to a dynamic process of ongoing manufactured relationships or "social engineering" that, not only takes time to build up, but also needs resources and strategies to frequently develop, cultivate, and maintain over time (Gold et al. 2002, 6; Bian and Zhang 2014, 424).

However, who is going to manufacture *guanxi* or *la guanxi*? The particularistic relationship between partners is not equal; it is always the weaker side that wants to build a closer relationship through gift-giving in exchange for service. The stronger side already has the information and resources in the dyadic relationship and, therefore, does not need to build *guanxi* with the weaker side. Thus, Guthrie (2002) argues that *guanxi* has to be investigated by the actor's structural position as to see whether, or to what extent, an individual perceives the necessity to cultivate *guanxi* ties. "Individuals who are positioned in *guanxi* networks of powerful individuals are unlikely to see a need to cultivate *guanxi* ties, as they already know and have relationships with the individuals in positions of power" (Guthrie 2002, 46).

Therefore, in this rigorous definition, *guanxi* is not just a social relationship, it is a particularistic and asymmetric relationship that is constructed on purpose. If *guanxi* is a socially constructed relationship, which is based upon a pre-existing relationship, this brings it to the concept of social capital. As mentioned above, social capital refers to resources that can be mobilized in purposive action and beneficial for individuals or collectivities derived from network structures (Bourdieu 1986; Coleman 1990; Burt 1992; Putnam 2000; Lin 2001). Social capital, thus, is a resource that resides in networks rather than resources itself; it needs to be unlocked by the actor. Indeed, social capital is a dynamic process of resource mobilization, which, as Lin (1999, 3) maintains, "the premise behind the notion of social capital is: investment in social relations with expected returns." It is in this sense that the term of *guanxi* is similar to the concept of social capital – *guanxi* as a form of social capital that people mobilize or facilitate to favor exchanges (Bian 2006). The favor exchange in the business world may facilitate acquiring information, financial capital, and other substantial resources that can make business-related matters happen. In this sense, *guanxi* is qualified as a corporate social capital through interpersonal networks for business purposes.

Guanxi *web and social network*

In a very general sense, a corporate social capital, more or less, exists at interpersonal networks, and the incumbent entrepreneur is able to mobilize the resources embedded in the networks. Although there is no consensus among academics regarding whether the concept of social capital is located at the individual or collective levels, for example, Coleman (1988), Putnam (2001), and Woolcock (2001) tend to regard social capital as collective assets at the group and community level (Anderson et al. 2012; Gedajlovic et al. 2013), whereas Lin (1999; 2001) regarded it as individual assets possessed at individually accessed networks. In this book, we regard social capital as a product of social interactions; it is embedded in social connections and networks of a group or a community where norms and trust have been generated. This network can effectively reduce transaction costs, enable knowledge learning, enhance financial capital collection, and reinforce collective action, and so forth. Although the concept of social capital does not exclude that individual property is important in generating economic effect, it nonetheless still stresses that individuals may have a high or low propensity to use or develop the resources that reside in the collectivity (Anderson et al. 2012; Gedajlovic et al. 2013).

Granovetter's (1985) idea of social embeddedness of economic activities laid the foundation for economic sociology in studying corporate social capital. His main argument maintains that social actors are embedded in macro social relations and network structures, through which mutual acquaintances, recognition, and trust are built and which provides them with a credential to mobilize necessary resources. This social embeddedness thesis is especially productive in studying the emergence and development of small and medium-sized enterprises (SMEs), which led to the investigation of relational assets of the incumbent entrepreneur's personal networks that may facilitate the establishment or development of their businesses

(Granovetter 1995; Thornton 1999; Aldrich 2005; Light and Dana 2013). It is also by this theoretical foundation that a significant number of studies on the emergence of entrepreneurship in East Asia has emerged (see Hamilton 1997; Tsui and Farh 1997; Hamilton et al. 2000; Batjargal and Liu 2004; Carlisle and Flynn 2005; Fong and Chen 2007; Lee and Anderson 2007; Guo and Miller 2010).

Nevertheless, it has to be mentioned that *guanxi* is a dyadic and interpersonal relationship, and therefore, it is not at the collective level. In Chinese society, as mentioned above, *guanxi* is "highly personalized" (Gold et al. 2002, 6; Bian and Zhang 2014, 424). The comparable concept to social networks is thus not *guanxi*, but *guanxi web* (Guo and Miller 2010, 270). *Guanxi* web in the Chinese context indicates the extension of a social relationship from the core family members to kinship ties and. further, to nonkinship networks. The core family ties are characterized by unconditional loyalty and obligation that are not reciprocal (Tsui and Farh 1997). However, these core family ties can be extended to kin and nonkin "quasi-familial" relations in which trust can be created, and nonkin members are then recruited to be treated as family members. *La guanxi* (pulling relationship) indicates that an actor tries to bring an outsider as close as possible to become a core family member, or vice versa: An outsider tries to become closer as a family member of another person. Those actions usually involve gift-giving or exchange. This extension of *guanxi* relations in Chinese society from the core family relations to outsiders, as Fei (1947/1992, 65) described, is like "ripples . . . spreading out from the center," which can be infinite. This is also the way in which most Chinese entrepreneurs start and run their business – by mobilizing resources from their social networks – beginning from family members and friends where trust is unconditional and obligation is asymmetrical. However, as the business expands, the entrepreneur needs other types of resources beyond the family ties (Guo and Miller 2010; see also chapter 7 by Hsung and Lin and chapter 8 by Wang, Wu, Chen). We discuss this in the following section.

Guanxi *and different forms of social capital*

An incumbent entrepreneur will try to mobilize their social capital as hard as possible to nurture the emergent firms, but not every social tie in the network is equally beneficial. There are two forms of social capital in the conventional sense: bonding and bridging (Woolcock 1998; Putnam 2001; Storper 2005; Knorringa and van Staveren 2006). Bonding social capital emerges from strong social ties (Granovetter 1985), which are based on similar backgrounds, for example, family, kinship, gender, ethnicity, community, and religion. Sometimes, this type of social capital can be referred to as an ascribed group, which has a strong social cohesion that can generate strong trust among individuals (Knorringa and van Staveren 2006, 19). Therefore, based on these strong social ties, many family businesses were able to raise their necessary funding to start their own businesses through their family-related networks.

In contrast to bonding social capital, bridging social capital emerges from weaker social ties across society that holds together through sharing the minimum of common values (Portes and Sensenbrenner 1993; Woolcock 2001; Burt 2004; Storper 2005; Knorringa and van Staveren 2006). Since weak ties exist among people who are heterogeneous, bridging social capital thus generates social contacts that are not redundant, and to that end, it can create new values. If bonding social capital is based on interpersonal and strong trust, then bridging social capital is based on a type of generalized trust, which occurs mostly at the meso- and macro-level. In terms of economic value, bonding social capital is beneficial for enhancing solidarity and reducing transaction costs but may create a lock-in effect; bridging social capital, in contrast, is beneficial for innovation and generating new ventures. Thus, scholars tend to regard bridging social capital as having a higher economic value than does bonding social capital (Burt 2005).

It is noteworthy to mention that *guanxi*, bonding, and bridging social capital are not "either-or" but "more-or-less" categories, into which social networks can be neatly divided. Indeed, as Knorringa and van Staveren (2006, 22) maintains,

> without bonding social capital there is no fertile ground for bridging social capital to develop. Bridging social capital requires that economic actors are familiar with the strong ties of bonding social capital, which provide them with the necessary social capabilities, particularly interpersonal capabilities of trust, sociability, organization, responsibility, and loyalty, to connect to other people.

Or, as Burt's (2004) concept of a structural hole describes, bonding social capital within the group provides people with the social basis to extend their relationships to others outside their group, while the benefits of the bridging social capital is built upon the bonding function that links two or more separate and isolated clusters together. The relationship among the three can be shown in Figure 1.1.

From the perspective of Chinese entrepreneurship, Guo and Miller (2010) found that an entrepreneur tends to use different kinds of *guanxi* strategy to develop their enterprises along with the growth of their business. It runs from the core family members and close friends at the initial stage, then enlarges the *guanxi* circle to

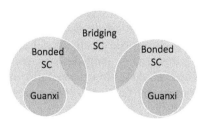

Figure 1.1 The mechanisms of *guanxi* and the social capital of bonding and bridging

more larger groups, such as business associations, and finally to nonkin friends when the business is stable. As they state,

> [A]n entrepreneurial *guanxi* network started with a small, core circle of *gan-qing* [affection]-based *guanxi* ties with the entrepreneurs' family members and close friends. As the entrepreneurial firm grows, this initial *guanxi* network was enlarged and included an intermediary and then a periphery circle composed, respectively, of *renqing* [reciprocity]- and *jiaoqing* [acquaintance]-based *guanxi* ties with other nonkin members to support the expanding needs and growth momentum of the new venture.

In other words, Chinese entrepreneurs tend to use different *guanxi* strategies to benefit the growth of their enterprises. Core members in *guanxi* networks are important at the initial stage, whereas bonding capital is important at its expanding stage; finally, bridging social capital is important as the enterprise wants to move forward into new ventures.

Entrepreneurship and social capital in Greater China

The above theoretical framework is generally applicable to the emergence and growth of enterprises in the Greater China area. Chinese people worldwide may adopt similar strategies to build and expand their enterprises. Nevertheless, as we will argue, due to the different historical times and the environmental contexts, the contents of social capital might be changed and the importance of *guanxi* may be diluted.

Entrepreneurship and transformation of social capital

Entrepreneurs are products of their social environment (Granovetter 1985), and the ways they perceive business opportunities are conditioned by that environment and their social background (Anderson et al. 2007, 250; Lee and Anderson 2007). Therefore, the resources embedded in the entrepreneur's social networks, and the ways in which the actor mobilizes the resources, will influence the development of the business. It is not our task to investigate the process in which resources in social networks are transformed into social capital (Gedajlovic et al. 2013), we regard the pre-existence of resources as an *antecedent*, which is an historical contingency. An individual may fortunately have better opportunities than others to acquire capital and information in a resourceful organization (or a rich family) where the person has worked (or belonged to) for a long period of time. But, most importantly, the ability to mobilize the resources in their networks is required; otherwise, their resources are useless.

On the other hand, the transformation of collectivities or institutions can also affect the properties or resources in social networks. As argued by some authors (i.e., Guthrie 1998; 2002; Li 2007), *guanxi* developed as a result of weak institutional regulations and high uncertainty; it is thus a proxy for actors to build high personal trust to minimize the risk and transform it into certainty. Guthrie (1998; 2002) thus argues that, when the controlling power of bureaucrats has been given away to market competition, and as economic reform progresses and more transparent institutional regulations are established in post-Mao's China, the necessity of *guanxi* networks may be largely reduced. As he stated that "the extent to which *guanxi* matters in China's transforming economy depends in crucial ways on the institutions that define economic and social action, and these institutions are changing in dramatic ways" (Guthrie 2002, 38). In a similar vein, Nee and Opper (2012) have recently argued that the rise of private enterprise economy in China has been due to the uncertainty in its initial reform stage, which facilitated the

> bottom-up construction of endogenous economic institutions" by private entrepreneurs through informal norms and social networks within close-knit business communities. As the private enterprise economy has become an irrepressible power, however, the Chinese state then began "to enact, *ex post*, the formal rule and policies that cumulatively conferred legitimacy formal legal rights, and equality to private firms.
>
> (Nee and Opper 2012, 16)

This theoretical position, although convincing from the institutionalist perspective, however, has not been widely hailed by scholars from a culturalist perspective. For example, Bian (1997; 2014) finds that the Chinese tend to favor strong ties (*guanxi*) to find jobs rather than relying on weak ties or bridging social capital, as is more common in Western societies (Granovetter 1985). The Chinese tend to trust people in familiar circles; therefore, building trust through *guanxi* networks is very important for an entrepreneur to do business. This finding also has been widely supported by many entrepreneurial studies that become aware of the prevalence of the *guanxi* practice in a Chinese context (Tsui and Farh 1997; Batjargal and Liu 2004; Carlisle and Flynn 2005; Lee and Anderson 2007; Guo and Miller 2010). This persistent finding indicates that *guanxi* may well be a cultural phenomenon, which is not necessarily conditioned by any formal institutional regulations.

The above two theories can be regarded as contesting hypotheses: The institutionalist argues that *guanxi* is merely the product of weak institutions; therefore, if formal institutional regulations are established, then people merely have to follow the rules rather than following personal relations or *guanxi*. The culturalist argues that *guanxi* is a cultural practice; therefore, it relates less to formal regulations but more directly with culturally conditioned daily practices. Which hypothesis can better explain the ongoing social and economic development? This needs to be empirically tested (also Gold et al. 2002; Bian and Zhang 2014).

This test can be done vertically and horizontally by using the historical and comparative methods as simulations to see the similarities and differences among firms' development trajectories in diverse contexts. These are the aims of our book, with the chapters endeavoring to show how social capital, especially *guanxi*, affects the emergence and development of private enterprises in the Greater China area – China, Taiwan, and Hong Kong. Specifically, we want to highlight the following: Do *guanxi* networks still play important roles in the emergence and development of an enterprise? Or have *guanxi* networks been diluted by former systems and regulations?

Moreover, enterprises in the areas of Greater China, with the exception of the short-term experiences of China's privately owned enterprises, have gone through many generations. The historical experiences of those firms, some having gone through four generations, and their evolutions, provide invaluable data for us to observe the historical trajectory of enterprise transformation. More importantly, in the age of globalization, capital and social relations can go beyond physical space and be extended to other places in a very short period of time. How have those different Chinese areas developed various forms of institutions to accommodate the new globalized environment? How have the Chinese capitalists in those areas developed new spatial strategies to conquer social and cultural limitations in order to rapidly accumulate their capital (i.e., Yeung 2009, 224–226)? Some of the chapters in this book will carefully deal with this cross-border issue, to see the transformation of the role of social capital in business development. Indeed, all the above issues are used to check whether the institutionalist or the cultur-alist explanations can better account for the relationship between social capital and entrepreneurship in the Greater China area by detailed cases and qualitative studies. We hope that through those comprehensive case studies, this book is able to compile a detailed comparison in order to highlight the similarities and dif-ferences among those three areas in Greater China and contribute to the existing knowledge on social capital and entrepreneurship.

Following the comparative study design, the first part of this book, "*Guanxi* and Entrepreneurship in China," deals with the importance of *guanxi* in the emergence and growth of enterprises in contemporary China. All the three chapters show, no matter whether the business is a small shop (chapter 2), a small to medium-sized enterprise (chapter 3), or a firm in the newly emergent venture capital business (chapter 4), China's businesspeople know that they have to mobilize resources in the *guanxi* web in order to start their businesses and survive the severe competi-tion. Simply put, will the current Chinese experience last for a very long time?

Due to the similar Chinese cultural backgrounds, and their earlier experiences of industrialization in the post-World War II era, cases from Taiwan and Hong Kong may be used as proxies for comparison. Indeed, while both Taiwan and Hong Kong have inherited similar Chinese cultural elements, their long-term experi-ences of industrialization may have resulted in different and formal institutional developments (see Hamilton 1997; Hamilton et al. 2000; Wong 2008). Whether these experiences have diluted the element of *guanxi*, or the role of bonding social capital, is one issue that deserves to be closely examined.

In the second part of the book, "Social Capital and Its Transformation," the authors use Taiwan and Hong Kong as examples to see the path of evolution of the enterprises. The issues discussed range from the transmission of social capital to second and third generations in Taiwan's extensive family businesses (chapter 5); to how a family business in Hong Kong nurtured and then continued to use social capital to enhance their business in a different historical context, surviving in the age of globalization (chapter 6); and to the transformation of types of social capital in high-tech industries like the semiconductor and biopharmaceutical firms in Taiwan (chapters 7 and 8). These chapters show some similar characteristics as to the workings of a family business in terms of *guanxi* and social capital mobilization with Chinese cases; however, with regard to industrial transformation into high-technology areas and business expansions to the global market, new mechanisms such as bridging social capital or structural holes, seems to be much more important than that of the strong bonding social capital and *guanxi* networks.

Therefore, as we will come to understand from the chapters in this book, the culturalist perspective seems to be still valid in terms of explaining the expansion of a family enterprise and its succession as a family firm. However, as the enterprise moves forward to meet severe market competition and wants to expand to other areas, the institutionist perspective seems better able to explain the transformation. As chapters on Taiwan's high-technology industry (chapter 7) and the pharmaceutical industry (chapter 8) show, a firm with better networking strategies with other firms in terms of joint ventures, an interlocking directorate, and technological collaborations can build up better corporate social capital within the environment of market-like competition. The argument has also been widely tested as competitive social capital in the financial market, semiconductor industry, and knowledge economy (*Burt 1992; 2005*; Podolny 1993; 2005; Tsai 1998; 2000) over the past two decades.

Entrepreneurship and cross-border social capital

More importantly, in the age of globalization in which social relations can go beyond physical space and be extended to other places, it is interesting to know how these Chinese enterprises, in three different Greater China areas, developed business models to accommodate the new globalized environment. In the past, studies on the cross-border investments from Taiwan to China have found that Taiwanese firms, on the one hand, have to use *guanxi* networks to build very close relationships with local bureaucrats (Hsing 1998) and bring with them a whole production network in order to reduce transaction costs and retain production efficiency for the global buyers (Wang and Lee 2007). Now, as China has transformed from a world factory to a world market, the current situation has dramatically changed. The production networks are beginning to localize, and the trade relations between China, Taiwan, and Hong Kong have also been transformed. As a recent publication has shown, border crossing in the Greater China area has changed from merely focusing on production, to a residential community formation, and finally to identity contesting (c.f. Wang 2014). These transformations, in effect, have come along with the change in the forms of social capital, in which an incumbent entrepreneur is able to mobilize.

Indeed, as the chapters in the third part of our book, "Social Capital and Cross-Border Linkages," show, some firms have already begun to establish local production networks via the new social networks in which Taiwanese entrepreneurs have now established in China (chapter 9), while some specific trades, such as the ancient jade trade, still retain very traditional high trust social relations even across the Taiwan Strait (chapter 10). In addition, the mobilization of social networks by Taiwanese businessmen to build a Mazu Temple in China is also illuminating, showing how these businesspeople persuaded both the high and low ranks of Chinese officials to accept the religious belief that the Communists had prohibited for decades (chapter 11).

In terms of enterprise mobilization to other places or industrial upgrading, Yeung's (2004) study on overseas Chinese enterprises in Southeast Asia is illuminating. He argues that overseas Chinese enterprises have specific characteristics, which are "because of geopolitical anxiety, in turn legitimizes their reliance on family based actor rather than host-country institutions to coordinate their social and economic activities" (Yeung 2004, 8). Although globalization leads to Chinese enterprises having to cope with various institutional requirements, they are able to find a way to compromise their management practices and external institutional demands. Thus he concludes, "Chinese capitalism has a certain degree of structural endurance and yet is subject to dynamic transformations overtime, this leads to a form of hybrid capitalism" (Yeung 2004, 42). The hybridity, indeed, is a negotiation process through which Chinese entrepreneurs are able to find ways to survive and become prosperous by combining various types of *guanxi* networks and social capital in different institutional contexts. This cross-border mobilization also shows in the Taiwanese businesspeople's ambitious action in establishing a foundation in linking the innovative capability of the Massachusetts Institute of Technology (MIT) with Taiwanese firms, in which the founders are able to mobilize their social networks to benefit Taiwanese industry as a whole (chapter 12). The example of the Epoch Foundation (Taiwan), shows how hybridity, as a bridge to link structural holes across borders, can be functioning exceedingly well for the innovation of enterprises.

Conclusion and discussion: *guanxi* matters but in specific times and spaces

This book aims to explore the issues related to the role of social capital or *guanxi* in the development of entrepreneurial activities in the Greater China area. We ask three key questions: To what extent is *guanxi*/social capital still important in China? Does social capital play similar roles in China, Taiwan, and Hong Kong? What are the contents of social capital being developed among these three Chinese areas as their trade and production networks have rapidly developed over recent decades? The design of this book is to use the emergence and development of China's privately owned enterprises as a primary model and employs Taiwan and Hong Kong counterparts as comparison cases to see the similarities and differences amongst them. Although each case presented here is not designed purposively for this book, the comparison, nonetheless, shows some significant theoretical meanings for the studies of social capital and the implications for future research.

We propose two contesting hypotheses about the role of *guanxi* in Chinese entrepreneurship. The institutionalist argues that *guanxi* is a product of weak institutional regulations (Guthrie 1998; 2002; Li 2007; Nee and Opper 2012), whereas the culturalist camp maintains that *guanxi* still plays an important role in economic transaction and enterprise activities (Bian 1997;Tsui and Farh 1997; Batjargal and Liu 2004; Carlisle and Flynn 2005; Lee and Anderson 2007; Guo and Miller 2010). Through the case studies presented in this book, we can rest assured that the presence of *guanxi* networks in entrepreneurship is not an either-or question but rather a question of degrees and extents.

Theoretical contributions

Through detailed case studies in China, Taiwan, and Hong Kong, this book has shown that *guanxi* still matters, but in specific times and spaces. Our cases in Taiwan and Hong Kong show that the continuity of a family business has still depended very much on *guanxi* networks or bonding social capital. However, when the business moves to high-tech areas, or when a family business intends to expand to other businesses outside of their original areas, weak ties and structural holes are important and are being stretched far beyond their original social networks.

Indeed, as Hsung and Lin show in chapter 7, because of the severe global competition and the uncertainty of the semiconductor industry, successful Taiwanese high-tech firms have to build up a variety of interorganizational and intraorganizational networks to deal with the market uncertainties. These interorganizational networks are far removed from personal *guanxi* and networks. Instead, their study proposes that the structural holes theory has better explanatory power (Burt 1992; 2005). Entrepreneurs should know how to exploit the opportunities of a brokerage firm. Brokers who connect more to disconnected persons and social circles, tend to create more social capital of information diffusion interest by controlling the interests of the conflicting actors.

In this sense, by comparing the development of the Taiwanese high-tech industry with the current Chinese cases, this book shows that, besides the succession of a family business, the intuitionalist account gains more empirical support as an enterprise expands to new product areas, especially the high-technology industry that needs new knowledge, and which is not available in the existing *guanxi* networks. This perspective thus supports the argument that maintains that *guanxi* is a product of institutional uncertainty, meaning the rules and regulations of economic transactions are ambiguous, nontransparent, and incompatible with one another. Thus, if institutional rules become more transparent, then *guanxi* is not really necessary.

Recently, Bian and Zhang (2014), proposed the idea that two elements are key determinants of *guanxi*-based corporate social capital. One is institutional uncertainty, and the other is market competition. Institutional uncertainty has previously been discussed. As to market competition, it refers to more competitors in the market and the high degree of competition (Bian and Zhang 2014,

431). Combining these two factors, they propose that "the higher the degree of the institutional uncertainty" and that "the higher the degree of market competition," "the greater the propensity that *guanxi*-based corporate social capital is used to strengthen corporate actors' comparative advantage" (Bian and Zhang 2014, 433). They, therefore, suggest that the combination of these two elements can comprehend the evolution of China's *guanxi*-based corporate social capital. Surprisingly, they argue that the current post-WTO era is expected to have higher degrees of institutional certainty because of new developments and mixed institutional arrangements; therefore, institutional uncertainty is expected to be persistent or rising; hence, *guanxi*-based social capital remains important (Bian and Zhang 2014, 433).

Bian and Zhang's thesis may not be applicable to others in the Greater China area. For one, Taiwan and Hong Kong have evolved differently in the post-WWII era due to different political regime rules; for another, both Taiwan and Hong Kong have been exposed to the capitalist market competition for more than half a century. Moreover, unlike China, they do not have those gigantic state-owned companies that have oligarchical power in the market that mainly served for the state's own purposes. Given these differences, therefore, the element of market competition may not be a forceful explanatory factor, or be useful, to account for both the Taiwan and Hong Kong cases.

Then, what element can account for the continuity of a family business in maintaining *guanxi* and personal networks in Taiwan and Hong Kong? Southeast Asian Chinese family businesses may provide a clue, because the family firm is the dominant form of Chinese business in Southeast Asia, or for overseas Chinese in general. In those places, Redding (1990) finds that Confucianism has been the core value that places great emphasis on paternalism, collectivism, personalism, social hierarchy, and familism, which in turn greatly influences the development of enterprises. Due to the fact that Chinese enterprises develop differently from the West, Redding calls it a new form of capitalism – Chinese capitalism.

Many studies on Chinese family businesses also show that the owners hold the continuity of the family's wealth and control as being more important than the development of the business itself (Wang and Chen 2011). In order to retain control, many family firms do not want to be listed on the stock market, as market expansion is not their ambition. Even when they want to expand, the owners tend to adopt very traditional ways of *guanxi* building and are very careful not to lose control in the boardroom. In this sense, it is very common for Chinese family firms to show their characteristics of strong networking and flexibility; however, they nonetheless show their weakness of technological and organizational capability in managing global affairs (Wang and Chen 2011). In this sense, the maintenance of the family business is directly related to cultural values.

If a family business wants to cope with the influence of globalization, it has to adopt a modern firm's management system that emphasizes impersonal and rational organizational characteristics and that puts the firm's development ahead of the family's own wealth and values. There are different ways to achieve this goal: One is to reduce the family ownership and become a publicly listed company, because in this way it is no longer considered a family business. The family firm can also own the majority of the stock shares and recruit a professional chief executive officer (CEO) to manage the company, and it thereby becomes a professionally run company. Finally, the family may send descendants to renowned business schools for professional training and then to return to run the company in a professional capacity. The last method has been mainly undertaken by the majority of family firms in the Greater China area, including Taiwan, Hong Kong, and even Singapore (Yeung 2004; Wang and Chen 2011).

In sum, by comparing social capital and entrepreneurship in China, Taiwan, and Hong Kong, we find that there is continuity and discontinuity of *guanxi* in the Greater China area. In terms of family business' continuity and succession, *guanxi* networks are still important; however, in terms of business development into new areas that need new knowledge, the weight of *guanxi* networks has been given to weak ties and structural holes. Finally, as a corollary, if a family business wants to expand to new areas, *guanxi* networks are not enough. Nurturing bridging social capital is more important than bonding social capital, although Chinese family firms prefer a hybrid form in which family control has been integrated with descendants' professional training and management.

Future research agenda

This book has contributed to the study of *guanxi* and social capital in relation to Chinese entrepreneurship. We have used China's emerging privately owned companies as exemplars to show the workings of *guanxi* networks from a Chinese context. Then we use Taiwan's and Hong Kong's cases as simulation for comparison to see the factors of *guanxi* networks in different institutional settings and at historical times. The chapters of this book have together shown the important and interesting findings as stated above, but there are still a few possible clues based on our findings for future research.

First of all, in order to test our findings, it is necessary to discover more cases from China. This can be done by obtaining two sets of cases: One is the family business; the other is high-technology firms. Family businesses in China are quite recent; however, some of them have already begun to hand over the reins to their second generation sons or daughters. It is therefore a good opportunity to investigate whether these firms will show similar patterns with those of Taiwan and Hong Kong. Moreover, as the high-tech privately owned firms are also emerging in China, it is also interesting to note the interlocking pattern of board members and their external linkages, which will show whether bridging social capital or structural holes are essential for the firms to develop in China as Taiwanese cases have shown.

Second, we maintain that globalization has only shortened physical distance, as it has not obliterated the impact of domestic institutions upon actors. It is therefore easy to understand why privately owned firms in China, Taiwan, and Hong Kong have developed in both similar and different manners. In this book, we have been mainly concerned with the side of similarities. We have paid less attention to the difference dimensions that may have been generated by different institutions. Therefore, questions regarding differences may be worthy of further studies, such as: How did the British and Japanese rulers shape Hong Kong's and Taiwan's business management in terms of *guanxi* building? This question applies to China versus Taiwan and Hong Kong.

Third, the current literature on Chinese entrepreneurship has paid a lot of attention to *guanxi* networks and its impact on business development (Chan 1992; Weidenbaum and Hughes 1996; Li 2007). However, a lot less attention has been paid towards the building of various *guanxi* ties with a firms' performance at those different stages? In fact, most of the social capital studies tend to describe what has happened rather than to ask questions regarding a firms' performance? (i.e., Bian and Zhang 2014). This also shows up in most of the chapters in our book, with the exception of chapter 7. In the future, it is necessary to ensure more research based on quantitative data to compare the performance of family and nonfamily firms, so as to see the contribution of different kinds of social capital in the Greater China area.

Fourth, it is very interesting to find that, due to a lack of institutional management in cross-border transactions, which is thus highly uncertain, purposive construction and maintenance of social capital becomes very important (as shown in chapters 9, 10, and 11). In the future, if contracts of cross-border trade and investments becomes more institutionalized and transparent, and whether this kind of bonding social capital is necessary, is a very thought-provoking issue to be observed and researched.

Fifth and finally, the chapters of our book have mainly focused on both individual and organizational levels, but very few have payed attention to the structural level. As chapter 12 shows, the Epoch Foundation plays an important role in linking Taiwan's high-tech firms with MIT's innovation capability; hence, the consequences have been beneficial for the industry as a whole. There are many similar organizations and foundations in the Greater China area that play important roles that are as significant as the EPOCH Foundation in nurturing cross-border collaborations that are also worthy of being studied in the future.

References

Adler, Paul, and Kwon Seok-Woo. 2002. "Social Capital: Prospects for a New Concept." *Academy of Management Review* 27 (1): 17–40.

Aldrich, Howard. 2005. "Entrepreneurship." In *The Handbook of Economic Sociology*, Second Edition, edited by Neil Smelser and Richard Swedberg, 451–477. Princeton, NJ: Princeton University Press.

Anderson, Alistair, John Park, and Sarah L. Jack. 2007. "Entrepreneurial Social Capital Conceptualizing Social Capital in New High-Tech Firms." *International Small Business Journal* 25 (3): 245–272.

Anderson, Alistair R., Sarah Drakopoulou Dodd, and Sarah L. Jack. 2012. "Entrepreneurship as Connecting: Some Implications for Theorising and Practice." *Management Decision* 50 (5): 958–971.

Batjargal, Bat, and Mannie Liu. 2004. "Entrepreneurs' Access to Private Equity in China: The Role of Social Capital." *Organization Science* 15 (2): 159–172.

Bian, Yanjie. 1997. "Bringing Strong Ties Back In: Indirect Ties, Network Bridges, and Job Searches in China." *American Sociological Review* 62 (3): 366–385.

Bian, Yanjie. 2006. "Guanxi." In *International Encyclopedia of Economic Sociology*, edited by J. Beckert and M. Zafirovski, 314–344. New York; London: Routledge.

Bian, Yanjie. Forthcoming. *On Guanxi.* Beijing: Social Science Academic Press (in Chinese).

Bian, Yanjie, and Lei Zhang. 2014. "Corporate Social Capital in Chinese Guanxi Culture." *Contemporary Perspectives on Organizational Social Networks* 40: 421–443.

Bourdieu, Pierre. 1986. "The Forms of Capital." In *Handbook of Theory and Research for the Sociology of Education*, edited by John Richardson, 241–258. New York: Greenwood.

Burt, Ronald S. 1992. *Structural Holes: The Social Structure of Competition.* Cambridge: Harvard University Press.

Burt, Ronald S. 2004. "Structural Holes and Good Ideas." *American Journal of Sociology* 110 (2): 349–399.

Burt, Ronald S. 2005. *Brokerage and Closure: An Introduction to Social Capital.* New York: Oxford University Press.

Carlisle, Elliot, and Dave Flynn. 2005. "Small Business Survival in China: Guanxi, Legitimacy, and Social Capital." *Journal of Developmental Entrepreneurship* 10 (1): 79–96.

Chan, Wellington. 1992. "Chinese Business Networking and the Pacific Rim." *Journal of American-East Asian Relations* 1 (2): 171–190.

Coleman, James S. 1988. "Social Capital in the Creation of Human Capital." *American Journal of Sociology* 94: 95–120.

Coleman, James S. 1990. *Foundations of Social Theories.* Cambridge, MA: Harvard University Press.

Fei, Xiaotong. 1947/1992. *From the Soil.* Berkeley, CA: University of California Press.

Fong, Eric, and Wenhong Chen. 2007. "Mobilization of Personal Social Networks and Institutional Resources of Private Entrepreneurs in China." *Canadian Review of Sociology and Anthropology* 44: 415–449.

Gedajlovic, Eric, Benson Hong, Curt B. Moore, G. Tyge Payne, and Mike Wright. 2013. "Social Capital and Entrepreneurship: A Schema and Research Agenda." *Entrepreneurship Theory and Practice* 37 (3): 455–478.

Gold, Thomas, Doug Guthrie, and David Wank. 2002. "An Introduction to the Study of Guanxi." In *Social Connections in China: Institutions, Culture, and the Changing Nature of Guanxi*, edited by Thomas Gold, Doug Guthrie and David Wank, 3–20. Cambridge: Cambridge University Press.

Granovetter, Mark. 1985. "Economic Action and Social Structure: The Problem of Embeddedness." *American Journal of Sociology* 91 (3): 481–510.

Granovetter, Mark. 1995. "The Economic Sociology of Firms and Entrepreneurs." In *The Economic Sociology of Immigration: Essays in Networks, Ethnicity, and Entrepreneurship*, edited by Alejandro Portes, 128–165. New York: Russell Sage Foundation.

Guo, Chun, and Jane K. Miller. 2010. "Guanxi Dynamics and Entrepreneurial Firm Creation and Development in China." *Management and Organization Review* 6 (2): 267–291.

Guthrie, Doug. 1998. "The Significance of the Declining Significance of Guanxi: How Networks Change in China's Market." *The China Quarterly* 154: 254–282.

Guthrie, Doug. 2002. "Information Asymmetries and the Problem of Perception: The Significance of Structural Position in Assessing the Importance of Guanxi in China." In *Social Connections in China: Institutions, Culture, and the Changing Nature of Guanxi*, edited by Thomas Gold, Doug Guthrie and David Wank, 37–56. Cambridge: Cambridge University Press.

Hamilton, Gary. 1997. "Organization and Market Process in Taiwan's Capitalist Economy." In *The Economic Organization of East Asian Capitalism*, edited by Marco Orru, Nicole Biggart, and Gary Hamilton, 237–295. New York: SAGE.

Hamilton, Gary, Robert Feenstra, Wongi Choe, Chung Ku Kim, and Eun Mie Lim. 2000. "Neither States Nor Markets: The Role of Economic Organization in Asian Development." *International Sociology* 15 (2): 291–308.

Hsing, You-tien. 1998. *Making Capitalism in China: The Taiwan Connection*. New York: Oxford University Press.

Hsu, Jinn-Yuh, and AnnaLee Saxenian. 2000. "The Limits of Guanxi Capitalism: Transnational Collaboration between Taiwan and the US." *Environment and Planning A* 32 (11): 1991–2005.

Knorringa, Peter, and Irene van Staveren. 2006. *Social Capital for Industrial Development: Operationalizing the Concept*. Geneva: United Nation Industrial Development Organization.

Lee, Edward Yiu-Chung, and Alistair R. Anderson. 2007. "The Role of Guanxi in Chinese Entrepreneurship." *Journal of Asia Entrepreneurship and Sustainability* 3 (3): 38–51.

Li, Peter Ping 2007. "Guanxi as the Chinese Norm for Personalized Social Capital: Toward an Integrated Duality Framework of Informal Exchange." In *Handbook of Research on Asian Business*, edited by Henry Wai-Chung Yeung, 62–83. London: Edward Elgar Publishing.

Light, Ivan, and *Léo*-Paul Dana. 2013. "Boundaries of Social Capital in Entrepreneurship." *Entrepreneurship: Theory and Practice* 37 (3): 603–624.

Lin, Nan. 1999. "Social Networks and Status Attainment." *Annual Review of Sociology* 25: 467–488.

Lin, Nan. 2001. *Social Capital: A Theory of Social Structure and Action*. New York: Cambridge University Press.

Nahapiet, Janine, and Sumantra Ghoshal. 1998. "Social Capital, Intellectual Capital and the Organizational Advantage." *Academy of Management Review* 23 (2): 242–266.

Nee, Victor, and Sonja Opper. 2012. *Capitalism from Below: Market and Institutional Change in China*. Cambridge, MA: Harvard University Press.

Payne, G. Tyge, Curt B. Moore, Stanley E. Griffis, and Chad W. Autry. 2011. "Multilevel Challenges and Opportunities in Social Capital Research." *Journal of Management* 37 (2): 491–520.

Podolny, Joel M. 1993. "A Status-based Model of Market Competition." *American Journal of Sociology* 98 (4): 829–872.

Podolny, Joel M. 2005. *Status Signals: A Sociological Study of Market Competition*. Princeton, NJ: Princeton University Press.

Portes, Alejandro, and Julia Sensenbrenner. 1993. "Embeddedness and Immigration: Notes on the Social Determinants of Economic Action." *American Journal of Sociology* 98 (6): 1320–1350.

Putnam, Robert D. 2000. *Bowling Alone: The Collapse and Revival of American Community*. New York: Simon and Schuster.

Putnam, Robert D. 2001. "Social Capital: Measurement and Consequences." *Isuma: Canadian Journal of Policy Research* 2 (1): 41–51.

Redding, Gordon. 1990. *The Spirit of Chinese Capitalism*. New York: Walter de Gruyter.

Storper, Michael. 2005. "Society, Community, and Economic Development." *Studies in Comparative International Development* 39 (4): 30–57.

Thornton, Patricia. 1999. "The Sociology of Entrepreneurship." *Annual Review of Sociology* 25: 19–46.

Tsai, Wenpin. 2000. "Social Capital, Strategic Relatedness and the Formation of Intraorganizational Linkages." *Strategic Management Journal* 21: 925–939.

Tsai, Wenpin, and Sumantra Ghoshal. 1998. "Social Capital and Value Creation: The Role of Intrafirm Networks." *Academy of Management Journal* 41: 464–476.

Tsui, Anne S., and Jing-Lih Farh. 1997. "Where Guanxi Matters: Relational Demography and Guanxi in the Chinese Context." *Work and Occupations* 24 (1): 56–79.

Wang, Jenn-hwan. Ed. 2014. *Border Crossing in Greater China: Production, Community and Identity*. London: Routledge.

Wang, Jenn-hwan, and Chuan-Kai Lee. 2007. "Global Production Networks and Local Institutional Building: The Development of the Information Technology Industry in Suzhou, China." *Environment and Planning A* 39 (8): 1873–1888.

Wang, Jenn-hwan, and Tsung-Yuan Chen. 2011. "Rethinking Family Business Studies in Taiwan: An Integrated Framework." In *Dose Family Business Still Matter?* edited by Jenn-hwan Wang and Chao-Tung Wen, 1–45. Taipei: Juliu Publishing Company (in Chinese).

Wank, David L. 1996. "The Institutional Process of Market Clientelism: Guanxi and Private Business in a South China City." *The China Quarterly* 147: 820–838.

Weidenbaum, Murray, and Samuel Hughes. 1996. *The Bamboo Network: How Expatriate Chinese Entrepreneurs are Creating a New Economic Superpower in Asia*. New York: Martin Kessler Books.

Wong, Raymond Sin-Kwok. 2008. "Contemporary Changes of Chinese Entrepreneurship in Hong Kong." In *Chinese Entrepreneurship in a Global Era*, edited by Raymond Sin-Kwok Wong, 59–80. London: Routledge.

Woolcock, Michael. 1998. "Social Capital and Economic Development: Toward a Theoretical Synthesis and Policy Framework." *Theory and Society* 27 (2): 151–208.

Woolcock, Michael. 2001. "The Place of Social Capital in Understanding Social and Economic Outcomes." *Isuma: Canadian Journal of Policy Research* 2 (1): 11–17.

Yang, Mayfair Mei-hui. 1994. *Gifts, Favors, and Banquets: The Art of Social Relationships in China*. Ithaca, NY: Cornell University Press.

Yeung, Henry Wai-Chung. 2004. *Chinese Capitalism in a Global Era: Towards Hybrid Capitalism*. New York: Routledge.

Yeung, Henry Wai-Chung. 2009. "Transnationalizing Entrepreneurship: A Critical Agenda for Economic Geography." *Progress in Human Geography* 33 (2): 210–235.

Part I

Guanxi and entrepreneurship in China

2 The social capital for self-employment in transitional China

Yanjie Bian and Wenbin Wang

Introduction

Self-employment provides a window into China's economic change and growth. Before the 1978 reforms, the self-employed accounted for less than 1 percent of the urban labor force, and it was near zero in the collectivized rural countryside. Then China's industrial and agricultural sectors were monopolized by the Communist party-state. However, in the initial stage of the reforms, self-employment was the very first of nonstate economic forms to emerge and grow, and during the later reforms, it became the cradle of the Chinese market economy and capitalism. Today, the nonstate sector is several times the size of the state sector in terms of both labor force and economic output, and self-employment remains a pivotal form of work and business in China. As of 2012, self-employment accounted for 18 percent of urban jobs in China (Xie 2014).

How does an individual become self-employed? Certainly, the growth of a market economy provides an expanding space for self-employment opportunities and other nonstate economic forms, and under a durable Communist party-state with an antiprivatization ideology, risk taking is by and large an important part of the spirit of entrepreneurship. While these issues have been well studied and understood in the literature of economics and management (Allen 2000; Barbieri 2003), in this chapter, we ask a sociological question: To what extent does social capital serve as a mechanism whereby socially constrained individuals turn to self-employment and succeed in it? In other words, what roles does social capital play in setting up a self-employment arrangement from which one can move to a sizable private business in China?

In the social sciences, social capital is a heuristic concept that is defined in multiple ways (Portes 1995). For our analytic purpose, we follow Burt (1992, 12) and define social capital as "the resources contacts hold and the structure of contacts in a network. The first term describes whom you reach. The second term describes how you reach." The first term of this definition applies almost universally to various situations in which Chinese individuals become self-employed: They need the social contacts that provide assistance and help with license applications, financial capital, business opportunities, and other matters in order to set up a self-employment arrangement and operate it well. We report case studies on how our self-employed informants received assistance and help from their social contacts. The second term of Burt's definition concerns *how* to reach the right kinds of social contacts, in other words, the networking process of social capital mobilization. We believe that a substantial cultural difference exists in this process between Western societies, in which the concept of social capital emerges and develops, and Chinese society in which we conducted our empirical research. Thus, theoretical thinking about the networking process of social capital mobilization in the Chinese context is needed in order to guide an interpretation of the data we collected from the self-employed.

This chapter first discusses some theoretical considerations about the use of social capital for self-employment in transitional China. Central to these considerations is an argument that the self-employed act both rationally and normatively in the social capital mobilization process. Briefly, the self-employed tend to have greater success in mobilizing social capital when they rationally use both strong ties and weak ties to obtain different kinds of resources and assistance, when they rationally utilize sector-crossing ties for various business opportunities, and when they normatively engage in social-eating activities through which they generate intended and unintended consequences for their business developments. In the research design section that follows, we describe how we approached these three dimensions of social capital mobilization: tie strength, sector crossing, and engagement in social eating. This is followed by a presentation of in-depth interviews and a large-scale household survey we conducted, which provide supporting evidence for our theoretical considerations. The conclusion discusses the implications of our empirical analysis for future research about social capital in Chinese self-employment and entrepreneurship.

Theoretical considerations

How can social capital be mobilized from the networks of social contacts in China or elsewhere? A point of departure is Granovetter's (1973) seminal work on the strength of weak ties. According to Granovetter, valuable and nonredundant information about economic opportunities is embedded in the networks of ongoing social relationships, and weak ties of infrequent interaction and low intimacy entail greater probabilities of transmitting such information to people with dissimilar attributes and social positions. In an empirical study on job searches in the United States, Granovetter (1974) shows that job seekers tend to obtain nonredundant job information from acquaintances rather than relatives and friends and thus get better jobs in terms of prestige and pay. This is the well-known strength-of-weak-ties hypothesis. Lin (1982) later extended this line of reasoning by arguing that weak ties connect people across ranks of a social hierarchy, and through weak ties, individuals reach out to higher-status people whose "social resources" will lead weak-tie users to obtain jobs of higher prestige. This is the core of Lin's theory on social resources and social capital (2001). While empirical studies have reported mixed results (Granovetter 1995; Lin 1999), posing a serious challenge to the network approach to labor market studies (Montgomery 1991; Mouw 2003), the most recent Chinese studies on job searches provide proof that the information and influence mobilized through *guanxi* networks of social contacts increase wages for Chinese workers, both at the entry level (Bian and Huang 2014) and during later career development (Bian et al. 2015).

Guanxi is the Chinese expression of social connections. Students of China around the world have found it so culturally contextualized that they share the consensus that "the Chinese *guanxi* is not a term that can adequately be expressed by an English-language equivalent of one word, the concept is too culture specific" (Parnell 2005, 35). By definition, "*guanxi* (or kuan-hsi) refers to a dyadic, particular, and sentimental tie that has the potential of facilitating favor exchange between the parties connected by the tie" (Bian 2006, 312). In China, any blood or marital relationship qualifies for this definition, and persons connected by a nonkin tie can develop *guanxi* between them if they repeatedly invest in sentiment in the tie and at the same time build up obligations to each other, making the tie mutually special and beneficial for both parties. It takes time, resources, and strategies to cultivate, maintain, develop, and redevelop *guanxi* ties (Yang 1994). Events of cultural significance, including festivals, holidays, weddings, birthdays, and occasions of social drinking and eating, provide opportunities for *guanxi* building (Bian 2001; Bian et al. 2005). The deeply understood, widely accepted, and sometimes explicitly spelled-out implication of *guanxi* building are future favor exchanges between parties tied by mutually recognized *guanxi*. In short, *guanxi* culture legitimizes the expected obligation to provide a favor to someone when it is sought after through a *guanxi* tie. Such reciprocal outcomes are believed to be the unintended consequences of social networking in Western cultures (Arrow 1998), although they are often generated by deliberate processes of *guanxi* building because *guanxi* ties in essence are "particular-instrumental ties" (Walder 1986).

Several elaborations about *guanxi* are in order. First, *guanxi* facilitates favor exchange. In the Chinese context, a favor means substantial help that produces a decisive outcome or influence on others to get things done. Informational help is considered less substantial unless the information transmitted is confidential and made available secretly (Bian 1997; Bian and Huang 2009). Second, *guanxi* is a particular tie combining acquaintance (*shu*), intimacy (*qin*), and trustworthiness (*xin*). Special favors are thus granted to targeted beneficiaries in special relationships and cannot be transferred (Yeung and Tung 1996; Bian 2010). Third, particularism is fortified by personalized sentiment, such as personal feelings (*renqing*), personal face (*mianzi*), and personal attachment (*ganqing*), which jointly impose relational obligation and exert social-psychological pressure on the favor granter and the favor receiver (King 1985; 1994). Finally, because *guanxi* ties provide multiple functions and accumulate reciprocal obligations between connected parties over time, they are multiplex ties (Mitchell 1969).

These elaborations indicate that *guanxi* networks present high reciprocal expectations and strong behavioral constraints on people living in Chinese culture and society. As such, some Westerners on their first trips to China feel that Chinese life is amazingly puzzling, awful, or bitter (Butterfield 1982). The particularistic nature of *guanxi* can be frustrating for foreign businesspeople investing in China, especially when they lack preexisting social ties in the country and try to use Western values to make ethical judgments about developing and utilizing social relationships for economic activities (Lovett et al. 1999). Nevertheless, for Chinese businesspeople, "the social relationship is a prerequisite to get involved in a business relationship" (Gomez Arias 1998, 150), maintaining *guanxi* with "the right individuals" is the key to long-term success (Wong 1988), and "tendering of favors" through preexisting interpersonal strong ties brings expected benefits (Yeung and Tung 1996).

One inference that can be drawn from this research on Chinese *guanxi* is that the process of social capital mobilization through *guanxi* networks of social contacts is culturally and institutionally contextualized in China. First, this process is sensitive to the strength of ties, and it is highly expected that stronger ties are more effective in mobilizing substantial resources relevant to favor exchanges. Second, the process is sensitive to China's dual economic context, and business opportunities are likely to be embedded in sector-crossing ties. Third, this is a normatively dynamic process in which social capital mobilization results from favoritism-prone social interactions such as social eating and drinking. We elaborate these three dimensions of social capital mobilization in the Chinese context below.

Tie strength

Granovetter's strength-of-weak-ties hypothesis basically points to the roles of weak ties as information bridges. Along this line of analysis, Bian (1997) proposes an alternative hypothesis in the Chinese context of *guanxi* culture: Strong ties of trust and obligation are more frequently and more effectively used than weak ties to facilitate exchanges of substantialized favoritism among people connected through kin and pseudokin relationships. Here, substantialized favoritism refers not just to information, although confidential information that entails valuable opportunities is one form of such favoritism. More commonly understood forms of substantialized favoritism include job opportunities in the pre-reform and postreform eras (Bian 1997; 2008; Bian et al. 2012) and those that lead to a successful self-employment arrangement, which is the focus of this chapter. The stories presented shortly imply that both weak ties and strong ties are used by Chinese self-employed informants, with the former used basically to gain nonredundant information that is not immediately available, and the latter more likely to be used to obtain substantial assistance in the forms of license applications, financial investments, and business contracts.

Sector crossing

Spanning structural boundaries is an inherent property of network bridges, and theory-informed examples include weak ties that bridge nonredundant information across social groups (Granovetter 1973), social resources that are channeled across levels of a social hierarchy (Lin 1982), and structural holes that generate information and control benefits from otherwise disconnected structurally equivalent positions (Burt 1992). In transitional China, the most salient institutional structure is the economic dualism of the state and nonstate sectors, each having distinctive resources and opportunities. A recent study shows that sector-crossing ties contain moonlighting job opportunities; with personal attributes held constant, crossers are found to have significantly higher personal and family annual incomes than their noncrosser counterparts (Bian et al. 2012). Here, we study the extent to which sector-crossing social capital plays an important role in becoming self-employed.

Social eating

In past and present China, *guanxi* building is a lifelong process (Fei 1949/1992), and favor exchanges have become a lifestyle for both villagers (Yan 1996) and urbanites (Yang 1994). One of the common occasions for *guanxi* building and rebuilding is social eating and drinking, and the roles of hosts, guests, and attendees are culturally understood and contextually referenced to the *guanxi* ethos. At social eating and drinking occasions, participants take the opportunity to exchange information about matters of mutual interest, share opinions on issues of common concern, offer advice that will benefit the other party, or talk about opportunities to do things together. While all of these can maintain and strengthen ties already established between the parties, one particular networking function is that the parties around the table have great flexibility to adjust socialization to the extent that it serves expressive and instrumental purposes, as described in Bian (2001), who conceptualizes the practices into an innovative measurement device of social-eating networks. Bian finds that the frequency of one's social-eating engagements is positively associated with one's political status and economic resources and increases one's social network diversity and resource mobilizing capacities. In this study of self-employment in China, our theoretical interest is in the role of social-eating activities in mobilizing social capital for self-employment: to what extent do individuals mobilize useful social capital through social eating to establish successful self-employment arrangements, which can then move toward the start of a sizable business?

Research design

Our empirical analysis is based on two sources of data. First, in-depth interviews were conducted with self-employed persons in various locations in China. This source of data helps us understand the importance of network-based social capital in certain aspects of the process of becoming self-employed and achieving success. The list of interviews is provided in Table 2.1. These informants are certainly not a representative sample. We identified several informants whose stories were theoretically informed. We then asked these informants to identify their friends or acquaintances if they believed these people could offer somewhat different stories about social capital's importance to their self-employment arrangements. Our

Table 2.1 Profile of informants

	Pseudonyms	Sex	Age	Occupation	Time of Interview
1	Dong	Male	40	Business owner	December 2012
2	Meng	Male	51	Party secretary	October 2012
3	Wu	Female	42	Worker	April 2013
4	Zeng	Female	39	Owner	December 2012
5	Zhang	Male	44	College teacher	February 2013
6	Zhao	Female	40	State official	February 2013
7	Zhou	Male	39	Business owner	April 2013

goal was to generate a diverse list of informants both in terms of their personal attributes and their self-employment arrangements.

The second source of data was a large-scale household survey conducted in the eight largest Chinese cities in 2009. While the survey used a probability sample and has a large number of randomly selected respondents (N = 7100), we focus our analytic attention on the 584 self-employed people. Details about this survey sample and the subsample of self-employed persons are available elsewhere (Wang and Zhao 2012); here, we note that the self-employed persons included in this subsample can be seen as an independent probability sample of self-employment in China's largest cities. In this sample self-employed respondents were asked to provide their personal attributes, the process of their self-employment arrangements, and the social contacts that provided various kinds of assistance in the process of setting up their self-employment or business ventures. Of most relevance are the measurements of the respondent's tie strengths to these social contacts, whether these social contacts work in the same or different economic sectors, and the frequency of joining them for social eating. These measures make it possible to estimate the effects of *guanxi* networks on the probability and success of self-employment.

Table 2.2 presents a profile of self-employed respondents as compared to employee respondents in the survey. First, compared to employees, the self-employed group tended to have more males than females, were younger, less educated, and had significantly fewer members of the Communist Party. Second, while a majority of employees worked in the state sector and all self-employed in the nonstate sector, the self-employed tended to have a much higher personal income, with a great variation within the group. Third, the two groups did not significantly differ in measures of tie strength (percentage of strong ties to New Year's visitors, a measure of Chinese *guanxi* networks) and sector-crossing ties (contacts from two sectors rather than one), but the self-employed engage in significantly more social-eating activities than employees.

In the next three sections, we analyze how tie strength, sector crossing, and social eating affect self-employment arrangements.

Table 2.2 Profiles of the self-employed and employees, 2009 JSNET Survey

Variables	Self-Employed		Employees	
	Mean	S.D.	Mean	S.D.
% male	0.57	0.49	0.46	0.50
Age	38.65	9.89	43.49	13.49
Year of schooling	11.31	3.32	12.35	3.29
% Communist Party membership	0.05	0.22	0.19	0.39
% Work in the state sector	0.00	0.00	0.69	0.46
Annual personal income (RMB¥)	66228	158328	28620	31872
% Strong ties to New Year's visitors	0.79	0.23	0.78	0.24
% Sector-crossing ties	0.65	0.47	0.63	0.48
Extensity of social eating (factor score)	0.27	1.05	−0.02	0.93
Number of respondents	584		6518	

Tie strength and self-employment

Let us consider a case study. Ms. Wu was laid off a few years ago and was given a modest cash payment as laid-off insurance. She planned to use this money to start a self-employed business to sustain her livelihood but had no opportunity to do so. In her many visits to the District Government to seek help, she became acquainted with a staff member who worked in the front office receiving visitors. This individual shared the information that there was a great demand for printing services near the government offices. Many people came to the government to apply for grants and projects, to file legal suits, and to make various requests to the government, and all of them would need printing and copying services, which the government did not provide. While Ms. Wu was highly motivated to open a printing and copying shop, she did not have sufficient funds to do so. Knowing of their daughter's financial need, Ms. Wu's parents tried to help. At the time, their home was located in an area under a governmental plan of reconstruction, and her parents received a good amount of reallocation fees. They decided to lend Ms. Wu the money to support her plan. The shop was subsequently opened, located in a convenient location for the people coming to the government for various reasons, and has operated very well thus far.

This story uncovers two different kinds of social ties that play different roles in starting a self-employment arrangement. The first was a weak tie to an acquaintance who worked in a government office and had access to valuable information about opening a printing and copying service shop. However, this information would not have been valuable if Ms. Wu had not had loving parents who lent her money as start-up capital. While the weak tie to a governmental staff member offered informational resources, the strong tie to her parents gave her the substantial resources in the form of money that enabled her to capitalize on the

Table 2.3 Start-up capital and business contracts by tie strength

	Source of Start-Up Capital (RMB¥)		
	>10,000	10,000–100,000	>100,000
Self or family	72.7%	58.2%	47.8%
Strong ties to lender	15.3%	19.9%	26.6%
Weak ties to lender	12.0%	21.9%	25.6%
Number of cases	234	237	113
	Source of First Business Contract		
	Frequency	%	
Self or family	150	25.68	
Mixed ties to providers	302	51.72	
Strong tie to providers	39	6.68	
Weak tie to providers	93	15.92	

information channeled through a weak tie. In the case of self-employment opportunities, strong ties and weak ties play different roles, supporting the hypothesis
about the strength of weak ties of low intimacy and infrequent interaction on
information flow (Granovetter 1973) and the hypothesis about the role of strong
ties of trust and obligation for obtaining substantial assistance in the absence of
market institutions (Bian 1997). The 2009 Chinese survey provides evidence of
these roles.

As can be seen in Table 2.3, capital investment for opening a self-employed
business came mostly from the self or family. However, the larger the capital
investment, the greater the probability that the capital investment had to be generated by social connections, with a roughly balanced dependence on strong ties and
weak ties. In our analysis, strong ties include relatives and close friends, and weak
ties include less-close friends and acquaintances. As for the sources of business
information and contracts, one-fourth came from within the family, more than
half from mixed ties, less than 7 percent from strong ties, and nearly 16 percent
from weak ties. Strong ties seem to play a greater role in financial and contract
relations.

Sector-crossing ties and self-employment

The fundamental point in Granovetter's strength-of-weak-ties hypothesis is that
weak ties cut across group boundaries and thus offer nonredundant information
and opportunities to social actors. In the Chinese context, Table 2.2 implies that
both strong ties and weak ties are important sources of business information and
contracts, and the combination of the two kinds of ties offers the strongest help for

Table 2.4 Capital investment by sector-crossing ties

		Start-Up Capital (RMB¥)		
		<10,000	*10,000–100,000*	*>100,000*
Social ties in one sector	35.0%	43.8%	34.2%	16.3%
Social ties across sectors	65.0%	56.2%	65.8%	83.8%
Number of cases	452	185	187	80
		Pearson Chi square = 18.6967, p. < 0.001		

capitalizing self-employment opportunities. This finding urges us to go beyond tie strength to ask whether boundary-crossing ties are more effective channels than within-boundary ties for the Chinese to capture self-employment opportunities. In transitional China, the most important structural boundary is that between the state and nonstate sectors, and those who have sector-crossing ties enjoy more earning opportunities than counterparts without them (Bian et al. 2012). Basically, the state is in control of governmental grants and projects, and the nonstate sector is a source of market-related resources and opportunities. The following two case studies offer interesting details about the value of social ties that combine the distinctive resources of the state and nonstate sectors.

Mr. Meng is the head of a state-owned enterprise. Although his enterprise had stable revenue, he was under strong pressure to generate extrabudgetary earnings in order to increase the income of his employees. Through his close connection to the executive vice president of a listed company, Mr. Meng developed a series of personnel training projects in collaboration with the listed company. Mr. Meng's enterprise supplied instructors for these projects, and the listed company operated them by using financially flexible arrangements. These collaborated projects became an impressive source of extrabudgetary income for Mr. Meng's enterprise and its employees.

Ms. Zeng is self-employed and operates an interior design and decoration company. Her most reliable business is a long-term contract with a large state-owned construction firm, where one of the executives is her close relative. She frequently obtains reliable internal information from this relative, which helps her win the competition for profitable interior design and decoration projects from this firm.

While the above stories discuss how people in the state and nonstate sectors seek and maintain earning opportunities through close social ties, the 2009 survey shows that sector-crossing ties are an important channel for raising the capital investments for starting a self-employed business. The results are presented in Table 2.4.

The 2009 survey included questions about how many visitors the respondents had received at home during the weeklong celebration of the previous Chinese New Year (Spring Festival) and whether these New Year's visitors worked for a state or nonstate employer. Among the 452 self-employed respondents who answered the questions, 35 percent had New Year's visitors who worked in one sector (state or nonstate), and 65 percent had some New Year's visitors who worked in the state sector while others worked in the nonstate sector. We consider the first group as having social ties in one sector, and the second group as having social ties across the sectors. Table 2.1 shows a clear pattern regarding the advantage of the sector-crossing group in mobilizing a greater amount of start-up investment capital.

Social-eating ties and self-employment

Extensive social contacts are potentially helpful to the business success of the self-employed, but these social contacts are not always available or willing to help. In the Chinese context, frequent interactions through social eating, drinking, and entertainment are important opportunities for maintaining, enhancing, elevating, and deepening the relational bonding, interpersonal trustworthiness, and mutual obligations among those who are connected to each other. In fact, social eating – eating a meal with significant others for the purpose of social activities – has been an important social network generator in the Chinese context (Bian 2001). The more social-eating activities in which one participates, the more capacity one has for mobilizing resources from social contacts, as the following case study demonstrates.

Mr. Zhang was a college teacher who became acquainted with a manager in charge of the logistics of the college. Over the years, Mr. Zhang frequently invited him to dinners, where his generosity, friendliness, and interpersonal strategies helped him to develop new friends, mostly introduced to him by the manager. Through social drinking and eating, these people became his friends. When they heard of his idea to open a Korean restaurant near the college, they all offered to help. One helped secure a good location with low rent, another helped find food supplies of high quality but at reasonable prices, and still others helped introduce chefs and skilled workers. The issues of official inspection and business emergencies also arose, but Zhang never needed to worry because his drinking and eating friends "voluntarily" offered help to solve these problems. By the time of the 2009 survey, Zhang's restaurant had been open for several years, and both his business and his social drinking and eating networks were increasing.

Mr. Zhang's story demonstrates that social capital tends to be mobilized through social activities. In the case of self-employed people, the capacity to mobilize resources through social activities is important for their business development. On the other hand, in order to maintain and develop business, the self-employed are much more willing to engage in such social interactions as social eating, drinking, or entertaining. The 2009 survey compares the features of the social networks of the self-employed and those of employees.

The first two variables in Table 2.5 about resource mobilizing capacities were developed through involvement in social eating. The indicators contributing to these two composite scores (the first is the factor score from a factor analysis

Table 2.5 Features of social networks for the self-employed and employees

Variables	a. Self-Employed		b. Employee		c. T-Test for
	Mean	S.D.	Mean	S.D.	a – b
Resource mobilizing capacity via social eating (factor score)	0.27	1.05	−0.02	0.93	p. < .001
Resource mobilizing capacity via social eating (Likert scale)	14.05	5.32	12.54	4.74	p. < .001
Number of New Year's visitors	31.72	38.85	26.79	34.84	p. < .001
Number of occupations in which New Year's visitors work	5.69	4.29	5.25	3.95	p. < .01
Highest prestige of New Year's visitors	−0.11	0.83	0.01.	0.74	p. < .001

and the second a Likert scale summing up the values of the contributing indicators) include frequency of social-eating involvement, frequency of being a social-eating host, frequency of being a social-eating invitee, and frequency of developing new friends through social eating. In these two variables, the higher the values, the greater the capacity one has to mobilize resources through social-eating networks. As can be seen, the self-employed are significantly higher in both variables than employees. The factor score is a standard score with the mean of 0 and a standard deviation of 1. Table 2.4 shows that the self-employed have a mean factor score of resource mobilizing capacity of 0.27, which is much higher than the −.02 obtained by employees. Similarly, the Likert-scale measure shows a mean of 14.05 for the self-employed, which is significantly higher than the mean of 12.54 for employees.

Other measures in Table 2.5 concern features of social networks based on New Year's visitations. As can be shown, the self-employed are significantly higher in the magnitudes of all three measures than employees. Specifically, the self-employed had an average of 31.72 visitors during the weeklong celebration of the previous Chinese New Year, significantly higher than the 26.79 for employees. This means that the self-employed have larger social networks than employees. Next, the 31.72 visitors for the self-employed group worked in 5.69 occupations on average (out of ten different occupations on the questionnaire), which is also significantly higher than the 5.25 occupations in which employees' visitors worked. This implies that the self-employed not only have larger social networks than employees but that their social networks are also occupationally more diverse. Finally, the highest occupational prestige of visitors for the self-employed group is −.11 (on a standard-score scale), which is significantly lower than the .01 for employees. This indicates that the self-employed are connected to more and diverse people, yet these people are somewhat lower in the occupational hierarchy than employees' visitors. Note that the employees comprise an occupationally diverse group of managers, professionals, and skilled and unskilled laborers.

Theoretical reflections and conclusions

The above case studies of a few self-employed informants and the 2009 survey show that social networks and social capital are important factors for the Chinese in starting and succeeding in self-employment. We have identified three dimensions of social networks and social capital – tie strength, boundary crossing, and resource mobilizing capacity, and each is relevant and useful for self-employment development. Here we discuss the theoretical plausibility of these dimensions in relation to self-employment.

Tie strength is a universal variable measuring personal social networks; start-up capital and business information are two kinds of important resources that can be mobilized from both strong ties and weak ties. We found that the strong ties of kin and pseudokin relations are important, not only in helping the self-employed to obtain a sufficient amount of start-up capital, but also in providing an important source of encouragement and emotional support for moving toward self-employment in the fast-changing and highly uncertain Chinese economy. Meanwhile, weak ties can help the self-employed obtain valuable information about self-employment and business opportunities, although capitalizing on the information and opportunities depends heavily on the financial and emotional support provided by strong ties. The combination of strong ties and weak ties presents the best social capital for the self-employed to move forward and realize their entrepreneurial dreams.

Both strong ties and weak ties are useful if they are boundary-spanning ties. Although Granovetter (1973) assumes that only weak ties can cut across group boundaries, the Chinese tend to have strong ties with their New Year's visitors, but two-thirds of them have strong-tie visitors from both the state and nonstate sectors. We found that self-employed individuals whose social ties cross the two sectors are more successful in securing start-up capital and in obtaining valuable business information for their business development. The sector-crossing social capital of the self-employed helps them to secure state-tailored resources and market-oriented opportunities. More generally, when information, opportunities, and resources are structured within economic sectors, sector-crossing social networks can mobilize them more effectively. In so doing, sector-crossing social networks are the most useful social capital for the self-employed in transitional China.

For the self-employed, tie strength and sector-crossing ties are instrumentally meant for one thing: to mobilize the resources (including information and opportunities) embedded in the networks of social contacts. However, tie strength and sector-crossing ties will not produce resource mobilization themselves; the self-employed individual must take action to mobilize embedded resources from these networks of social ties. Our study shows that the self-employed have greater resource mobilizing capacities through their social drinking and eating networks than employees precisely because they have an instrumental goal to achieve: They want to maintain and develop their businesses. During China's economic transformation, business laws and market regulations are not being effectively enforced by the state or other formal institutions, contributing to high institutional and market uncertainties. These uncertainties open up the space in which resources are by and large mobilized through the networks of social contacts. While this feature of Chinese economic growth has been characterized in a model of "network capitalism" (Boisot and Child 1996; Lin 2011), our analysis of the self-employed presents further evidence on the resource mobilizing capacities of social-eating networks.

These theoretical discussions lead to two conclusions. First, while the Schumpeterian term "entrepreneurship" points to the importance of the capitalist spirit of risk taking and innovation, our study shows that the process of becoming an entrepreneur occurs in a social environment in which information, opportunity, and relevant resources can be obtained without structural and cultural constraints. Networks of social contacts are an important force of social capital for the self-employed because they help them obtain these kinds of resources when starting a self-employment arrangement. Second, Confucian culture advocates conformity with the norms and does not encourage adventure, risk taking, or entrepreneurship. Yet China's market reforms present real opportunities for self-employment, and moving toward an entrepreneurial work life is realized by the mobilization of social capital resources through the networks of social contacts (Bian and Zhang 2014). These networks are multidimensional and can be captured by the variables of tie strength, boundary-crossing ties, and the resource mobilizing capacities of the self-employed through social interactions. The opportunities and success of a self-employment arrangement are partly the manifestation of these social networking dynamics.

References

Allen, David. 2000. "Social Networks and Self-Employment." *Journal of Social-Economics* 29 (5): 487–501.

Arrow, K. 1998. "What Has Economics to Say about Racial Discrimination." *Journal of Economic Perspectives* 12: 91–100.

Barbieri, Paolo. 2003. "Social Capital and Self-Employment." *International Sociology* 18 (4): 681–701.

Bian, Yanjie. 1997. "Bringing Strong Ties Back In: Indirect Ties, Network Bridges, and Job Searches in China." *American Sociological Review* 62 (3): 366–385.

Bian, Yanjie. 2001. "*Guanxi* Capital and Social Eating: Theoretical Models and Empirical Analyses." In *Social Capital: Theory and Research*, edited by Nan Lin, Karen Cook, and Ronald Burt, 275–295. New York: Aldine de Gruyter.

Bian, Yanjie. 2006. "Guanxi." In *International Encyclopedia of Economic Sociology*, edited by J. Beckert and M. Zafirovski, 312–314. London: Routledge.

Bian, Yanjie. 2008. "Born out of Networks: A Sociological Analysis of the Emergence of the Firm." In *Chinese Entrepreneurship in a Global Era*, edited by R. Wong, 166–182. London and New York: Routledge.

Bian, Yanjie. 2010. "Relational Sociology and Its Academic Significance." *Journal of Xi'an Jiaotong University (Social Sciences)* 30 (May): 1–6.

Bian, Yanjie, and Lei Zhang. 2014. "Corporate Social Capital in Chinese Guanxi Culture." *Research in the Sociology of Organizations* 40: 417–439.

Bian, Yanjie, R. Breiger, D. Davis, and J. Galaskiewicz. 2005. "Occupation, Class, and Social Networks in Urban China." *Social Forces* 83: 1443–1468.

Bian, Yanjie, Wenbin Wang, Lei Zhang, and Cheng Cheng. 2012. "Sector-Crossing Social Capital and Its Impact on Wage Income." *Chinese Social Sciences* 2: 110–126.

Bian, Yanjie, and X. Huang. 2009. "Network Resources and Job Mobility in China's Transitional Economy." *Research in the Sociology of Work* 19: 255–282.

Bian, Yanjie, Xianbi Huang, and Lei Zhang. 2015. "Information and Favoritism: The Network Effect on Wage Income in China." *Social Networks* 40: 129–138.

Boisot, Max, and John Child. 1996. "From Fiefs to Clans and Network Capitalism: Explaining China's Emerging Economic Order." *Administrative Science Quarterly* 41: 600–628.

Burt, R. 1992. *Structural Holes: The Social Structure of Competition*. Cambridge, MA: Harvard University Press.

Butterfield, F. 1982. *China: Alive in the Bitter Sea*. New York: Bantam Books.

Carlisle, E., and D. Flynn. 2005. "Small Business Survival in China: *Guanxi*, Legitimacy, and Social Capital." *Journal of Developmental Entrepreneurship* 10: 79–96.

Fei, X. 1949/1992. *From the Soil, the Foundations of Chinese Society*. A Translation of Fei Xiaotong's *Xiangtu Zhongguo*, with an Introduction and Epilogue by G. Hamilton and W. Zheng. Berkeley: University of California Press.

Gold, T., D. Guthrie, and D. Wank. 2002. *Social Connections: Institutions, Culture, and the Changing Nature of Guanxi*. New York: Cambridge University Press.

Gomez Arias, J. 1998. "A Relationship Marketing Approach to *Guanxi*." *European Journal of Marketing* 32: 145–156.

Granovetter, Mark. 1973. "The Strength of Weak Ties." *American Journal of Sociology* 78 (6): 1360–1380.

Granovetter, Mark. 1974. *Getting a Job: A Study of Contacts and Careers*. Cambridge, MA: Harvard University Press.

Granovetter, Mark, 1995. Afterword: Reconsiderations and a New Agenda. In *Getting a Job*, pp.139–182. Chicago: University of Chicago Press.

King, A. 1985. "The Individual and Group in Confucianism: A Relational Perspective." In *Individualism and Holism: Studies in Confucian and Taoist Values*, edited by D. Munro, 57–70. Ann Arbor, MI: Center for Chinese Studies, University of Michigan.

King, A. 1994. "Kuan-his and Network Building: A Sociological Interpretation." In *The Living Tree: The Changing Meaning of Being Chinese Today*, edited by W. Tu, 109–126. Stanford, CA: Stanford University Press.

Lin, Nan. 1982. "Social Resources and Instrumental Action." In *Social Structure and Network Analysis*, edited by W. Tu, P. V. Marsden, and N. Lin, 131–145. Beverly Hills, CA: Sage.

Lin, Nan. 1999. Social networks and status attainment. *Annual Review of Sociology* 25: 467–488.

Lin, Nan. 2001. "Guanxi: A Conceptual Analysis." In *The Chinese Triangle of Mainland, Taiwan, and Hong Kong: Comparative Institutional Analysis*, edited by W. Tu, A. So, N. Lin, and D. Poston, 153–166. Westport, CT: Greenwood.

Lin, Nan. 2011. "Capitalism in China: A Centrally Managed Capitalism (CMC) and Its Future." *Management and Organization Review* 7: 63–96.

Lovett, S., L. Simmons, and R. Kali. 1999. "*Guanxi* Versus the Market: Ethics and Efficiency." *Journal of International Business Studies* 30: 231–247.

Mitchell, J. 1969. "The Concept and Use of Social Networks." In *Social Networks in Urban Situations: Analyses of Personal Relationships in Central African Towns*, edited by J. Mitchell, 1–50. New York: Humanities Press, Inc.

Montgomery, J.D. 1991. "Job Search and Network Composition: Implications of the Strength-of-Weak-Ties Hypothesis." *American Sociological Review* 57: 586–596.

Mouw, T. 2003. "Social Capital and Finding a Job: Do Contacts Matter?" *American Sociological Review* 68: 868–898.

Parnell, M. 2005. "Chinese Business *Guanxi*: An Organization or Non-organization?" *Journal of Organisational Transformation and Social Change* 2: 29–47.

Portes, A. 1995. "Economic Sociology and the Sociology of Immigration: A Conceptual Overview." In *The Economic Sociology of Immigration Essays on Networks, Ethnicity, and Entrepreneurship*, edited by A. Portes, 1–41. New York: Russell Sage Foundation.

Walder, A. 1986. *Communist Neo-Traditionalism: Work and Authority in Chinese Society.* Berkeley: University of California Press.

Wang, Wenbin, and Yandong Zhao. 2012. "A Social Network Analysis of One's Becoming Self-Employed." *Chinese Journal of Sociology* 3: 78–97.

Wong, S. 1988. *Emigrant Entrepreneurs: Shanghai Industrialists in Hong Kong.* New York: Oxford University Press.

Xie, Yu. 2014. "The Chinese People's Livelihood Development Report 2014." Beijing: Peking University Press.

Yan, Y. 1996. *The Flow of Gifts: Reciprocity and Social Networks in a Chinese Village.* Stanford, CA: Stanford University Press.

Yang, M. 1994. *Gifts, Favors, and Banquets: The Art of Social Relationships in China.* Ithaca, NY: Cornell University Press.

Yeung, I., and R. Tung. 1996. "Achieving Business Success in Confucian Societies: The Importance of Guanxi (Connections)." *Organizational Dynamics* 25: 54–65.

3 *Guanxi*-based corporate social capital and Chinese entrepreneurship

Lei Zhang

How can we explain the business success of private enterprises in China? What makes this issue more challenging is the fact that "private-sector growth in China has taken place in an environment that is openly hostile to entrepreneurs and private businesses" (Tsai 2002). Among all possible interpretations, the social networks and social capital explanations are believed to be more powerful and convincing (Fong and Chen 2007; Nee and Opper 2012). In this chapter, I contribute to this stream of relational explanations by conceptualizing Chinese *guanxi*-based corporate social capital as an isotopic substitution of Western weak-tie-based corporate social capital and using it to explain the establishment, development, and prosperity of small and medium-sized enterprises (SMEs) in contemporary China.

To demonstrate the explanation power of *guanxi*-based corporate social capital, I incorporate four interview stories as supporting materials for my propositions. This chapter concludes with a methodological discussion on how Western researchers measure *guanxi*-based corporate social capital and differentiate it from similar concepts of friendship, *ganqing*, *mianzi*, and *renqing*.

Definition and benefits of corporate social capital

Social capital refers to productive benefits (Coleman 1988; 1990) derived from structures and resources in networks (Bourdieu 1986; Baker 1990; 2000; Burt 1992; Lin 2001a; 2001b) composed of durable interpersonal connections (Granovetter 1985) and membership affiliations (Putnam 2000). Following the idea of network-embedded economic activities (Granovetter 1985; 1992; Moran 2005), in this research I define the corporate social capital of SMEs as productive benefits that are derived from entrepreneurs' personal social networks and facilitate business establishment, development, and performance. The productive benefits of corporate social capital include (1) information sharing and resource mobilization and (2) trust, shared norms, and commitment.

Information sharing and resource mobilization

Social capital theory predicts that social ties linking a focal entrepreneur to his/her resourceful peers act as "channels or conduits through which 'market stuff' flows"

(Podolny 2001, 33). The "market stuff" refers to any business-related information and resource, yet not all social ties are equally effective to channel "market stuff." A widely accepted theoretical prediction is that weak ties connecting heterogeneous network members are more capable of sharing nonredundant and diversified information and resources (Granovetter 1973). In addition to being channels, weak ties bridging structural holes generate a structural advantage to better synthesize information and control resource flows, which in turn promotes productivity (Burt 2005).

Empirical studies in Western societies largely confirm the power of weak ties. First, studies on network information sharing show that weak ties provide cost-effective channels for diffusing highly diversified knowledge across organizational borders in both domestic (Bouty 2000; Walter et al. 2007) and international (Presutti et al. 2007) markets. A recent meta-analysis of 258 research articles on the knowledge transfer of small organizations (Macpherson and Holt 2007) again confirms the information benefit of weak ties. Second, besides information sharing, weak ties also connect focal entrepreneurs to actors in formal capital markets, such as commercial banks (Uzzi 1999), venture capital firms and investment banks (Gulati and Higgins 2003), and seed investors (Shane and Cable 2002), and to members in informal friendship networks (e.g., Bates 1997) to extract financial resources. Third, among all weak ties, a special kind of weak tie that bridges network structural holes not only channel more diversified resources (e.g., Burt 2004; Uzzi and Spiro 2005) but also provide tie holders with stronger bargaining power, more choices to manipulate resource flows, more effective ways to reinforce strategic alliances, and as a result better business performance (Mizruchi and Glaskiewicz 1993; Powell et al. 1999).

Trust, shared norms, and commitment

Weak ties not only transfer information and resources but also carry social values such as trust, norms, and commitment to long-term interactions. These social values gradually attach to social ties via repeated economic interactions and stable membership (Bourdieu 1986) and lubricate resource flows (Moran 2005). First, trust attached to social ties secures economic transactions by reducing opportunistic behaviors and unforeseeable uncertainties (Coase 1937; Williamson 1981), and trust self-reinforces during repeated interactions (Buskens and Weesie 2000). As a critical component of social capital (Putnam 1993; 2000), trust makes social capital an effective governance structure for controlling moral risks and related transaction costs (Ring and Van de Ven 1992; Powell and Smith-Doerr 1994; Provan and Kenis 2008).

Next, productive norms diffusing across social ties generate solidarity, smooth coordination, and a public good of "value-based business integration" that benefits all network members (Cousins et al. 2006). Research demonstrates some important productive norms are diffused through social networks, such as common goals and mutual interests, community responsibilty (Grangsjo and Gummesson 2006), willingness to collaborate (Rottman 2008), and moral expectations of acceptable business behaviors (Biggart and Castanias 2001). Among all norms, social capital particularly emphasizes commitment to long-term and stable social connections among business actors. Strong commitments lower the costs of buyers (Krause et al. 2007), increase the market reputation of suppliers (Luo et al. 2004), and foster reciprocity in future transactions (Carney 2005).

Dimensions and isotopes of corporate social capital

As reviewed above, findings in Western societies largely confirm that corporate social capital derived from weak ties promotes business performance. This theory is labeled the "weak-tie-based corporate social capital theory." Is weak-tie theory the only workable explanation of business performance in the relational perspective? Is establishing weak ties a universally effective solution to exert the productive power of social capital for all kinds of businesses across time and nations?

My answer is "No" because empirical counterexamples clearly show that weak-tie theory is conditional. For example, recent research has already questioned the validity of weak-tie theory by demonstrating the contingent efficiency of weak ties at different developing stages of companies (*timing contingency*) (Maurer and Ebers 2006), for companies of different ownership and size (*demographic contingency*) (Peng and Luo 2000), in economies with different levels of marketization (*environmental contingency*) (Batjargal 2003; Martinsons 2008), and so on (see Adler and Kwon 2002 for other contingencies). In addition to these challenges, Confucian traditions of strong-tie preference, person- and situation-specific moral standards, and the reluctance to take advantage of network members via brokering ties has already been identified as a *cultural contingency* of the weak-tie theory that cannot be ignored (Bian 1997; 2008; Burt et al. 2000; Xiao and Tsui 2007).

These contingencies lead to an inspiring question: Is weak-tie theory just one special case of all possible social capital theories? An analytical decomposition of the concept of social capital is the first step to answer this theoretical question.

Social capital "clearly is not a unidimensional concept" (Putnam 1995, 76); this concept contains at least three analytical dimensions: the relational dimension, the structural dimension, and the moral dimension (Nahapiet and Ghoshal 1998). The relational dimension of social capital comes from the idea of "relational embeddedness" (Granovetter 1992) and refers to the concrete and ongoing content of social ties, such as levels of "being particular," levels of trust and trustworthiness, and other emotional attachments. Tie strength is a direct measurement of this dimension. Strong relations are so mutually particular and are more powerful in mobilizing resources and influence and less likely to decay. In contrast, weak relations are less mutually particular, less irreplaceable, and more likely to decay but have the power to connect more diversified contacts. The structural dimension of social capital is rooted in the idea of "structural embeddedness" (Granovetter 1992) and refers to impersonal network structures that can be measured by tie simplexity versus tie multiplexity. A social tie is simplex if it carries only one function or fulfills only one purpose; a social tie is multiplex if it carries multiple functions (Coleman 1988; Shipilov and Li 2014). The origin of the moral dimension of social capital can be traced back to Bourdieu's observation on the durable obligations of network members that entitle them to credit "the collectivity-owned capital" (1986, 249). The variation in feeling obliged to provide resources to network members is a direct measure of this dimension. Some networks have a strong culture of reciprocity, and members in such networks are subjected to a socially coercive power to be reciprocal. Other networks do not carry such a culture; reciprocal behaviors in these networks are largely optional and usually based on rational calculations of investments versus gains.

Different combinations of these three dimensions generate social capital based on different network configurations (Nahapiet and Ghoshal 1998) and bring different benefits to socially embedded actors. In this research, I push this idea one step further to define isotopes of social capital in the following way:

> Social capitals with *different* dimensional configurations are *isotopes* of each other if they fulfill the *same* set of functions.

Theories relating *isotopic* social capitals to a given outcome are competing social capital theories in the relational perspective. These theories share one identical proposition: Social networks are productive. These theories differ in determining which social networks are more productive in what context. For example, weak-tie-based corporate social capital has a configuration of low particularism, simplexity, and low obligations, and weak-tie theory explains the business performance of some enterprises in Western societies. In China's cultural context, *guanxi*-based corporate social capital has a configuration of high particularism, multiplexity, and strong obligations, and it fulfills the same business functions in China as weak ties do in the West. Therefore, *guanxi*-based corporate social capital and weak-tie-based corporate social capital are isotopes, and a theory of how *guanxi* facilitates business performance in China qualifies as a social capital theory in a relational perspective that competes with weak-tie theory.

In the second half of this chapter, I will elaborate a theoretical framework to show how *guanxi*-based corporate social capital acts as an isotope of weak-tie-based corporate social capital in a Chinese context. In addition, I accommodate interview stories as supportive materials.

Guanxi-based corporate social capital

A social network definition of guanxi

The term *guanxi* is a cultural concept that is commonly used in Chinese everyday language; its meaning is similar to "relationships" or "connections" in English.[1] However, the exact meaning of *guanxi* cannot "adequately be expressed by an English-language equivalent of one word, the concept is too culture specific" (Parnell 2005, 35). To incorporate this cultural concept into the discourse of social capital theories, a *guanxi* tie is defined as a particular instrumental tie (Walder 1986; Hwang 1987; 2001; Yang 1994) or "a dyadic, particular and sentimental tie that has potential of facilitating favor exchanges between the parties connected by the tie" (Bian 2006, 312).

Several key words in Bian's definition of *guanxi* deserve a much closer look. First, *guanxi* ties in either situation are "mutually special and beneficial for both parties" (Bian and Zhang 2014, 424). In China, strong ties among family members and relatives are culturally defined as particular ties. In addition, nonkin weak ties also have the potential to become strong and pseudokin ties if both parties decide to conduct frequent and long-term interactions, during which kinlike sentiments accumulate over those ties. Next, various interpersonal sentiments are crucial components of *guanxi*, such as personal face (*mianzi*), personal feeling (*renqing*), and personal attachment (*ganqing*) (Hwang 1987; Kipnis 1997; Lee and Dawes 2005). The accumulation of those sentiments continuously increases the level of "being particular" over time.

Lastly, *guanxi* ties are used to channel favors, which refers to "substantial help that produces decisive outcome or influence on others to get things done" (Bian and Zhang 2014, 425). In Chinese culture, favors are an extremely valuable resource that can be exchanged exclusively through *guanxi* ties in a reciprocal manner. In this research, favors observed in interviews include interest-free borrowing, insider-only market information and business opportunities, exclusive technical know-how, franchised marketing channels, highly discounted logistic services, and government purchases. Favor exchanges are reciprocal in nature— favor receivers carry moral obligations and psychological pressure to repay favor granters, and granters expect obligated favor paybacks from receivers in the future (King 1985; 1994).

Guanxi-*based corporate social capital: theory, propositions, and empirical supports*

I define *guanxi*-based corporate social capital as productive benefits derived from entrepreneurs' *guanxi* ties that facilitate business establishment, development, and performance. As an isotope of Western weak-tie corporate social capital, *guanxi*-based corporate social capital fulfills functions of information/resource sharing and moral value injections in Chinese business. Empirical studies show that Chinese *guanxi*-based corporate social capital acts as a conduit for information and resource flows (Parnell 2005), which are crucial to business performance (Luo and Chen 1997). At the same time, *guanxi*-based corporate social capital promotes trust among kin and pseudokin network members, defuses shared norms of proper behaviors, and generates commitment to long-term reciprocal obligations (Cheng 1995; Li and Liang 2002; Wang and Liu 2002; Bu 2003). Empirical studies also show that these productive benefits cannot be effectively fulfilled by Western-style weak-tie-based corporate capital (Standifird and Marshall 2000; Carlisle and Flynn 2005).

In addition to functional similarities, the analytical dimensions of *guanxi*-based corporate social capital qualify *guanxi*-based corporate social capital as an isotopic substitution of its Western weak-tie-based counterpart. The corporate social capital that prevails in Western societies tends to be based on weak ties of simplex productive functions and low mutual obligations. In contrast, Chinese *guanxi*-based corporate social capital contains particular strong ties, and each strong tie tends to fulfill multiple functions and carries strong moral obligations of reciprocal favor exchanges.

Particularism

High particularism differentiates *guanxi*-based corporate social capital from weak-tie-based corporate social capital in the relational dimension of social capital. *Guanxi* ties meet the definition of ties that are strong in "emotional intensity, the intimacy (mutual confiding), and the reciprocal services" (Granovetter 1973, 1361). But the term "strong tie" cannot fully capture the particular nature of *guanxi* ties because *guanxi* is more complicated in its social meanings and much richer in functions than Westerners' understanding of strong ties.

First, *guanxi* ties are strong ties connecting egos to diversified network members and resources. In Western societies, the term "strong ties" refers to kinship ties among family members and relatives. As a result, the attributes of network members tend to be homophilous. *Guanxi* ties are strong but contain not only relatives but also a large number of pseudokin members. Pseudokin is a unique aspect of the Chinese culture of "differential mode of association" (*cha xu ge ju*) (Fei 1947/1992). *Guanxi* represents a special type of strong ties that gradually emerge from actively attaching kinlike sentiment, intimacy, and various moral expectations to nonblood relationships. In China, pseudokin ties usually include ties among classmates (people socialized in the same environment from childhood to early adulthood), *laoxiang* (people born and/or raised up in the same geographic area and share the same cultural identities), comrades-in-arms (people who share the same collective memories of harsh conditions or even of life-or-death experiences), and patron-client relationships in the workplace (traditional Confucian ideology expects the leader-subordinate or teacher-student relation to follow similar moral standards as father-son and king-subject relations). *Guanxi* culture has a tendency to continuously turn more and more heterogeneous network members into pseudokin so that the diversified needs of exchanging insider-only favors can be met. The exclusive nature of favors requires a certain level of particularism as a precondition to initiating exchanges. As a result, the process of "pseudokinization" that enables subsequent flows of favors eventually leads to an expanding inner circle of one's *guanxi* network to include resourcefully diversified contacts. Therefore, the Western definition of "strong tie" only captures ties between relatives in a *guanxi* network and ignores pseudokin ties.

Second, *guanxi* generates person-specific moral standards. The differential mode of association, as a cultural tradition and a value system, prevents Chinese from establishing a universal moral standard (especially general trust) that is applicable to general others. Instead, Chinese culture generates different norms for treating people of different social distances, and conditions Chinese people to be very sensitive to slight differences in social distance. For example, taking advantage of core network members cannot be tolerated and will result in severe social sanctions, while playing opportunistic tricks on network outsiders is accepted as a clever move for the collective interests of insiders. As a result, higher levels of particularism in China lead to stronger person-specific trust and trustworthiness, which can later be used to facilitate business transactions. The lack of particularism brings higher moral risks in business transactions and harms performance.

The particularism of *guanxi* demonstrates the power of strong ties in China. This feature of *guanxi* ties contradicts the theoretical conclusion of weak ties (Granovetter 1973; Burt 2005). The ultimate reason for this difference in theoretical predictions is the difference in the nature of resource exchangeability across network boundaries. The power of weak ties is a true prediction only when resources are exchangeable across network boundaries. If this precondition is not true, strong ties will become the only network solution for mobilizing insider-only resources. Take information as an example. In the West, codified information can be easily transferred through strong and weak ties. Compared to strong-tie contacts in Western contexts, weak-tie contacts are more heterogeneous and therefore are more capable of providing diversified information. This is the power of weak ties. In contrast, in China, codified and reliable information is very rare in the public domain (Martinsons 2008). Instead, high-quality information that is timely, reliable, and accurate is isolated in inner circles of networks, and the circulation of such productive information is considered as favor exchanges.

Proposition 1: In China, the high level of particularism facilitates business performance because such relational advantage provides guanxi network insiders with (1) the capability of mobilizing members-only favors of high-quality resources and information that can substantially fulfill diversified instrumental needs and (2) a high level of trust and trustworthiness guaranteed by kinlike sentiment in guanxi ties.

THE STORY OF MR. W

Mr. W, a forty-seven-year-old in 2002, was previously a farmer in the rural outskirts of Town D. He had only a primary school education. In 1982, he established a small furniture workshop in Town D. Although Mr. W grew up in a rural area, he had a strong global vision even at the early stages of his business. After twenty years of promoting traditional Chinese rosewood furniture overseas, Mr. W's company expanded from a tiny backyard workshop to a 20,000 square-meter R&D and manufacturing compound with more than 500 employees. By 2002, Mr. W's company had become the leading competitor in the local rosewood furniture industry in Town D. With over 180 different designs in five production lines, Mr. W earned an outstanding reputation in the overseas luxury furniture markets in the United States, Singapore, Malaysia, Hong Kong, Macau, and Taiwan.

In 1982, when opening and reforming policies took effect in Town D, Mr. W decided to start his own business. At that time, the initial funds of around RMB¥4,000 represented a huge amount of money for an ordinary rural family.

Almost all of his initial investments came from his brothers and sisters, particularly his close relatives in Hong Kong who had enough money to invest and strong incentives to help relatives who were fighting against poverty. The money Mr. W obtained from relatives in Hong Kong carried no interest, and there was no repayment date. Both Mr. W and his relatives in Hong Kong treated the investment funds as family support with strong kinship sentiment rather than a for-profit investment.

In addition to these initial investments, *guanxi* with relatives and close friends in Town D also provided Mr. W with skilled labor. In the early stages of Mr. W's business, none of the workers had experience in organizing and running a small family-owned furniture workshop. A strong feeling of belonging and a shared vision to significantly improve family living standards generated a persistently high level of work incentives. In this learning-by-doing stage, the workers in Mr. W's small factory worked like a family and eventually overcame difficulties in product design, manufacturing, and marketing.

Years later, some of these founding members left W's company and started their own businesses in various industries. Starting their own businesses did not cut their strong ties with Mr. W. Instead, these founding members became crucial in the later developmental stages of Mr. W's company. First, these strong ties guaranteed frequent face-to-face communication, which provided Mr. W with up-to-date, diversified, and trustworthy insider-only information about good ideas for production designs, latest market demands, new business orders, and so on. Second, during the expansion of their own businesses, these founding members also established new network ties and then connected Mr. W to their new friends with more diversified resources. At one point, Mr. W faced an unexpected shortage of diesel fuel for his machines and did not have enough cash to buy fuel from the market. One of the founding members knew of Mr. W's difficulty and quickly introduced Mr. W to a factory owner in his new network who happened to have some extra diesel fuel reserves. Mr. W immediately signed a borrowing contract with this new friend and agreed to repay the same amount of diesel fuel in a few months at no interest. Finally, when founding members successfully expanded their own businesses, they were more capable of providing more frequent and stronger financial support to Mr. W. It was a constant challenge for luxury rosewood furniture companies to maintain enough cash flow, but the interest rate of short-term loans from commercial banks tended to be very high. It was therefore very common for Mr. W to borrow money from strong-tie network members for an interval of several months to buy raw materials, pay wages, and cover other related expenses before receiving payments from his customers. Such short-term borrowing was treated as a favor exchange since strong-tie network members have the obligation to help one another. Usually these short-term loans carried no or a very low interest rates due to the high level of pseudokin sentiment.

Strong *guanxi* culture in Town D and frequent face-to-face interactions and favor exchanges among entrepreneurs gave birth to a trade association for local rosewood furniture industry. As the elected deputy chairman of this association, Mr. W benefitted a lot. First, taking such a central position in this formal organization was a strong market signal that further promoted the trustworthiness and reputation of Mr. W's company in the domestic rosewood industry. Second, the local trade association demonstrated the power of collective bargaining based on strong solidarity and close coordination. Due to the lack of trust between furniture companies and logistic service providers, shipping costs used to be very high, and severe damages even complete loss of very expensive furniture happened frequently. After the local trade association came to be, this formal organization signed long-term bulk-shipping contracts with several highly trustworthy shipping companies. Instead of negotiating and paying deposits individually for each shipment, the shipping companies paid the association a highly discounted amount of deposit at once, and any damages or contract defaults would be deducted and paid to the shipper directly from this pool of deposits. That formal arrangement lowered shipping costs significantly and effectively avoided opportunistic behaviors of logistic companies.

Multiplexity

Multiplexity differentiates *guanxi*-based corporate social capital from its weak-tie-based counterparts in the structural dimension. Multiplexed ties, or "multi-stranded ties," were first studied by anthropologists (e.g., Mitchell 1969; Verbrugge 1979, 1287) and defined as "the overlap of roles, exchanges, or affiliations in a social relationship" (Verbrugge 1979, 1286). Among social network analysts, Coleman's (1988) term of "appropriability" (social ties of one kind can be used to achieve other purposes), Hwang's concept of "mixed ties" (1987), and a more recent study on multiplexity (Shipilov and Li 2014) demonstrate how this phenomenon can be integrated into social capital theories.

Guanxi ties tend to be multiplexed. A *guanxi* tie usually fulfills diversified functions that "mix qualitatively different norms of exchange, namely, expressive with instrumental, social with economic, symbolic with material, personal with public, friendship with businesslike, [and] familial with collegial"[2] (Bian and Zhang 2014, 427). First, tie multiplexity increases functional diversity for a given network size and represents a more efficient way to excavate network resources. Since *guanxi* ties are very costly and time-consuming to establish and maintain, multiplexity therefore becomes critically important in mobilizing resources with a limited number of core *guanxi* network members. Next, when a tie is multiplexed by both instrumental and emotional functions, trust and trustworthiness start to accumulate on that tie. The multiplexity nature of *guanxi* ties explains why Chinese entrepreneurs often conduct business via kin and pseudokin ties and actively attach emotional functions to important business relationships (Wong 1988). Finally, compared to people linked by simplex ties, "people in a multi-stranded relationship interact with one another in many different contexts and are therefore less likely to be able to withdraw completely from contact with one another" (Mitchell 1969, 23). That is, multiplexity provides an additional safeguard against tie decay.

Multiplexity has two implications for how *guanxi*-based corporate social capital matters to the performance of Chinese SMEs. First, multiplexed *guanxi* ties carry instrumental interests and emotional values at the same time, which increases the social cost of opportunist behaviors (people usually cannot handle the price of cheating a business partner who is also a close relative or pseudokin) so that multiplexity effectively controls transaction cost. Second, the enduring nature of multiplexed ties increases the stability of long-term business relationships. Combining these two implications results in *Proposition 2: In China, highly multiplexed guanxi ties generate structural advantages to control opportunistic behaviors and secure long-term and stable business relations, all of which facilitate performance.*

THE STORY OF MR. X

Mr. X, forty years old in 2002, was a junior high school graduate. He established his furniture company in the early 1980s in Town D. By the end of 2002, his company provided at least 200 jobs locally and reached an after-tax profit of RMB¥4.7 million. As a very profitable business specializing in designing and selling high-end rosewood furniture in the domestic luxury furniture market, his company earned a good reputation as a top-ten brand in the local furniture industry of Town D.

Guanxi provided the initial investments for Mr. X's business. Besides personal savings, Mr. X managed to obtain additional starting investments mainly from relatives and close friends. Only a small proportion of investment came from local bank loans. It was not easy to obtain financial support from state-owned banks in the early 1980s. The interest rate was very high, and the amount of loan was limited—around RMB¥2000. Local banks also required reliable guarantors as a nonnegotiable precondition to endorse the private borrower's creditworthiness. To meet this precondition, Mr. X depended heavily on close friends and relatives in his village who had known him for a long time, trusted him, and were willing to take unpredictable risks.

After Mr. X's business entered a stage of rapid expansion, informal financial support from family members, relatives, and close friends could no longer sustain the needs of constant cash flow and larger amount of hardware investment. Formal and institutionalized sources of financial supports from banks and credit unions then became crucial for the development of Mr. X's company. However, informal social connections still played an important role in obtaining loans more quickly and cheaply. Mr. X mentioned Brother[3] San (*San ge*) repeatedly during our face-to-face interview as a crucial figure who connected Mr. X to highly competitive commercial loan offers. Brother San had a strong tie with the local branch manager of state-owned Bank A. By mobilizing this tie, Mr. X obtained low-interest loans from Bank A with a much simplified and quicker loan-approval process. This special *guanxi* with Brother San, Mr. X admitted, was the first key advantage for his business success.

In addition to providing loan offers, Brother San also channeled the latest governmental policies and government purchasing opportunities to Mr. X. Brother San had close friends who worked for the local government, and some of his friends were officials who were decision makers for local commercial policies and governmental purchases. Mr. X and Brother San met frequently, and during their casual conversations, insider-only information flowed naturally from Brother San to Mr. X. More importantly, the help of Brother San and his friends in the local government were not limited to information sharing. Substantial favor exchanges could lead to highly profitable business. For example, as governmental support for the development of the local private economy, local policy loans were usually much cheaper, and their payment terms were much longer than commercial loans. However, not all private companies in the local market had equal opportunity to be financed by this policy. Help from the inside, connected through Brother San, became a competitive advantage for Mr. X.

Strong moral obligation

Levels of feeling obliged to do something that is culturally proper to do contrast *guanxi*-based corporate social capital with weak-tie-based corporate social capital in the moral dimension. Strong obligations among *guanxi* network members are culturally constructed and are deeply rooted in Confucian traditions. The core idea of moral obligations is that when interacting with *guanxi* insiders, doing things that are morally "proper" always takes priority over doing things that are rationally "correct." An extreme example is provided in the moral teaching of Confucius:

> The Duke of She informed Confucius, saying, "Among us here there are those who may be styled upright in their conduct. If their father has stolen a sheep, they will bear witness to the fact." Confucius said, "Among us, in our part of the country, those who are upright are different from this. The father conceals the misconduct of the son, and the son conceals the misconduct of the father. Uprightness is to be found in this.[4]

In this story, rather than following the legal duty of a citizen (and also a rational calculation to avoid severe punishment for concealing the truth) to report crimes honestly to officials, it is the moral obligation of the son to conceal the crime of his father. Rational calculation is not part of the son's decision-making process. Of course, this is an extreme case of practicing moral obligation. In daily business activities, practicing moral obligations is usually observed as prioritizing the interests of *guanxi* partners over selfish rational calculations. In another words, moral obligations include a set of culturally defined and mutually expected norms to provide reciprocal and unselfish favors to other *guanxi* network insiders in need. Following such moral standards also broadcasts the good reputation of helpers across the *guanxi* network and credits helpers with a moral advantage to receive larger favors in the future. Therefore, *Proposition 3: In China, culturally defined and socially coercive moral obligations provide entrepreneurs with safety nets against unpredictable market fluctuations and ensure continuous favor exchanges in the future, all of which improve performance.*

THE STORY OF MR. Y

Focusing mainly on lower-end furniture markets, Mr. Y's company in Town D was a small and young business established in 2001. By the end of 2002, around sixty full-time employees worked for Mr. Y's business, assembling cheap wooden furniture. The majority of his business orders came from domestic markets.

Compared to Mr. W and Mr. X, Mr. Y had more experience in running a private business before he established his current factory in Town D. Thirty-six years old in 2002 with a junior high school education, Mr. Y was one of the earliest to leave his hometown in Zhejiang Province to take advantage of market reforms in southeast China beginning in the early 1980s. Mobilizing *guanxi* with local administrative officials, Mr. Y began in self-employment in Shenzhen as an agent for Chung Ying Street Closed Area Entry Permits. Years later, one of his weak-tie friends invited him to join in starting a furniture factory in Zhuhai, but this business soon ran into trouble due to serious wage disputes between his friend and the workers. When Mr. Y was facing huge pressure and deciding to quit, one of his *laoxiang* in his inner *guanxi* circle, Mr. K, provided him with a huge favor. Mr. K first helped Mr. Y establish a rosewood-painting workshop in Town D then started to outsource painting and finishing projects from his furniture company to Mr. Y. To help Mr. Y out in those years, Mr. K continued to pay him outsourcing prices higher than market average. Gradually, Mr. Y not only fully recovered from his investment failure in Zhuhai but also accumulated enough money to open a new rosewood furniture showroom in Town D in the early 1990s. In the late 1990s, the profit margin of running a showroom declined dramatically, and Mr. Y decided to begin his own furniture manufacturing business in 2001.

Switching his business focus from the furniture retailing industry to furniture manufacturing was a difficult transition, but Mr. Y was very lucky. He maintained a dense *laoxiang* network in Town D (members in this network were all from Zhejiang Province and worked in Town D), and this network advantage connected him to the needed human capital and technical know-how. Several *laoxiang* in his *guanxi* network were highly experienced carpenters with high salaries and widespread reputations in Town D. They were the first group of helpers willing to quit their current jobs and switch to Y's newly established company. Quitting jobs from fully established companies to join Mr. Y's new venture was not a very rational choice—they faced the possibility of lower wages and higher risk, but "as *laoxiang*, we are obliged to help each other out." After Mr. Y's new business started to grow, he began to hire more and more *laoxiang* in Town D or from his hometown a thousand miles away.

> Most of the skilled workers, all R&D, and all managerial staff are my *laoxiang*. We speak the same language. We have similar taste in designing. We trust each other and work together like a family. Besides, we always feel mutually supported since *laoxiang* are supposed to help each other out.

Interview stories directly support three *guanxi* propositions. *Guanxi* ties that are high in particularism, heavy in multiplexity, and strong in moral obligations construct an effective corporate social capital for Chinese entrepreneurs. *Guanxi* facilitates business performance by mobilizing resources and substantial favors through particularistic strong-ties between network insiders and generates an exclusive resource advantage. *Guanxi* also improves business performance through multifunctional ties, which provide enough resource diversity and which stabilize channels for resource exchanges. Strong moral obligation attached to *guanxi* ties establishes solid relational embeddedness, increases mutual trust and trustworthiness, and acts as a safety net for both parties connected by a *guanxi* tie. Before we jump to conclusions and discussions, another interview story may serve as a contrasting example, showing that, in the current Chinese market environment, an SME relies mainly at arm's length and weak ties tends to face more challenges.

THE STORY OF MR. Z

Mr. Z, fifty-nine years old in 2012 with a BA in Economics, had a small health product company running into deep trouble. Mr. Z had around fifteen years of experience in self-employment and running small businesses. "But nothing ever went smoothly." Before becoming a business owner, Mr. Z had a middle-level managerial position in state-owned Company L. Compared to Mr. W, Mr. X, and Mr. Y, Mr. Z was less skillful in managing interpersonal relationships, and as he admitted, the lack of social networking skills was one of several reasons pushing him to leave Company L and start his own business in 1996. Mr. Z started his first interior design business in 1998 with two acquaintances that used to be clients of Company L. Since this business was not profitable as they once expected due to the lack of continual business orders in this almost saturated and highly competitive market, in 2000, it was closed for good with a huge loss of investment, most of which were borrowed from Mr. Z's family members and relatives. More horrifying experiences happened in 2004, and this time, one of Mr. Z's acquaintances introduced him to several "potential" business partners who were actually swindlers and eventually skipped off with all his investments.

After six years of recovery, in 2010, Mr. Z got a new chance to establish a small business making superoxide dismutase (SOD) liquor as a health product. Due to limited social resources with local government, it was not possible for this small business to get a distillery license. So, the only option was to bulk-buy spirit from the market. This supply-chain worked well for one and half years, and his small business was ready to see a brighter future. But, in the middle of 2011, two major spirit suppliers decided to shrink down the supply and to increase prices substantially. As a downstream firm, there was little bargaining space left for Mr. Z, and now, his small business, once again, was facing a shut down. This is the story of Mr. Z's unfortunate experiences in his fifteen years of entrepreneurship. But this is not a completely sad story. Just like Mr. Z said, "I'm still kicking. I'm adjusting myself and searching for new business partners. I won't give up."

Conclusions and discussions

Interview stories generate a clear and convincing image – Chinese *guanxi* have played indispensable roles for the establishment, development, and eventual prosperity of private-owned small and medium-sized enterprises in the past thirty years of economic reform. It is theoretically important to conceptualize Chinese *guanxi*-based corporate social capital as an isotope of corporate social capital in the Chinese cultural context and compare it to Western weak-tie corporate social capital. As a social capital derived from multifunctional strong-ties with moral obligations attached, *guanxi* make diversified and insider-only resources mobilizable through strong-tie-dominated networks, generate governance structure based on traditional moral values and with effective social sanctions to prevent opportunistic behaviors, promote mutual trust and trustworthiness, sustain long-term business exchanges, and therefore facilitate business performance. Besides its explanatory power for the business performance of SMEs, conceptualizing *guanxi* as an isotope of corporate social capital is also theoretically significant. By doing so, this unique social phenomenon in Chinese culture can be included into mainstream discourse of social capital theories and can enrich our understanding of the contingency nature and internal complexity of social capital.

Table 3.1 summarizes this conclusion that corporate social capital based on *guanxi* in the Chinese context and on old-boy networks in the West are high in particularism, multiplexity, and obligations. They clearly contrast to weak-tie and structural-hole-based corporate social capital, which carry low particularism, simplex functions, and almost no moral obligations. All these types of corporate social capital fulfill very similar productive functions, but their internal analytical dimensions take opposite values (high in three dimensions versus low in those dimensions). Besides, we can also expect to see social capital based on associational/elite networks and on kinship/ethnic networks. Those forms of social capital, with different configurations in three dimensions, are also isotopes of Western weak-tie social capital. I suggest that future social capital research pay more attention on those isotopes so that the theoretical framework of social capital can be further completed.

The concept and dimensions of *guanxi*-based corporate social capital in this chapter is closely related to friendship, *ganqing*, *mianzi*, and *renqing*. Methodologically speaking, these four related concepts *per se* are not *guanxi*, but their analytical components can be used as measurements of three *guanxi* dimensions. Friendship and *ganqing* (personal attachment) make a social tie particular for

Table 3.1 Three dimensions of corporate social capital with examples

Tie Multiplexity	Relational Particularism	
	High	*Low*
High	Extremely strong obligation *Guanxi* networks Old-boy networks	Moderate obligation Associational networks Elite networks
Low	Strong obligation Kinship networks Ethnic networks	Weak obligation Weak-tie networks Structural hole networks

Table 3.1 is a revision of Bian and Zhang's Table 1 (2014, 428).

both parties. And strong friendship between close friends as well as deep *ganqing* between kin and psuedokin increase the level of particularism. In this sense, duration and intensity of friendship and perceived personal attachment are measures of partiuclarism. In addition to the relational dimension, Chinese *guanxi* has a structural dimension that is conceptualized as multiplexity in this chapter. *Mianzi* (face) as "perceived social position and prestige within one's social network" (Hwang 1987, 961) derives from various signals of ascribed and achieved personal attributes as well as relational activities in *guanxi* networks. A person who is capable and willing to provide diversified resources to his/her network contacts accumulates more *mianzi* and obtains a higher and more critical structural position in a *guanxi* network. That is to say that *mianzi*-saving activities that increase the diversity of resource exchanges are qualified measures of structural dimension of *guanxi*. *Renqing* (personal feeling) emphasizes obligations to help network contacts in need. And measures of *renqing* can be used directly as measures of the moral dimension of *guanxi*.

Another two related theoretical issues need to be discussed. First, are *guanxi* effects diminishing as Guthrie (1998) has suggested? It is true that Chinese cultural, economic, and political institutions have been under ongoing reforms since late 1970s. And during this process, how people do business may also change across time. Particularly after 2000, the Chinese market and its enterprises started to face a new round of fast and deep globalization, which inevitably accelerates the establishment of a more institutionalized and more free-competing market environment. I argue that, in this process, large companies with more international marketing and financing needs have to face shocking waves of globalization directly and adjust their social networking strategies to better integrate themselves into this global market dominated by Western rules and cultural habits. In contrast, SMEs have been and will be embedded deeply into local and grassroots *guanxi* networks so that they can survive constant discrimination and marginalization in domestic markets. Given this long history of *guanxi* embeddedness and given fewer urgent demands of global connections, it is not easy and not necessary in the near future for SMEs to divert from *guanxi*-based marketing, financing, and other daily operations to the Western weak-tie dominated networking strategy. Therefore, I believe that, even if the diminishing significance of *guanxi* is inevitable, it is still the long-run forecast for the fate of *guanxi*.

Second, are *guanxi* ties unique in China? I think that the prevailing existence of *guanxi* ties and strong preference on using *guanxi* ties are unique in China and some other East Asian societies. A study on overseas Chinese business networking strategies in Singapore (Zang 2001) domonstrates *guanxi*-based social capital and weak-tie-based social capital are equally important for financing and marketing in Singapore where Eastern and Western cultures coexist. However, particular and multifunctional ties *per se* are not unique to China. As what my literature review suggests, even if strong-tie resources are more redundant than weak-tie resources, it is more likely to actually mobilize resources via strong ties. And financing business start-ups via strong ties is not a rare phenomenon in the West. Multiplexity is also observed in Western societies, and its theoretical significance has been revived recently. At the same time, strong moral obligation is also available in the West, such as values of brotherhood and old-boy networks. So, all components of *guanxi* exist in the West, and we can safely assume that *guanxi* as an isotope of social capital is not unique in China, but we just don't observe this isotopic social capital to be prevailing in the West.

Notes

1 In the Chinese grammatical system, there is no difference between plural and singular forms of a countable noun. As a countable noun, *guanxi* can refer to "a connection" or "a set of connections" depending on context. This linguistic difference between Chinese and English further increases the difficulty of translation. In this chapter, I use "a *guanxi* tie" to refer to "one/a connection" or "one/a tie" and "*guanxi*" as a plural-only noun that refers to "connections" or "ties."

2 This multiplex nature of *guanxi* provides a theoretical explanation of the social phenomenon that Chinese people often cannot clarify the different norms of exchanges across social domains when they are connected by *guanxi*, as widely observed by China researchers (Smart 1993; Yang 1994; Yan 1996; Kipnis 1997; Gold et al. 2002).

3 In Chinese culture, "brotherhood" represents a typical pseudokin *guanxi*. San and Mr. X were not relatives, but strong interpersonal sentiment and emotional functions were later attached to their instrumental relations.

4 Translated by James Legge (http://ctext.org/analects/zi-lu).

References

Adler, P. S., and S. W. Kwon. 2002. "Social Capital: Prospects for a New Concept." *Academy of Management Review* 27 (1): 17–40.

Baker, W. E. 1990. "Market Networks and Corporate Behavior." *American Journal of Sociology* 96 (3): 589–625.

Baker, W. E. 2000. *Achieving Success Through Social Capital Tapping the Hidden Resources in Your Personal and Business Networks*. San Francisco: JOSSEY-BASS.

Bates, T. 1997. "Financing Small Business Creation: The Case of Chinese and Korean Immigrant Entrepreneurs." *Journal of Business Venturing* 12: 109–124.

Batjargal, B. 2003. "Social Capital and Entrepreneurial Performance in Russia: A Longitudinal Study." *Organization Studies* 24 (4): 535–556.

Bian, Y. 1997. "Bringing Strong Ties Back In: Indirect Ties, Network Bridges, and Job Searches in China." *American Sociological Review* 62 (3): 366–385.

Bian, Y. 2006. "Guanxi." In *International Encyclopedia of Economic Sociology*, edited by J. Beckert and M. Zafirovski, 312–314. London: Routledge.

Bian, Y. 2008. "Born out of Networks: A Sociological Analysis of the Emergence of the Firm." In *Chinese Entrepreneurship in a Global Era*, edited by R. Wong, 166–182. London and New York: Routledge.

Bian, Y., and L. Zhang. 2014. "Corporate Social Capital in Chinese Guanxi Culture." *Research in the Sociology of Organizations* 40: 421–443.

Biggart, N. W., and R. P. Castanias. 2001. "Collateralized Social Relations: The Social in Economic Calculation." *American Journal of Economics and Sociology* 60 (2): 471–500.

Bourdieu, P. 1986. "The Forms of Capital." In *Handbook of Theory and Research in the Sociology of Education*, edited by J. G. Richardson, 241–258. New York: Greenwald Press.

Bouty, I. 2000. "Interpersonal and Interaction Influences on Informal Resource Exchanges between R&D Researchers across Organizational Boundaries." *Academy of Management Journal* 43 (1): 50–65.

Bu, C. 2003. "The Theoretical Explanation and Modern Content of the Structure of Grade." *Sociological Research* 1: 21–29 (in Chinese).

Burt, R. S. 1992. *Structural Holes: The Social Structure of Competition*. Cambridge, MA: Harvard University Press.

Burt, R. S. 2004. "Structural Holes and Good Ideas." *American Journal of Sociology* 110 (2): 349–399.

Burt, R. S. 2005. *Brokerage and Closure: An Introduction to Social Capital*. New York: Oxford University Press.

Burt, R. S., R. M. Hogarth, and C. Michaud. 2000. "The Social Capital of French and American Managers." *Organization Science* 11 (2): 123–147.

Buskens, V., and J. Weesie. 2000. "An Experiment on the Effects of Embeddedness in Trust Situations: Buying a Used Car." *Rationality and Society* 12: 227–253.

Carlisle, E., and D. Flynn. 2005. "Small Business Survival In China: Guanxi, Legitimacy, and Social Capital." *Journal of Developmental Entrepreneurship* 10 (1): 79–96.

Carney, M. 2005. "Corporate Governance and Competitive Advantage in Family-Controlled Firms." *Entrepreneurship Theory and Practice* 29 (3): 249–265.

Cheng, P. H. 1995. "Differential Mode of Association and Organizational Behaviors of Chinese." *Chinese Indigenous Psychology Research* 3: 142–219.

Coase, R. H. 1937. "The Nature of the Firm." *Economica* 4 (16): 386–405.

Coleman, J. 1988. "Social Capital in the Creation of Human Capital." *American Journal of Sociology* 94: S95–S120.

Coleman, J. 1990. *Foundations of Social Theory*. Cambridge: Harvard University Press.

Cousins, P. D., R. B. Handfield, B. Lawson, and K. J. Petersen. 2006. "Creating Supply Chain Relational Capital: The Impact of Formal and Informal Socialization Processes." *Journal of Operations Management* 24 (6): 851–863.

Fei, X. 1947/1992. *From the Soil: The Foundations of Chinese Society. A Translation of Fei Xiaotong's Xiangtu Zhongguo*, translated by G. G. Hamilton and W. Zheng. Berkeley, CA: University of California Press.

Fong, E., and W. Chen. 2007. "Mobilization of Personal Social Networks and Institutional Resources of Private Entrepreneurs in China." *Canadian Review of Sociology and Anthropology* 44: 415–449.

Gold, T., D. Guthrie, and D. L. Wank. 2002. *Social Connections in China Institutions, Culture, and the Changing Nature of Guanxi*. Cambridge, UK; New York: Cambridge University Press.

Grangsjo, Y. F., and E. Gummesson. 2006. "Hotel Networks and Social Capital in Destination Marketing." *International Journal of Service Industry Management* 17 (1): 58–75.

Granovetter, M. S. 1973. "The Strength of Weak Ties." *American Journal of Sociology* 78: 1360–1380.

Granovetter, M. S. 1985. "Economic Action And Social Structure: The Problem of Embeddedness." *American Journal of Sociology* 91: 481–510.

Granovetter, M. S. 1992. "Networks and Organizations: Structure, Form and Action." In *Problems of Explanation in Economic Sociology*, edited by N. Nohria and R. Eccles, 25–56. Boston: Harvard Business School Press.

Gulati, R., and M. C. Higgins. 2003. "Which Ties Matter When? The Contingent Effects of Interorganizational Partnerships on IPO Success." *Strategic Management Journal* 24 (2): 127–144.

Guthrie, D. 1998. "The Declining Significance of Guanxi in China's Economic Transition." *The China Quarterly* 154: 254–282.

Hwang, K.K. 1987. "Face and Favor: The Chinese Power Game." *American Journal of Sociology* 92 (4): 944–974.

Hwang, K.K. 2001. "Theory Construction and Methodological Foundation of Confucious Relationalism." *Research of Education and Society* 2: 1–34 (in Chinese).King, A. 1985. "The Individual and Group in Confucianism: A Relational Perspective." In *Individualism and Holism: Studies in Confucian and Taoist Values*, edited by D. Munro, 57–69. Ann Arbor: Center for Chinese Studies, University of Michigan.

King, A. 1994. "Kuan-hsi and Network Building: A Sociological Interpretation." In *The Living Tree: The Changing Meaning of Being Chinese Today*, edited by W. Tu, 63–84. Cambridge, MA: The MIT Press.

Kipnis, A.B. 1997. *Producing Guanxi: Sentiment, Self, and Subculture in a North China Village*. Durham, NC: Duke University Press.

Krause, D.R., R.B. Handfield, and B.B. Tyler. 2007. "The Relationships between Supplier Development, Commitment, Social Capital Accumulation and Performance Improvement." *Journal of Operations Management* 25 (2): 528–545.

Lee, D.Y., and P.L. Dawes. 2005. "Guanxi, Trust, and Long-Term Orientation in Chinese Business Markets." *Journal of International Marketing* 13 (2): 28–56.

Li, W., and Liang, Y. 2002. "Special Trust and Universal Trust: The Structure and Characteristics of Chinese Trust." *Sociological Research* 3: 11–22 (in Chinese).

Lin, N. 2001a. "Social Capital." In *Social Capital: A Theory of Social Structure and Action*, edited by N. Lin, 19–28. Cambridge: Cambridge University Press.

Lin, N. 2001b. "The Theory and Theoretical Propositions." In *Social Capital: A Theory of Social Structure and Action*, edited by N. Lin, 55–77. New York: Cambridge University Press.

Luo, X., D.A. Griffith, S.S. Liu, and Y. Shi. 2004. "The Effects of Customer Relationships and Social Capital on Firm Performance: A Chinese Business Illustration." *Journal of International Marketing* 12 (4): 25–45.

Luo, Y., and M. Chen. 1997. "Does *Guanxi* Influence Firm Performance?" *Asia Pacific Journal of Management* 14: 1–16.

Macpherson, A., and R. Holt. 2007. "Knowledge, Learning and Small Firm Growth: A Systematic Review of the Evidence." *Research Policy* 36 (2): 172–192.

Martinsons, M. 2008. "Relationship-Based E-Commerce: Theory and Evidence from China." *Information Systems Journal* 18: 331–356.

Maurer, I., and M. Ebers. 2006. "Dynamics of Social Capital and Their Performance Implications: Lessons from Biotechnology Start-Ups." *Administrative Science Quarterly* 51 (2): 262–292.

Mitchell, J.C. 1969. "The Concept and Use of Social Networks." In *Social Networks in Urban Situations: Analyses of Personal Relationships in Central African Towns*, edited by J.C. Mitchell, 1–50. New York, NY: Humanities Press, Inc.

Mizruchi, M.S., and J. Glaskiewicz. 1993. "Networks of Interorganizational Relations." *Sociological Methods and Research* 22: 46–70.

Moran, P. 2005. "Structural vs. Relational Embeddedness: Social Capital and Managerial Performance." *Strategic Management Journal* 26 (12): 1129–1151.

Nahapiet, J., and S. Ghoshal. 1998. "Social Capital, Intellectual Capital, and the Organizational Advantage." *Academy of Management Review* 23 (2): 242–266.

Nee, V., and S. Opper. 2012. *Capitalism from Below: Markets and Institutional Change in China*. Cambridge, MA: Harvard University Press.

Parnell, M. F. 2005. "Chinese Business Guanxi: An Organization or Non-organization?" *Journal of Organisational Transformation and Social Change* 2 (1): 29–47.

Peng, M. W., and Y. Luo. 2000. "Managerial Ties and Firm Performance in a Transition Economy: The Nature of a Micro-Macro Link." *Academy of Management Journal* 43 (3): 486–501.

Podolny, J. M. 2001. "Networks as the Pipes and Prisms of the Market." *American Journal of Sociology* 107: 33–60.

Powell, W. W., K. W. Koput, L. Smith-Doerr, and J. Owen-Smith. 1999. "Network Position and Firm Performance: Organizational Returns to Collaboration in Biotechnology Industry." *California Management Review* 40: 228–240.

Powell, W. W., and L. Smith-Doerr. 1994. "Networks and Economic Life." In *The Handbook of Economic Sociology*, edited by N. J. Smelser and R. Swedberg, 368–402. Princeton: Princeton University Press.

Presutti, M., C. Boari, and L. Fratocchi. 2007. "Knowledge Acquisition and the Foreign Development of High-Tech Start-Ups: A Social Capital Approach." *International Business Review* 16 (1): 23–46.

Provan, K. C., and P. Kenis. 2008. "Modes of Network Governance: Structure, Management, and Effectiveness." *Journal of Public Administration Research and Theory,* 18: 229–252.

Putnam, R. 1993. "The Prosperous Community: Social Capital and Public Life." *The American Prospect* 13: 35–42.

Putnam, R. 1995. "Bowling Alone: America's Declining Social Capital." *Journal of Democracy*: 6 (1): 65–78.

Putnam, R. 2000. *Bowling Alone. The Collapse and Revival of American Community*. New York: Simon & Schuster.

Ring, P., and A. Van de Ven. 1992. "Structuring Cooperative Relationships between Organizations." *Strategic Management Journal* 13 (7): 483–498.

Rottman, J. W. 2008. "Successful Knowledge Transfer within Offshore Supplier Networks: A Case Study Exploring Social Capital in Strategic Alliances." *Journal of Information Technology* 23 (1): 31–43.

Shane, S., and D. Cable. 2002. "Network Ties, Reputation, and the Financing of New Ventures." *Management Science* 48 (3): 364–381.

Shipilov, A., and S. Li. 2014. "Toward a Strategic Multiplexity Perspective on Interfirm Networks." In *Research in the Sociology of Organizations: Contemporary Perspectives on Organizational Social Networks*, edited by D. J. Brass, G. Labianca, A. Mehra, D. S. Halgin, and S. P. Borgatti, 40: 95–110. Bingley, UK: Emerald Group Publishing Limited.

Smart, A. 1993. "Gifts, Bribes, and Guanxi – A Reconsideration of Bourdieu Social Capital." *Cultural Anthropology* 8 (3): 388–408.

Standifird, S. S., and R. S. Marshall. 2000. "The Transaction Cost Advantage of Guanxi-Based Business Practices." *Journal of World Business* 35 (1): 21–42.

Tsai, K. S. 2002. *Back-Alley Banking: Private Entrepreneurs in China*. Ithaca: Cornell University Press.

Uzzi, B. 1999. "Embeddedness in the Making of Financial Capital: How Social Relations and Networks Benefit Firms Seeking Financing." *American Sociological Review* 64 (4): 481–505.

Uzzi, B., and J. Spiro. 2005. "Collaboration and Creativity: The Small World Problem." *American Journal of Sociology* 111: 447–504.

Verbrugge, L. M. 1979. "Multiplexity in Adult Friendships." *Social Forces* 57 (4): 1286–1309.

Walder, A. G. 1986. *Communist Neo-Traditionalism: Work and Authority in Chinese Industry*. Berkeley, CA: University of California Press.

Walter, J., C. Lechner, and F. W. Kellermanns. 2007. "Knowledge Transfer between and within Alliance Partners: Private versus Collective Benefits of Social Capital." *Journal of Business Research* 60 (7): 698–710.

Wang, S., and X. Liu. 2002. "The Base of Trust: A Rationalist Interpretation." *Sociological Research* 3: 23–39 (in Chinese).

Williamson, O. 1981. "The Economics of Organization: The Transaction Cost Approach." *American Journal of Sociology* 87: 548–577.

Wong, S. L. 1988. *Emigrant Entrepreneurs: Shanghai Industrialists in Hong Kong*. New York: Oxford University Press.

Xiao, Z. X., and A. S. Tsui. 2007. "When Brokers May Not Work: The Cultural Contingency of Social Capital in Chinese High-Tech Firms." *Administrative Science Quarterly* 52 (1): 1–31.

Yan, Y. 1996. *The Flow of Gifts: Reciprocity and Social Networks in a Chinese Village*. Stanford, CA: Stanford University Press.

Yang, M.M.H. 1994. *Gifts, Favors, and Banquets: The Art of Social Relationships in China*. Ithaca, NY: Cornell University Press.

Zang, X. 2001. "Resource Dependency, Chinese Capitalism, and Intercorporate Ties in Singapore." In *SEARC Working Paper Series*, edited by K. Hewison, 6: 1–20. Hong Kong: Southeast Asia Research Centre of the City University of Hong Kong.

4 The *guanxi* circle phenomenon in the Chinese venture capital industry

Jar-Der Luo[1]

Introduction: the Chinese VC industry

Beginning in 1986 with state-owned company China Venturetech Investment Corp, the Chinese venture capital (VC) industry was born. In the next thirty years, the industry experienced three periods of development. From the mid-1980s to the early stage of the 1990s, it was the central government that actively cultivated VC firms. The Ministry of Science and Technology and the Ministry of Finance passed a series of laws to build the institutional base for VC registration. In addition, the central government also provided financial support for these new high-tech firms, such as the Torch High Technology Industry Development Plan and the 863 Plan. In 1987, local governments were also encouraged to support the development of high-tech firms in local industrial districts, so local government-owned VC firms began to appear. However, the industry had very slow growth during the first decade.

In the early 1990s, many industrial-district-based and university-based VC firms started up. The Chinese stock market was established in 1990, and the return on investment of VCs could be attributed to their going public. In addition, foreign investors were allowed to enter into the Chinese market, although they were prohibited from collecting money in China. At the same time, the central government passed many laws to build the institutional infrastructure for supporting a market economy, and policies were made to encourage the development of the VC industry. As a result, the number of private VC firms boomed in this period. This industry experienced a surge in the late 1990s, especially during the period of Internet investment fever. As shown in Table 4.1, the number of new entrants was about 10 each year before 1997, but it quickly grew to 121 in 2001. The investment fever declined in later years.

Due to rapid growth of the economy and a series of modifications to business laws in regard to corporations, the stock market, partnerships, and technology development, Chinese venture capital once again boomed after 2004. Each year after 2005 saw more than 200 new investors entering the industry, and the growth rate was at least 20 percent, with the exception of 2009, according to statistics from the SiMuTon database shown in Table 4.1.

However, the industry faced difficulties in development due to its institutional structure. On one hand, the central and local governments make regulations for

Table 4.1 Number of new venture capital firms by year

Year	Number of New Investors	Cumulative Number of Investors
1995	15	15
1996	8	18
1997	12	25
1998	26	48
1999	68	89
2000	117	164
2001	121	221
2002	98	261
2003	131	314
2004	168	377
2005	208	470
2006	266	657
2007	401	895
2008	541	1158
2009	512	1386
2010	635	1678
2011	757	2078

Source: Based on data from the SiMuTon database

and provide financial support to VC firms; on the other hand, local governments are major players in this market. Thus, these complications include insufficient governmental regulations, weak implementation of formal rules, interference from local governments, and serious moral hazard, all of which create a highly uncertain environment for investors (Williamson 1985).

Environmental uncertainty creates high transaction costs among trading partners, and market mechanisms will be insufficient to govern transactions of this sort (Williamson 1996). Instead, actors will use relational contracts to hedge against such an uncertainty (Granovetter 1985; Williamson 1996). In addition, VC investors often form various types of syndications for sharing risk (Wilson 1968; Lerner 1994), controlling opportunistic behaviors (Admati and Pfleiderer 1994), and compensating for each other's insufficiency (Lockett and Wright 2001; Tykvov´a 2007). The role of *guanxi* thus comes into our research agenda.

The purpose of this chapter is to use the network approach to study the Chinese VC industry; in this research, we propose a type of network structure called the "*guanxi* circle," and in the chapter, we will analyze how *guanxi* circles can work as a governance mechanism of transactions in such an uncertain environment. We employed qualitative methods to collect data and conducted eight interviews with seven experts in the VC industry, as listed in Table 4.2. We first asked them

Table 4.2 List of interviewees

Interviewee	Occupation	Time	Location	
Mrs. X	An entrepreneur of a start-up VC firm	July 2012	Chengdu	
Mr. L	A junior manager in state-owned VC firm	August 2012	Beijing	With recording
Mr. Z	A junior partner of a private VC investor	July 2012	Tianjin	
Mr. Y	A senior partner of a private VC investor	July 2012 and April 2013	Beijing	With recording
Mr. C	A CEO of a state-owned VC firm	October 2013	Tianjin	With recording
Mr. X	A general manager of a branch of a large VC investor	July 2012	Tianjin	
Mr. S	A senior manager of local government-owned VC in the field of green energy	August 2012	Tianjin	

for a general observation of this industry and their firms' business, and then they delineated the history and major partners of joint ventures. Finally, the interviews focus on why and how they formed such syndications. At times, a major investor may introduce its followers to us, so that we can trace different viewpoints from both a central ego and his or her followers.

In the following, we will first introduce what a *guanxi* circle is. Subsequently, this chapter will illustrate the five types of uncertainties that Chinese VC investors face and finally discuss how *guanxi* circles act as governance mechanisms to make joint ventures function in such an uncertain environment.

What is a *guanxi* circle?[2]

A *guanxi* circle is a group of people bound together for a common identity and shared interests. It can refer to a large community, such as circles of engineers, lawyers, or professors, for examples. But more often, it refers to a small clique in which group members know and interact with each other. This chapter defines the term "*guanxi* circle" according to its narrow meaning, thus including only small cliques rather than large communities.

A *guanxi* circle often has a central person as its leader, so it may be named after someone, such as manager Chang's circle, CEO Lin's circle, and so forth. That means a leading person accompanied by his/her strong ties forms a *guanxi* circle in which members share common interests and struggle for these interests together (Luo and Yeh 2012). Two important Chinese characteristics construct the cultural and normative bases for the *guanxi* circle phenomenon. First, as indigenous sociologist Fei (1992) called "the differential mode of association" (in

Chinese, *cha xu ge ju*), a Chinese ego-centered network is comprised of multiple layers of rings in which different behavioral and moral standards are applied for each of these different rings of *guanxi*.

Second, family ethics is the base for a Chinese person to build and maintain his or her *guanxi* (Liang 1983; Bond and Hwang 1986). *Guanxi* circles are actually imitated as pseudofamilies in his or her working life. Through the process of "family-ization" (i.e., turning an outsider to be a family member; Chua et al. 2009), a central ego may recruit outsiders into his or her pseudofamily in the workplace.

Egocentric and the differential modes of association

A Chinese person divides his or her social ties into several rings, and different rings imply different moral standards. It is common for indigenous Chinese research to categorize three types of *guanxi*. For example, *guanxi* may be classified as expressive, mixed, or instrumental ties, based on the continuum between expressive and instrumental elements (Hwang 1987; 1988). Or, *guanxi* may be divided into obligatory, reciprocal, and utilitarian ties, according to the degree of obligation (Zhang and Zhang 2006).

Based on Fei's framework of differential modes of association (1992) and Yang's three categories of Chinese social relations (1993), we propose a framework of differential relationships (Luo 2005; 2011). Acquaintance ties fit in the outermost ring of an ego-centered network under the "rules of equity" (Hwang 1987) and may come to be trusted based on general ethical principles of fairness and the conservative process of repeated exchanges. *Guanxi* of this sort is defined by its short-term duration and rational behaviors.

There are two types of strong ties included in a person's *guanxi* circle. The innermost ring generally consists of family members and fictive kin (Chen 1994). Chinese psychologist Yang (1993) calls the most inner ring of an ego-centered social network *chia ren*, which translates as "family ties," including real family and pseudofamily ties, since they may include special intimate relations other than family members (Chen 1994; Luo 2005).

Familiar ties, including good friends and persons to whom one feels particularly close, fit in the next ring under the "rules of favor exchange," by which relational trust can be built up from frequent exchange of favors (Hwang 1987; Tsui and Farh 1997). Familiar ties generally involve instrumental exchanges, but pure rational choice account cannot explain the behaviors in this ring well.

An actor's motivation is mixed (Granovetter 2002) since historical, cultural, and normative factors are intertwined with self-interest calculations (Granovetter 1999). While family ties place emphasis on expressive and normative concerns, and while acquaintance ties take care of instrumental interests, familiar ties need to balance the two different motivations – expressive and instrumental concerns. A familiar tie by definition is a strong tie (Granovetter 1973; Marsden and Campbell 1984). Yet, familiar ties are different from family ties, since they are concerned more with instrumental interests and can be broken if there is a lack of trustworthy behavior.

For a central ego, the ring of acquaintance ties provides abundant opportunities and resources that may be accessed by weak ties (Granovetter 1973; Burt 1992). However, the resources in this ring are not guaranteed for successful mobilization. So, acquaintance ties of this sort are outsiders for the *guanxi* circle's central ego.

The ring of family ties constructs the core of a *guanxi* circle. This core may be called the "basic team" (Chen 1998) or "confidant" (Chi 1996), since it includes the basic forces and most intimate relations for the central ego.

The ring of familiar ties is the interface between a circle core and the outside world, as shown in Figure 4.1. They are more flexible and open than the core but much stronger in mobilizing resources than acquaintance ties. Thus, an important benefit of maintaining familiar ties as the periphery members of a *guanxi* circle is to keep circle operations flexible and the circle boundary open to the outside world.

The open boundary of a **guanxi** *circle*

For a circle leader, any acquaintance tie may be a future familiar tie, so preserving the norms of reciprocity is beneficial for expanding a person's *guanxi* circle. By the same token, the core of a *guanxi* circle is not closed either, and familiar

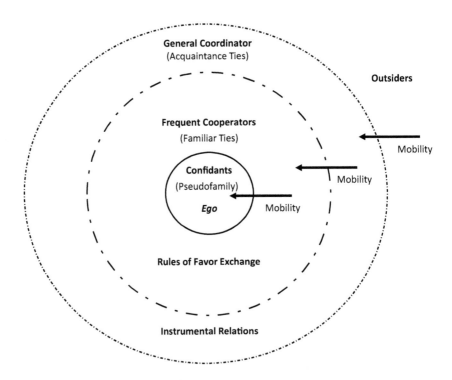

Figure 4.1 Diagram of a *guanxi* circle

ties may join in the focal person's "basic and confidential" team (Chen 1994; Chi 1996). The institution of familiar ties makes the boundary of a *guanxi* circle blurred and provides more structural room for flexible operations in coupling and decoupling network ties.

In Chinese daily life, the principle of similarity introduces a stranger into a person's ring of acquaintance ties. Tsui and Farh (1997) assert that Chinese form trust networks based on social demographic factors, in which the principle of similarity is applied to profession, work tenure, socio-economic class, sex, cohort group, birthplace, and family name. Similarity of Chinese role-identities signals trustworthiness. Perceiving similarity is the first step for a Chinese person to build *guanxi*. *Guanxi* of this sort may not lead to engagement in a long-term favor exchange but may lead to being treated more fairly. The rule of equity (Hwang 1987) emphasizes the morality of fairness through exchange among members of one's ring of acquaintance ties.

Familiar ties construct the main base of a Chinese's *guanxi* circle. Carrying valuable exchange relations from the outer group into a *guanxi* circle is a central part of Chinese culture. Most Chinese tend to dynamically shift their *guanxi* into or out of these categories of *guanxi*. A valuable and trustworthy acquaintance can be brought into the ring of familiar ties. As a result, the principles guiding social interaction are "upgraded" to a new standard.

The reciprocity of favor exchanges introduces an acquaintance tie into a person's ring of familiar ties. Favor exchanges have several features. First, it is important personalized help for the favor receiver. Second, a favor giver asks no payment under the name of "brotherhood," but the favor receiver will not forget the favor done for him and needs to pay back whenever an opportunity to do so is found. Third, there must be a "favor account" for a pair of familiar ties, and this account will remain as long as the friendship continues.

Some role-identities introduce a familiar tie into a person's innermost *guanxi* circle of family ties. Chinese societies treat many identity-counter-identity relationships as family ties (Chen 1994). Persons who would be considered outsiders in Western societies might be more easily introduced into a family tie in Chinese societies through salient pseudofamily role-identities (Chen 1994; Luo 2005), which create strong ties with such bases as fictive kin, blood brothers, and adopted relatives. This category is not limited to family members, and that is why it can be named "pseudofamily ties" (Chen 1994; Luo 2005).

Finding similarity to initiate *guanxi*, demonstrate trustworthy behaviors in repeated exchanges, return favors to fulfill the expectation of partners, and show brotherhood to maintain intimacy are all a part of daily life for Chinese in the workplace. As a result, a *guanxi* circle is possibly open to acquaintance ties.

Through this dynamic process, a Chinese person will learn who can be included in his or her *guanxi* circle and what kind of resources can be mobilized from circle members. A person with good *guanxi* generally mobilizes a group to achieve his/ her goals, and he or she certainly needs to help group members to accomplish their goals in return. How to maintain the mutual trust within this *guanxi* circle is often the chief concern of a circle leader in his or her workplace.

Summarizing the arguments stated above, there are some static features of a *guanxi* circle. First, a *guanxi* circle is centered on an ego. Second, it has a structure with differential modes of association including an innermost core, which is indicated by loyal, unbreakable, and intimate relationships, and periphery members, mainly composed of long-term relations with limited liability in frequent favor exchanges. Third, the boundary of a *guanxi* circle is usually open, and thus there may be overlapping areas among several *guanxi* circles. In the dynamic process, a *guanxi* circle may absorb outsiders into the inner group and also move trustworthy periphery members into the core. In other words, the boundaries within and outside a *guanxi* circle are blurred.

Guanxi circles and uncertainty in the Chinese VC industry

The uncertainty of finding investment opportunities

Network theories insist that business opportunities come from structural holes (Burt 1992) in which a bridging tie connecting two originally separated groups can utilize information asymmetry to broker the trades between the two groups. It is especially true for VC investors. Even in a mature market environment, VC investors still face much information asymmetry between investors and investees, and social connections indeed aid in overcoming the information gap.

In China, the problem of information asymmetry is especially serious, since many investees do not reveal information honestly and since government regulations are insufficient in regulating these opportunistic behaviors. In addition, the institutional designs, including accounting systems, auditing methods, government inspections, and mutual monitoring in the industrial community are not able to guarantee trustworthy information provided by the investees. Utilizing *guanxi* to obtain accurate information is thus a good way of discovering valuable investment opportunities. As a partner of VC investor, Mr. Z, stated, "[Good projects] all come from the mediation of good friends."

Uncertainty of zero-sum games

Due to the highly uncertain environment, VC investments have a high possibly of failing and losing money. If the main investor in the syndication wishes to have a fallback in a bad joint venture, then the other side of the partnership could be sacrificed for the interest of the main investor. In other words, it is a zero-sum game in the case of this sort, in which it is better to incorporate new and unfamiliar partners into the syndication. That is why it is found in our field studies that familiar ties are not always welcome, and at times, friends of friends are the best choices. For the sake of maintaining a friendship, the focal person will at times avoid inviting familiar partners to join in a new high-risk investment; as a senior partner of a VC investor, Mr. Y, puts it:

> The familiar partners [those who have joint venture with the interviewee in the past] are hard to negotiate with; sometimes, we disagree with each

other due to self-interest, but it is hard to talk straight . . . we are friends, you know. . . . One side may need to be sacrificed for the other side's interest . . . in the cooperation of Eastern type [i.e., zero-sum game]. [My habit is] . . . don't cooperate with familiar partners in one industry twice.

The insufficiency of credible commitment

In addition to the highly uncertain environment, a transaction itself in the VC industry, either among cooperating VC investors or between an investor and an investee, has the features of a long-term contract, with high asset specification and high behavioral uncertainty (Williamson 1985; 1996). In such a risky transaction, hostage taking in a formal contract is often offered as a credible commitment for hedging against possible opportunistic behaviors (Williamson 1996). However, such a deterrence method is often not accepted by Chinese actors. On the one hand, it hurts face and feelings of syndication partners. On the other hand, seizing hostages as a punishment is also generally not possible due to the weak implementation of formal regulations.

An alternative credible commitment is a person's reputation based on the mutual monitoring in a small community. Closure, dense network structure, intimate internal relations, and frequent interactions create a small social network full of committed relations (Coleman 1990; Yamagishi et al. 1998). Such a network accompanied by strong community norms will provide mutual monitoring, which ensures community members comply with group norms (Yamagishi and Yamagishi 1994). An actor with high centrality in such a network earns a reputation as a credible commitment, which enlarges his or her scale of cooperation and successfully reduces risk as a return. As a senior partner of private VC investor, Mr. Y, puts it:

[For a successful VC investor] it is not good to make any one side unhappy, . . . since someone sometime loses money, the central person [those who have a high degree of centrality in the VC community] can balance [the gain and loss; in other words, peripheral persons may not be able to find opportunities to balance the loss]. . . . In China, we earn reputation due to cooperation, rather than acquisition and merging.

The lack of a trustworthy third party

In a complex transaction like the VC investor's, contracts are often incomplete (Macaulay 1963), so information asymmetry and moral hazards bring about many disputes. In what Williamson (1985) called the "neoclassical contract," such a transaction needs the trustworthy third party as an arbitrator for the safety of trading. However, the Chinese legal system often cannot bear the burden to arbitrate disputes in the VC industry. Even worse, local governments generally take the role of players in the market, rather than arbitrators. As a result, formal contracts are far from protecting transaction safety.

Chinese VC investors generally bring these complex transactions into a small group so that mutual monitoring in such a closed and dense network can play the role of arbitrator. Especially, those central persons with good reputations in the group are the trustworthy third parties for most group members, and they may take on the burden to settle disputes. Mr. Y comments on this type of intimate network in the following way:

> First of all, firms [Chinese VCs] generally get bored with these [overly detailed contracts and calculative financial arrangements]. . . . Foreign investors pay too much attention on short-term profit . . . We are not like this. In China, we tend to foster something [over a long period], especially friendship.

Frequent changes in public policy

There are some reasons that leave room for rent-seeking behavior from government officers. First, the Chinese government continues to modify its policies so as to follow the fast-changing societal and economic environments in a transition economy. Second, local governments often interrupt investment activities for the purpose of developing local economies, so state-owned VC investors often directly subsidize certain industries or products. Third, the special designs of public administration in China often ask a private startup to obtain many licenses from government before it can operate (Wu et al. 2009).

A VC investor thus needs to seek strong governmental relations so as to hedge against these rent-seeking behaviors, on the one hand, and benefit from timely information about changing polices on the other hand. A senior investor in the field of green energy, Mr. S, stated that governmental relations are as follows:

> In this field [green energy] . . . we would like to invite government officers provide us with consultation, and help studying the investees. If it helps [the policy encourages] . . . then we will go on investing on the firm. The risk is small. If they don't favorite it, then we must be careful, since the governmental policies don't care this area.

The phenomenon of guanxi circles

Summarizing the above, we find that a successful Chinese VC needs to establish four types of *guanxi*. First, familiar ties are important for finding good investment opportunities. Second, bonding ties are necessary to build up a closed and dense network so as to provide credible commitment and trustworthy third parties in hedging the uncertainty in a transaction. Third, new weak ties are at times very useful in a zero-sum game. Finally, governmental ties are the key to avoiding the risk caused by fast-changing policies.

How does a successful VC leader, generally the owner of a successful VC firm, organize these types of *guanxi*? What is the structure of his or her ego-centered network? In our interviews with the senior investor Mr. Y, we find that there is a three-layer network structure. As he puts it:

There are few investors in the first layer [in terms of power and number of projects] . . . they have unique resources. . . . In the second layer, some famous PE [private equity] are in this layer. . . . Those in the third layer are generally not famous nationwide, but even some globally famous investors sometime need their cooperation, [since they may have special resources] such as local government relations, local market knowledge, etc.

The most powerful VC leaders in the first layer are often the centers of various groups of investors. Each of these investors controls many good investment opportunities and generally by itself launches a series of investment projects. An investor organizes various types of *guanxi* to form a network structure shown in Figure 4.1. The center may or may not have a group of brotherhood partners, who are confidants and always bound together to find all possible investment opportunities. The second ring is composed of frequent cooperators, who follow the center's investment projects. In general, they invest money rather than participate in decision-making. As Mr. Y said:

[Investors in the second ring] just ask me to take their money. Many VC investors are like this . . . . Money sellers [what he called those frequent followers] invest for only investment.

Those in the third ring are new weak ties for the center. They may have suitable resources for a certain project, such as money, local knowledge, local governmental relations, and industrial tacit knowledge, and so forth, and thus occasionally engage in instrumental exchanges with the center. This type of network structure is typically a sort of "*guanxi* circle" as stated above (Luo and Yeh 2012).

How *guanxi* circles work in the Chinese VC industry

Just as a *guanxi* circle is composed of three rings, that is, pseudofamily ties, familiar ties, and acquaintance ties, a successful Chinese VC leader organizes its various types of *guanxi* in the same way, namely, the brother-like confidants, frequent cooperators composed of familiar ties, and general coordinator coming from new weak ties. Thus, how can such a static structure accompanied by network dynamics of *guanxi* circles help a Chinese VC investor hedge against the five types of uncertainties stated in the third section?

The importance of closure

First, a successful VC investor organizes his or her confidants and frequent cooperators into a closed and dense network. As stated above, such a network provides trustworthy third parties as arbitrators in disputes and guarantees credible commitment for a complex and risky transaction in joint ventures. It is not easy to build up partnership relations among strangers in such a highly risky environment created by moral hazard. Good friends are thus the trustworthy third parties to provide secret and valuable information. As a result, most VCs search for investment opportunities in a group composed familiar ties, rather than engage in joint venture directly with strangers, as a junior partner of VC investor Mr. Z puts it:

> We [Mr. Z and another VC investor] met together several times in differ-ent projects. but we are not familiar with each other that time. . . . One day, a common friend of ours invited us to have a dinner . . . then we decide to invest jointly.

A successful VC leader knows how to organize those confidants and frequent cooperators into such a closed and dense group. He or she, as the center in a syndication network, thus needs to play the role of a trustworthy third party and enforce strong mutual monitoring as credible commitment in the group. In return, this central person garners a good reputation and further opportunities (Podolny 1993; Tykvov´a 2007). Reputation helps attract more members to join in the cir-cle, and they may bring in more resources and investment opportunities. In addi-tion, the central position can exercise influence on circle members so as to have more investment opportunities to choose and more control on investment projects. These benefits guarantee the profit and survival of the center.

Struggling for the center position in a syndication network tends to be an important target; this means a Chinese VC is equipped with a certain attitude, what we call "*guanxi*-orientation thinking," toward joint ventures. The VC may sacrifice the profit in one or two transactions for the sake of maintaining rela-tions, so that it can harvest a better position in the network. If this focal person forms a small *guanxi* circle of his or her own, or if he or she gains the center position in a sub-field community, then safety and profit will follow this posi-tion. One single transaction is fragile, but a series of investments in the collec-tive actions of a network is robust. As a junior partner of a Chinese VC, Mr. Z, stated:

> *Guanxi* is indeed important . . . some projects fail, but it is O.K., since *guanxi* is there. It [a successful project] is the result of process of collective actions . . . some things are good for *guanxi* building.

The importance of an open boundary

However, cooperation in a small closed and dense network is not enough, espe-cially when a new joint venture may be a zero-sum game in a highly uncertain environment. At this moment, the familiar partners may not be a good choice in some joint ventures, and new partners should be introduced by friends.

But why does a Chinese VC tend to cooperate with new entrants? In a joint venture, a powerful, central person in a circle in general initiates an investment project and other members follow. So he or she may control the whole process of investment and make the decision to distribute earned profit or the burden of loss. The new entrants always play the role of silent partners, who often contribute more money and share less profit in the project.

In addition to providing "surplus money" to the centered VCs in a network, new entrants may also bring new information, local governmental relations, local knowledge, and new opportunities into a network. These resources are keys for forming new projects. As a manager of a VC investor, Mr. X, articulated:

> Cooperation with new VCs for sure is profitable. Money, local knowledge, new information of projects . . . but I will not allow them to say too much [new VCs can't manage the project].

Then why does a new entrant wish to cooperate with the already closed and dense network? The dynamics of *guanxi* circles propose the possible answer, which will be discussed in the following section.

The importance of balancing openness and closure

There is a dilemma that a central ego faces in his or her *guanxi* circle. On one hand, a successful VC leader needs to build up a closed and dense network, but on the other hand, new entrants and new, necessary governmental ties always make this network open to the outside world. If a centered leader opens his or her *guanxi* circle to the outside too quickly and widely, this strategy will dilute the interests of old circle members, and the circle may fall apart. On the contrary, if this successful VC pays too little attention to the needs of these new weak ties, then he or she will sooner or later lose his or her reputation, and no new entrants will want to participate in such an ego-centered network. How to balance the openness and closure of this network is a challenge for the central person and requires the art of balancing the interests within and outside a *guanxi* circle.

In the practice of *guanxi* circle operations, the central person knows how to convince the new partners to sacrifice their short-term profit, but in return, he or she will offer long-term benefits to the sacrificed sides. As a CEO of a state-owned VC firm, Mr. C, said:

> A big brother has reputation and good investment portfolio to support this reputation. . . . A little brother likes the big brother, because he can use money to exchange reputation. He directly gets reputation from cooperating with a big name. . . . In addition, a little brother may manipulate *guanxi* [in the big brother's *guanxi* circle], and gradually move into the inner rings. It is possible for the little brother someday somehow to become a big brother [the center of his own *guanxi* circle].

In other words, a successful VC leader recognizes the long-term interests of a new entrant, that is, entering into a trustworthy *guanxi* circle, moving to the inner rings of the network gradually, building up his or her own *guanxi*, finding good opportunities to launch investment projects, and finally forming a *guanxi* circle of his or her own. Mr. Y stated as follows:

> For example, VC firm H focuses in one industry, which is in fashion now. H originally is only a follower. . . . But after the cooperation with some big guys . . . he chooses cases very carefully, so the investment performance is pretty good. Now, G launches some investment projects of his own. His harsh time has gone.

In the dynamics of *guanxi* operations, a smart, central person knows how to attract new partners to join his or her *guanxi* circle and keep old circle members profitable, even at the cost of sacrificing the new partners. But at the same time, the circle leader helps the sacrificed sides move into inner rings so as to build up their own *guanxi* circle as a return. In this way, a VC leader may solve the dilemma of openness and closure of a *guanxi* circle.

Conclusions and discussions

Many Chinese psychological studies have illustrated some special features of Chinese *guanxi* (Hwang 1987; 1988; Yang 1993; Zhai 2012). The question put in this chapter is what are the structural outcomes of *guanxi*? All of these studies help us to better understand the features of Chinese behavior, but the answer to this question should rely on the analysis of network structure and its dynamic process.

This chapter reveals the structural dimension of *guanxi* and describes a special structural phenomenon, the "*guanxi* circle" in the Chinese VC industry. The circle is a comparatively closed and dense social network (generally a sub-network of the whole VC industrial network) centered on one or several persons. On the one hand, a smart VC investor knows to build a *guanxi* circle so that he or she can provide credible commitment and trustworthy third parties for joint ventures in the network, since the formal institutions in China can hardly be used to hedge against the high uncertainty caused by opportunistic behavior and business disputes. In addition, those familiar ties in the network also help mobilize more partners to join in and introduce good investment opportunities. On the other hand, the boundary of a circle is not closed, so new entrants can enter into this network by networking with circle members, especially those in central roles. Since new entrants bring in money, local knowledge, emergent or needed governmental ties, and industrial knowledge, openness is also necessary for a healthy *guanxi* circle.

How can a circle leader balance the closure and openness of a *guanxi* circle? In the process of balancing the interests within and outside the *guanxi* circle, he or she generally sacrifices new entrants' short-term profits but provides long-term interests as a return. As shown in Figure 4.1, new entrants may move from outsiders to the peripheral rings of a circle and then to the core in a series of favor exchanges. By sacrificing short-term profit in single transactions, this new entrant may build up his or her own network of partners and even form a circle centered on him- or herself. A successful leader of a syndication network uses this way to open his or her circle boundary to new entrants. At the same time, the "surplus" extracted from new entrants' short-term profits can be used to subsidize old partners, so that the leader can maintain a comparatively closed and dense core of the circle. That is why the central person in a *guanxi* circle can balance the openness and closure of a circle.

This is only an initial study touching on this structural phenomenon of the Chinese VC industry. More issues deserve our attention in the future. In dynamic *guanxi* circle operations, a circle leader at times needs to couple in more networks and decouple some relations (Granovetter 1995). A successful entrepreneur should be skilled at balancing coupling and decoupling (Granovetter 2002). How and when a central person decouples relations challenges our future studies, since this chapter touches only on the issue of coupling.

In the long-term operation of a *guanxi* circle, some formal and informal rules as governance mechanisms may appear in the syndication network (Ostrom 1990; 2008). What are these governance mechanisms in the Chinese VC community? Political and societal environments in a changing China deeply influence the way to balance openness and closure and the model of internal governance mechanisms in a *guanxi* circle. The interactions between macro-level factors in outside environment and micro-level behaviors in a circle thus come into the spotlight of our research. This chapter initiates the analysis of "*guanxi* circle" in the Chinese VC industry but leaves many questions awaiting future studies.

Notes

1 The author is grateful for the financial support of Center for Social Network Research, Tsinghua University and Tsinghua's research project "Trust and Guanxi Studies on Internet", Project Number: 20121088015, as well as the support of Chinese Natural Science Foundation Project "Social Network in Big Data Analysis: A Case in Investment Network", Project number: 71372053.
2 Part of the section "What is a *guanxi* circle" is also used in the following book chapter: Jar-Der Luo, FangDa Fan, and Jie Tang. forthcoming. "Mining Data for Analyzing *Guanxi* Circle Formation in Chinese Venture Capitals' Joint Investment." In *Interdisciplinary Social Network Analysis*, edited by Xiaoming Fu, Margret Boos, and Jar-Der Luo. New York: Taylor & Francis Group.

References

Admati, A., and P. Pfleiderer. 1994. "Robust Financial Contracting and the Role of Venture Capitalists." *Journal of Finance* 49 (2): 371–403.

Bond, M. H., and K. K. Hwang. 1986. "The Social Psychology of Chinese People." In *The Psychology of the Chinese People*, edited by M. H. Bond, 213–266. Hong Kong: Oxford University Press.

Burt, R. 1992. *Structural Holes: The Social Structure of Competition*. Cambridge: Harvard University Press.

Chen, Chieh-Hsuan. 1994. *Subcontracting Networks and Social Life*. Taipei: Lien-Jin Press (In Chinese).

Chen, Chieh-Hsuan. 1998. *Sociological Perspectives on Taiwan's Industries – Transformation of Small and Medium-sized Firms*. Taipei: Lien-Jin Press (in Chinese).

Chi, S.C. 1996. "The Empirical Study in Roles of Leader's Confidant." *Management Review* 15 (1): 37–59.

Chua, R., M. Morris, and P. Ingram. 2009. "Guanxi vs. Networking: Distinctive Configurations of Affect- and Cognition-based Trust in the Networks of Chinese vs. American Managers." *Journal of International Business Studies* 40: 490–508.

Coleman, James. 1990. *Foundations of Social Theory.* Cambridge: The Belknap Press.

Fei, H.T. 1992. *From the Soil: The Foundations of Chinese Society.* Berkeley: University of California Press.

Granovetter, Mark. 1973. "The Strength of Weak Tie." *American Journal of Sociology* 78: 1360–1380.

Granovetter, Mark. 1985. "Economic Action and Social Structure: The Problem of Embeddedness." *American Journal of Sociology* 91: 481–510.

Granovetter, Mark. 1995. "The Economic Sociology of Firms and Entrepreneurs." In *The Economic Sociology of Immigration: Essays in Networks, Ethnicity and Entrepreneurship*, edited by A. Portes, 128–165. New York: Russell Sage Foundation.

Granovetter, Mark. 1999. "Coase Encounters and Formal Models: Taking Gibbons Seriously." *Administrative Science Quarterly* 44: 158–162.

Granovetter, Mark. 2002. "A Theoretical Agenda for Economic Sociology." In *The New Economic Sociology: Developments in An Emerging Field*, edited by M. Guillen, R. Collins, P. England and M. Meyer, 35–59. New York: Russell Sage Foundation.

Hwang, K.K. 1987. "Face and Favor: The Chinese Power Game." *American Journal of Sociology* 92: 944–974.

Hwang, K.K. 1988. *The Chinese Power Game.* Taipei: Lien-Jin Press (in Chinese).

Lerner, J. 1994. "The Syndication of Venture Capital Investments." *Financial Management* 23 (3): 16–27.

Liang, Shu-Ming. 1983. *The Comparison between Chinese and Western Cultures.* Taipei: Li-Ren Publishing House (in Chinese).

Lockett, A., and M. Wright. 2001. "The Syndication of Venture Capital Investments." *Omega* 29: 375–390.

Luo, Jar-Der. 2005. "Particularistic Trust and General Trust – A Network Analysis in Chinese Organizations." *Management and Organizational Review* 3: 437–458.

Luo, Jar-Der. 2011. "Guanxi Revisited – An Exploratory Study of Familiar Ties in a Chinese Workplace." *Management and Organizational Review* 7 (2): 329–351.

Luo, Jar-Der, and Kevin Yeh. 2012. "Neither Collectivism Nor Individualism – Trust in Chinese Guanxi Circles." *Journal of Trust Research* 2 (1): 53–70.

Macaulay, Steward. 1963. "Non-Contractual Relations in Business: A Preliminary Study." *American Sociological Review* 28 (1): 55–67.

Marsden, P., and K. Campbell. 1984. "Measuring Tie Strength." *Social Forces* 63 (2): 483–501.

Ostrom, E. 1990. *Governing the Commons: The Evolution of Institutions for Collective Action.* New York: Cambridge University Press.

Ostrom, E. 2008. "Building Trust to Solve Commons Dilemmas: Taking Small Steps to Test an Evolving Theory of Collective Action." In *Games, Groups, and the Global Goody*, edited by S. Levin, 211–216. New York: Springer.

Podolny, J.M. 1993. "A Status-Based Model of Market Competition." *American Journal of Sociology* 98: 829–72.

Tsui, Anne S., and Jiing-Lih Farh. 1997. "Where Guanxi Matters – Relational Demography and Guanxi and Technology." *Work and Occupations* 24 (1): 57–79.

Tykvov´a, T. 2007. "Who Chooses Whom? Syndication, Skills and Reputation." *Review of Financial Economics* 16 (1): 5–28.

Williamson, Oliver. 1985. *The Economic Institutions of Capitalism*. New York: The Free Press.

Williamson, Oliver. 1996. *The Mechanisms of Governance*. New York: Oxford University Press.

Wilson, R. 1968. "The Theory of Syndicates." *Econometrica* 36 (1): 119–132.

Wu, W.F., C.F. Wu, and M. Rui. 2009. "Between the Special Connections that High-ranking Managers of Some of China's Listed Companies have with Government and Tax Preference Afforded to them." *Management World* 3: 134–142 (in Chinese).

Yamagishi, T., and M. Yamagishi. 1994. "Trust and Commitment in the United States and Japan." *Motivation and Emotion* 18 (2): 129–166.

Yamagishi, T., K. Cook, and M. Watabe. 1998. "Uncertainty, Trust, and Commitment Formation in the United States and Japan." *American Journal of Sociology* 104: 165–195.

Yang, G.S. 1993. "Chinese Social Orientation." In *Chinese Psychology and Behavior,* edited by G.S. Yang and A.B. Yu, 87–142. Taipei: Laureate Press.

Zhai, X.W. 2012. *Favors, Face, and the Reproduction of Power*. Beijing: Beijing University Press.

Zhang, Y. and Z. Zhang. 2006. "Guanxi and Organizational Dynamics in China: A Link between Individual and Organizational Levels." *Journal of Business Ethics* 67 (4): 375–392.

Part II

Social capital and its transformation

Taiwan and Hong Kong

5 The social capital and entrepreneurship of succeeding generations

The case of the Koo family in Taiwan

Tsai-man C. Ho[1]

Introduction

Research on the succession of family businesses have focused largely on discussing whether the capabilities of family members should be considered as suitable for carrying on the businesses their fathers have founded. Relatively little attention has been devoted to exploring how family members become successors. For the founders, their spirit of innovation justifies their leadership. In contrast, for succeeding generations who aspire or are expected to take over the family business, their succession requires social recognition. Fan and his research group (2007) examined 217 succession cases from Hong Kong, Singapore, and Taiwan during the period from 1987–2005. They attribute the failure of some Hong Kong family firms to the founders' reputations and networks being nonfungible. They also indicate that the success of the first founders was based on their political connectivity and that social and personal ties are specific assets that are directly nontransferable to the inheritors. Their research even holds that the predecessors in Hong Kong, when compared to those in Singapore and Taiwan, just refused to relinquish their businesses. As a result, their descendants have fewer opportunities to train themselves to be successors (Fan et al. 2007). Their research raises interesting questions: Can social capital be transferred? Does entrepreneurship have anything to do with social capital?

Social capital represents one of the least tangible and fungible assets. In many societies, surnames (family names) indicate precisely the attributes of social capital that are not easily transferable, bought, sold, or traded (Coleman 1988). A surname comes to represent one specific kind of asset called "social capital," and this asset is exclusively possessed by its family members and is definitely passed on to the next generation. People outside of the family perceive that a particular surname comes within a class ranking system of social relationships. Because of such a perception, business opportunities might be created, and an entrepreneurial spirit might thus be generated. Other than the surname, what else is a family required to have or to do in order to legitimize or empower their descendants to become successors of the family business and thereby facilitate entrepreneurship? It is less about the descendants' individual willingness and more about the process of discipleship and fostering. This process helps family members to take part in a set of social relations that tend to foster a spirit of individuality, as well as to often provide opportunities for moving forward.

Relying mainly on archival research and the analysis of a secondary source of materials to generate data, I will now attempt to help readers understand how a family business endures and how its succeeding generations become entrepreneurs by examining the Koos' history. The Koo family has been thriving for four generations, mainly focusing on cement and financial industries. Leslie Koo, a representative of one branch of the family, currently chairs the Taiwan Cement Corp. The company is one of Asia's largest cement producers and had revenues of NT$116.1 billion in the year 2013. The other branch of the family is in charge of the CTBC Financial Holding Co. Ltd, formerly known as the Chinatrust Financial Holding Co. Ltd, until its name was later changed in mid-2013.

The following will first examine the relationship between social capital and entrepreneurship and the possibility of transference. The second section will then briefly introduce the history of the Koo family. The third section focuses on issues related to the patterns showing how social capital has been transferred, managed, utilized, and nurtured by the Koos. Finally, I will discuss the implications and conclusions of this case.

Literature review: social capital and entrepreneurship

Many researchers have examined the connotations between social relationships and entrepreneurship. Based on the concept of embeddedness, Granovetter (1985) has pointed out that individual behavior is not atomized and that the relationships between economic action and resources are embedded in the social context. Further studies have developed this concept and suggested that social capital, observed from the different levels of analysis (including individual, organizational, interorganizational, and societal), can be expected to be added to the form of returns from the abovementioned levels of relationships (Lin 2002). The concept of social capital, applied in business, usually implies that the success and survival of a firm relies very much on an entrepreneur's ability to establish a network of supportive relationships (Burt 1992; Lin 2002). Other scholars also argue that entrepreneurs have a wide range of contacts that help to further develop entrepreneurial ideas. They explain that these various correlations are necessary for the actors to gain resources when starting a new business (Shane 2000; Shane and Cable 2002).

Social capital and entrepreneurship can be viewed as aspects of a family's attempt to ensure that their successors will keep their business flourishing – that is, social capital provides resources in helping the family firm to survive and to continue to succeed. According to Burt, social capital contains resources: "Social capital is at once the resources contacts hold and the structure of contact in a network. The first term describes whom you reach. The second term describes how you reach [them]" (Burt 1992, 12). Some scholars emphasize that a set of conditions promote a knowledgeable transfer for different network types (Inkpen and

Tsang 2005). Network capital is regarded as an instrument to transfer knowledge. Certainly, the family will attempt to expose their successors, as much as possible, to an environment in which the successors' entrepreneurship would be more likely to emerge. However, "whom and how you reach" would be a challenge, first to the family before the network comes into play as an instrument: In particular, when there is a structural hole, by which Burt refers to the absence of a tie among a pair of nodes. Binding and bridging becomes significant when the family attempts to break through these structural holes.

Bourdieu's seminal work on cultural reproduction and social reproduction sheds light on the handing-down of social capital (Bourdieu 1973). Through education, social capital can be translated into wealth and power. Success in life relies on earlier accomplishments in life; that is, primary schools are the best time to start on the road to success. For example, children from the dominant classes internalize the skills and knowledge of their predominant culture during their youth. In the meantime, the habitus – that is, the lifestyle, the values, the dispositions, and the expectations – of a particular social group is developed. Bourdieu further points out that the role of education in society is, in fact, a contribution to social reproduction, rather than social mobility (Bourdieu 1984, 466–484). Bourdieu's concepts of habitus and social reproduction help one to understand the process by which social capital can be passed on to successors. At an interpersonal level, bridging and binding social capital could also be seen as signifying social class distinction (Bourdieu 1986).

Based on the previous theoretical and empirical research, this article aims to explore how a family fosters entrepreneurship for the next generation by binding and bridging networks. In addition, to cope with uncertainty encountered at different stages, the predecessors have also given considerable attention to developing a well-planned access to social capital for their children.

Brief introduction of the Koo family

The rise of Taiwan's Koo family started in 1895, when Japan took away the jurisdiction of Taiwan from China. The founder of the family, Koo Hsien-jung (辜顯榮 1866–1937), in exchange for his services to the Japanese colonial government, was appointed as the chief executive officer of a wholesale salt distributor and was granted many monopolistic rights (Yanaihara 1956, 14). In 1934, he was elevated to be a congressman of Imperial Japan's Upper House of the Diet. Koo Hsien-jung plowed the profits of his ventures into purchasing land in Taiwan for the benefit of his heirs. However, Koo Hsien-jung's biological first son, Koo Yue-fu (辜岳甫), died at an early age in 1936. Therefore, after Koo Hsien-jung's death in 1937, his second biological son, Koo Chen-fu (辜振甫 1917–2005), still a college student at the time, was obliged to take over the seven companies his father had left behind. When the Chiang Kai-shek government retreated to Taiwan in 1949, the Koos were already among the largest landowners on the island. In order to legitimize his regime in Taiwan, Chiang Kai-shek implemented the "land to tiller" reform program and arranged with the Koos, and other elite families, to

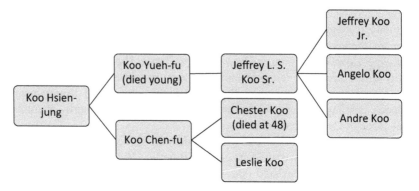

Figure 5.1 The main heirs of the Koo family

swap their land for shares in newly privatized businesses. In 1954, the Koos and four other families acquired the crown jewel: Taiwan Cement, the nation's leading cement company. Serving first as president and then chairman, Koo Chen-fu, the second-generation head of the family, established the company as one of Taiwan's blue-chip enterprises. During the Kuomintang (KMT) era, Koo Chen-fu built a more extensive business empire than his father's while maintaining the family tradition of staying close to those in power. This chapter focuses on two of the Koo family branches: the family of Koo Chen-fu and the family of his nephew Jeffrey L. S. Koo (辜濂松 1933–2012), as seen in Figure 5.1.

From 1961–1994, Koo Chen-fu chaired the Chinese National Association of Industry and Commerce (CNAIC), one of the primary links between business and government in Taiwan. In 1966, together with his nephew Jeffrey Len-Song Koo (辜濂松), whose father died young in 1936, Koo Chen-fu founded the China Securities Investment Co., which was renamed the Chinatrust Investment Co. in 1971, and was converted into the Chinatrust Commercial Bank in 1992, when the government ended the moratorium on new banks. Jeffrey L. S. Koo and his uncle worked together closely and made many joint investments. Over the years, the business empire of the Koo family has developed into a multinational business that includes interests in cement, securities, real estate, petrochemicals, telecommunications, and transportation. What distinguishes the Koos from other eminent families in Taiwan is not only the scope of their wealth accumulation but also their roles in both the business and political sectors.

Being fluent in two important foreign languages – Japanese and English – and having cultivated gracious manners, Koo Chen-fu devoted himself to helping Taiwan's diplomatic relations. When cross-strait relations between China and Taiwan were rapidly moving forward from the end of the 1980s, Koo Chen-fu was the top negotiator, chairing the Straits Exchange Foundation, which handled the relations between Taiwan and China. In that position, he held two historic talks with his counterpart from mainland China. Until his death in 2005, Koo Chen-fu remained the key decision-maker in the Koo's business group.

Another important person in the family is Jeffrey L. S. Koo, who is from the other branch of the family. He accepted the CNAIC chair bequeathed to him by his uncle and served from 1994–2002. Like his uncle, he was an ambassador-at-large, actively helping to expand Taiwan's international relations. He acted as an advisor to three Taiwanese presidents – Lee Teng-hui, Chen Shui-bian, and Ma Ying-jeou. In this way, both Jeffery L. S. Koo and Koo Chen-fu cultivated close relations with countless foreign political and business leaders for over four decades.

Regardless of who was in power, the Koo family has managed to maintain advantageous connections with the government of Taiwan. Despite that ability, both older and younger generations of the Koo family have encountered many challenges. Moreover, some of the younger ones have suffered major setbacks. Following the death of Chester Chi-yun Koo (辜啟允, Koo Chen-fu's first son, 1953–2001), a number of risky "landmine" (i.e., financially fragile) companies that Chester had invested in over the previous ten years began "exploding" (i.e., falling apart financially). This led to the division of the Koo group. Although reluctant to change its original succession plan, the group amicably divided into two subgroups: One is composed of the Taiwan Cement Corporation (TCC), focusing on the cement and other nonfinancial-sector businesses, and the other is Jeffrey L. S. Koo's branch, now known as the Chinatrust Group. At that time, both branches were challenged financially and legally.

One problem for the TCC group was repayment of over NT$25 billion in debt that Chester Koo had left behind. Another major challenge was a series of scandals involving Chester's younger brother, Leslie Cheng-yun Koo (辜成允 1954–). However, moving forward to the present, Leslie seems to have successfully survived this turmoil. Moreover, bolstered with his mother's (Cecilia Yen Cho-yun 嚴倬雲 1926–) mainland Chinese relationships and the legacy that his maternal grandfather Yen Fu (嚴復) left, the TCC has risen to the position of being the fourth-largest cement provider in all of China.

As for the other branch, Jeffrey Koo Jr. (辜仲諒, Koo Chung-ling, 1964–), the older son of Jeffrey L. S. Koo Sr., stepped down as chairman of the Chinatrust Commercial Bank in 2006 after the bank was heavily fined and reprimanded by Taiwan's Financial Supervisory Commission (FSC). The stated offense was his misuse of overseas funds when buying a stake in the Mega Financial Holding Co. Other investigations were also launched into three cases of suspected breach of trust and illegal trading by Chinatrust Financial, whose president is Jeffrey Koo Jr.'s, younger brother, Angelo Koo (辜仲瑩, 1965–). Although Taiwan's judicial system has considered some of the Koos' practices to be inappropriate, analysts in foreign investment companies have viewed these as a "normal way of conducting business" (Lin 2006) and stated,

> Perhaps because of their relatively young ages, as well as their aggressive manner and controversial close ties with the family of president Chen Shui-bian, the Koo brothers have faced strong criticism, undermining the positive social image that their father had cultivated for the group.
>
> (Lin 2008)

The Koos' story illustrates at least two points. First, a venturing spirit is a necessary, but not a sufficient, condition for continuing a business empire; it does not always guarantee success for each generation. Second, risks closely follow innovation; that is, not every new economic action will be legitimized, sanctioned, and welcomed by a government and society. The emergence of entrepreneurship is usually related to the process of institutional redefinition and the discussion on the legitimacy of entrepreneurial behavior that may confront possible resistance not only from the government but also from within a society. As the proverb says, "Fire is a good servant, but a bad master." In other words, the social capital that the older Koos had gained and invested in might not be so effective in their later stages and in different social contexts. Furthermore, surviving over a period of time that covers two or more generations requires various sources of social capital. Probing into the development of the Koos' business empire, one would discover that social capital might still be the most important of useful assets when facing the risks generated by entrepreneurial activities.

Marriage and social capital at different stages

Koo Chen-fu's first marriage during the era of Japanese rule in Taiwan successfully reinforced and expanded the social capital his father had bestowed. In November 1940, Koo Chen-fu married Ms. Huang Chao-hua, niece of Huang Hsin, a member of the Governor's Advisory Council. The wedding was held in the Hibiya Hotel of Tokyo. Kodama Tomō, Taiwan's military commander from 1937 to 1939, was the couple's matchmaker. Tomō was the son of Kodama Gentarō, the fourth governor of Taiwan under the Japanese government, who previously had ties with Koo Chen-fu's father.[2]

In a book published by Japanese journalist Itō Kinjiro in 1948, Koo Chen-fu was described as follows:

> Trim and courtly, featured with aristocratic bearing, Koo Chen-fu from his kindergarten years onward, has been educated and cultivated in the Japanese system. When interacting with others, his graceful manner and attitude is full of charm. His role is indispensable for a Japanese civil- and military-centered community. If Japan had not lost the war, he would have been a great figure in the future.[3]

The aspect of social capital discussed here is that the Koos' network with the Japanese was not only maintained but was even further consolidated and enlarged. However, in the event of a regime change would the established social capital still function? In the case of the Koos, their previous close relationship with the Japanese government was severely challenged after World War II, with changes occurring in an atmosphere filled with the rising heat of nationalism simmering around the island after the war. Following Japan's surrender, an unexpected episode took place in Koo Chen-fu's life. In 1946, Koo Chen-fu was incarcerated for treason by the KMT government for his involvement in the so-called "Taiwan Independence Plot" and was sentenced to nineteen months in prison.

Structural hole: marriage, bridging networks to solve political and business crises

Destiny is like a double-edged sword. Koo Chen-fu's wife died before the end of World War II, and he lapsed into a state of great sorrow. Nonetheless, this loss brought him a new opportunity when he met Cecilia Yen Cho-yun, who was the granddaughter of Yen Fu, a member of a prominent mainland family of intellectuals with roots in the Qing dynasty. After his release from jail, Koo Chen-fu married Cecilia. This family background later proved to be helpful to the third generation of Koos in expanding their business in China. At the time and just after the marriage, Cecilia's brother-in-law, Yeh Ming-Shun (葉明勳) played a key role in helping Koo survive under the KMT regime and even become a key figure in national affairs.

While taking refuge in Hong Kong with his new bride Cecilia, Koo Chen-fu rekindled his interest in Peking Opera, a fascination held since childhood. Koo Chen-fu regarded learning opera as being the best fruit he was able to cultivate in Hong Kong. His elegance in singing opera helped him become an amateur actor. His practice of this art form became a very significant means by which his career benefited in enhancing his relationships with key KMT members, thereby nurturing social capital in the society ruled by the KMT regime.

Long before the end of WWII, the Koo family had become one of the three largest landlord families in Taiwan. Koo Chen-fu's business, his property, and all his networks were in Taiwan, which now was under the control of the KMT. Koo Chen-fu, who was in self-imposed exile in Hong Kong, wanted to return, but the political atmosphere intimidated him. Cecilia's brother-in law, Yeh Ming-Shun, was at that time head of the Central News Agency (中央社) of the Republic of China (ROC). He cautiously made inquiries to General Peng Meng-Chi (彭孟緝), the garrison commander, about the possibility of allowing Koo Chen-fu to safely return to Taiwan. After being granted a letter of guarantee, Koo returned to Taiwan at the age of thirty-five.

Later, it is via Yeh again that Koo became acquainted with Secretary of the Executive Yuan Huang Shao-ku (黃少谷); that relationship proved to be beneficial. Coincidentally, Huang was also a devotee of the Peking Opera, so Huang and Koo would practice Peking Opera at Koo's house two to three times a week. At the age of 39, Koo made his on-stage debut in a performance of Peking Opera. In 1953, the KMT government started a specific program called "Land to the Tiller." The purpose of this program was to consolidate agricultural production and simultaneously to allow for talent and resources to be inserted into the industrial sector. Huang Shao-ku then introduced Koo Chen-fu to Minister of Economic Affairs Chang Tzu-kai (張茲闓) and was invited to be an advisory counselor to the program. With social affiliation and recognition from these networks, Koo began to overcome the incompleteness of his social contacts, and this directly helped him to subsequently take charge of the Taiwan Cement Corporation.

The social affiliation from his wife's family helped Koo resume his business status and gave him a chance to transform his prestige and that of his family

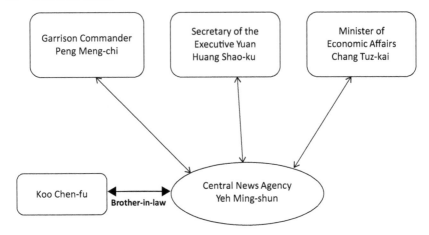

Figure 5.2 Network bridging

business from being a landowner into a capitalist with industrial plants. The excellent ties that Koo Chen-fu's father, Koo Hsien-jung, had established with important people in Japanese society during the colonial period are reflected in the ties Koo Chen-fu managed to revive. Members of the Koo family frequently helped to extricate the Taiwanese government out of diplomatic tangles, and the family contributed much to elevating Taiwan's profile in the international arena while the ROC government was struggling to maintain its international status vis-à-vis the People's Republic of China. Because the government turned to the Koos for support in its diplomatic efforts, the government, in return, helped the Koos with critical elections towards becoming board members of the Taiwan Cement Corporation.

Forming a bond between their social ties – to embed their heirs into associations

Although scholars have acknowledged the relationship between social capital and entrepreneurial activities and have recognized that an expected return is the driving force for one to invest in social capital, very few studies have tackled the question about how a social network is constructed and maintained over generations. The Koo family displays their excellence in this, as they are particularly skillful at establishing or using organizations to institutionalize personal ties so as to multiply power, resources, and influence in every aspect. In contrast to the establishment of a social network that is merely generated by personal relationships (*guanxi*), the Koo family prefers more organized connections. For example, Koo Chen-fu started the Taiwan Institute of Economic Research (TIER) in 1976, which was the first private, independent think-tank in Taiwan. The main purpose of the institute is to provide consultations to the government and enterprises through intensive research on domestic and foreign macroeconomics. Huang Shao-ku, who helped Koo align with the KMT, was then invited by Koo to be an honorary director of the institute when Huang was senior advisor to President Chiang Kai-shek. In this way, the social tie was maintained.

Diplomatic relations also played a role in the growth of the Koo family. The US had full diplomatic relations with the Republic of China (ROC) on Taiwan from 1949 to 1979. However, in case there were any changes in diplomatic relations between the ROC on Taiwan and the US, a group of business leaders and other social elites, proactively in 1976, in the US, launched the USA-ROC Economic Council (which in 1998 was renamed the USA-Taiwan Economic Council). David Kennedy was the first chairman of the USA-Taiwan Economic Council. He had also been Secretary of the Treasury in the first two years of the Nixon administration and then appointed Ambassador to NATO.

In 1977, Taiwan set up the ROC-USA Business Council with the full support of former ROC Minister of Economic Affairs Sun Yun-hsien (孫運璿). The council acts as a nongovernmental channel in order to facilitate Taiwan's bilateral business relations with the US. Chang Tzu-Kai was the first chairman of the ROC-USA Business Council, Koo Chen-Fu took over the position in 1981 and remained chairman for twelve years. In 1993, the position was filled by his nephew, Jeffrey L. S. Koo (at that time, chairman of the Chinatrust Commercial Bank). Jeffrey L. S. led the organization for two terms. Table 5.1 presents a list of the chairpersons.

Historically, the ROC-USA Business Council maintains close contacts with Taiwan's economic and trade offices in the United States, with the American Institute in Taiwan (AIT) and with the 17 US state trade offices currently operating in Taiwan. The council's purpose is "to promote Taiwan's bilateral links with the USA in the areas of trade, investment, and technology transfer."[4] This council consists of a board of thirty-one directors and nine supervisors. In 2012, the current chairperson of the ROC-USA Business Council, C. Y. Wang (王鍾渝), was invited by the Koo family and then appointed as the independent director of one

Table 5.1 List of chairpersons, ROC-USA Business Council

Chairmen from 1977 to the Present	
February 26, 1977–May 29, 1981	T. K. Chang
May 29, 1981–May 14, 1993	C. F. Koo
May 14, 1993–May 24, 1999	Jeffrey L. S. Koo
May 24, 1999–September 27, 2005	C. Y. Wang
September 28, 2005– September 15, 2008	Mu Tsai Chen
September 16, 2008–February 8, 2012	Jeffrey L. S. Koo
February 8, 2012–present	C. Y. Wang

Source: http://www.rocusabc.org.tw

of the family's businesses, Chinatrust Financial Holding Company. In return, Jeffrey L. S. Koo's firstborn son – Jeffrey Koo Jr. – became the vice chairman of the council with the help of C. Y. Wang. Although Jeffrey Koo Jr. was given this position, he has been accused of involvement in a scam known locally as the "Red Fire Case" in 2006. It is important to note that two other members of the Koo family – one from each branch of the family group – have their own roles within this council: Leslie Cheng-yun Koo (辜成允, Koo Chen-fu's younger son, now in charge of TCC) is a member of the board, and Angelo Koo (辜仲瑩, the second son of Jeffrey Koo Sr.) is a supervisor within the council.

To summarize, via personal ties, the Koos introduce their family members into formal associations in a sophisticated way. Consequently, their positions in these associations will create and facilitate even more external relationships that will, in turn, make them prominent whilst generating possible business opportunities. In a memorial service to mourn the passing of Jeffrey Koo Sr., David Laux (a previous president of the council) said,

> Jeffrey Koo did a lot to bring Taiwan into useful international connections and to promote their business possibilities. He introduced credit cards to Taiwan in 1974. He kept contacts up with the World Bank and the International Monetary Fund and was an advisor to three Taiwan Presidents: Lee Teng-hui, Chen Shui-bian, and Ma Ying-jeou. Importantly, he advocated for and supported closer economic cooperation with China, a key tenet of the administration of President Ma.[5]

This description accurately highlights the family's capabilities regarding entrepreneurship and networking.

Converting relationship into institutionalized social capital

The Koo family can be said to bestow favors when they invite former government officials to take part in the family's business groups. Many cabinet officials have been conspicuously invited, and subsequently have received positions, within the groups. This shows how the family invests in social capital (probably in the hope that someday these actions would bring returns, either in helping their successors or in the form of direct economic benefits). Table 5.2 provides more examples.

To illustrate this point, some examples are further explained. Samuel Shieh was the chairman of the Bank of Communication (1983–1989) and the governor of the Central Bank (1989–1994). The Koos created a "decision-making committee" within the Chinatrust Commercial Bank, specifically for Samuel Shieh, and it did not take very long before some returns became obvious. In 1996, the Asian Development Bank (ADB) came to Taiwan to issue their bonds. For many years, it had always been the Bank of Communication that gained the underwriting business regarding equities and bonds for the ADB. Samuel Shieh had, during his career, worked for both of these banks (see Table 5.2). This time, thanks to Samuel Shieh's mediation, the business went to the Chinatrust Commercial

Table 5.2 Converting relationships into institutionalized social capital

Name of Government Official	Post in Government	Position in the Koos Group
Sean Chen （陳沖）	• Ex-Prime Minister of Executive Yuan (2012–2013)	• Ex-President of KGI Securities (2007–2008)
Christina Liu （劉憶如）	• Ex- Minister of Finance	• Chief Economic Consultant of Chinatrust Financial Holding Company
Samuel C. Shieh （謝森中）	• Central Bank Governor (1989–1994) • Director of the Projects Department at the Asian Development Bank (1967–1981)	• President of Decision-Making • Committee in Chinatrust Commercial Bank
Lu Yu-jun （盧毓鈞）	• Former National Police Agency Director-General	• President of Chinatrust Security Company
Hsueh Hsiang-chuan （薛香川）	• Former Secretary-General of Executive Yuan	• Director of Chinatrust Financial Holding Company • Chairman of the Taiwan Lottery Co.
Wang Chih-kang （王志剛）	• Former Minister of Economic Affairs	• Consultant of Chinatrust Commercial Bank
Chiang Pin-kung Chiang （江丙坤）	• Ex-Director of Straits Exchange Foundation • Vice President of the Legislative Yuan	• Chief Advisor to Chinatrust Financial Holding Co., • Chairman of the Board of TIER
C.Y. Wang （王鍾渝）	• Lawmaker of the Legislative Yuan	• Independent Director of Chinatrust Financial Holding Co.,

Bank. Furthermore, because of this favorable outcome and interactive experience, Samuel Shieh then became the vice-chairman of the Straits Exchange Foundation to assist the chairman, Koo Chen-fu.

Another example concerns the establishment of the *San San Fe* (Third Wednesday Club), which was proposed by Chiang Pin-kung (江丙坤). At the time, he was the chairperson of the Council for Economic Planning (a unit of the government) and wanted the Club to be established in order to meet the challenges of Taiwan's economic transition in early 1999. The minimum qualification for membership requires a Taiwanese enterprise to be financially healthy and to have at least NT$20 billion in annual sales volume. Koo Chen-fu was elected the first chairperson. His nephew, Jeffrey Koo Sr., not surprisingly, took over this post from Koo Chen-fu and continued to serve in this position for three terms until his recent demise. Leslie, Jeffrey Sr.'s cousin, is now on the board of directors. It is important to note that the Koo family members have always remained in the Club from its commencement.

By means of periodic luncheon parties, the Third Wednesday Club promotes relations between members, strengthens communications between international enterprises, and boosts international investment. From 2000 onwards, Koo Chen-fu and Jeffrey Koo Sr., respectively, have led as many as fifteen group trips to Japan to visit forty-eight substantial enterprises (e.g., Mitsui, Mitsubishi, Sony), twelve organizations, and three industrial parks. From the companies visited, one can conclude that this reflects the Koos' continuing strong ties with Japanese business organizations. Since 2002, they have extended their reach into mainland China and have even signed a memorandum for economic and trade cooperation with the "Capital Enterprise Association" of Beijing, and later with the Shanghai Federation of Economic Organizations. Currently, there are fifty-eighth member-enterprises in the Club, and the net revenue of these enterprises exceeded US$320 billion and accounted for 62 percent of the GNP of Taiwan in 2011.[6]

Assurance of their reproduction

In his book, *The State Nobility*, Bourdieu reveals that, via various institutionalized practices of daily life and social situations, the noble class finishes their consecration of being "different." This process of social alchemy legitimizes their distinction and domination, bolsters their distance from other classes, and thereby ensures that their status will be reproduced and reinforced. Bourdieu argues that the field of power is a field of forces structurally determined by the state of relations of power, among the holders – a gaming space where those agents and institutions possessing enough specific capital to be able to occupy the dominant positions within their respective fields confront each other using strategies aimed at preserving or transforming these relations of power (Bourdieu 1996). Relatively speaking, economic capital – especially the "exchange rate" – is easier to observe than social capital. One of the consequences of economic capital is that the reproduction of social capital needs much more skillful manipulation.

Jeffrey L. S. Koo displayed his ability to establish connections with renowned foundations. He was named an Eisenhower Fellow in 1971 and became a trustee of the fellowship in 1980. The Eisenhower Fellowship claims to be different from other existing international scholarship and exchange programs: This fellowship is not granted to students or faculty but to mid-career professionals who have already achieved leadership positions. Each fellow receives an individualized, five-to-seven-week program of consultations with experts and senior officials in government, industry, academia, the arts, and the nonprofit sector. As a result, Jeffrey L. S. Koo met with many top government officials and banking executives during his visits to the US for over forty years. He also engaged with Eisenhower Fellows from other countries and formed many international friendships.

Here, once again, Jeffrey L. S. Koo fully presented his networking capabilities by setting up organizations. By building bridges that enabled his family members to move more prominently into the global arena, he helped the Koos be noted for having a more global perspective. In 1973, Koo and nine other Taiwanese Eisenhower Fellows, set up a domestic appeal for the Taiwanese to emulate the international exchange program by the founding of the Eisenhower Fellows Association of China (Taiwan) (EFACT). Jeffrey L. S. Koo served as the founding president of the association and became its chairman in 2002. In fact, the Chinatrust Group has assisted the EFACT with its affairs for decades. From 1954 until now, there have been more than forty Eisenhower Fellows from Taiwan. In the history of the Koo family, Jeffrey L. S. Koo was the first to be awarded an Eisenhower Fellowship. In 1999, his cousin Leslie Koo (of Koo Chen-fu's branch) was awarded a fellowship, and then Jeffrey L. S. Koo's first son, Jeffrey Koo Jr. was awarded one in 2006.

The prominence of family members could be partly ascribed to the work performed by the EFACT, which is believed to have contributed greatly to the Eisenhower Fellowship, particularly through the efforts of Jeffrey L. S. Koo Sr. (e.g., donations and fund-raising).[7] The nomination process includes the participation of "binational committees abroad from fields identified by the country representatives as critical to national needs." The EFACT is also responsible for the nominations. In 2011, US retired general and former Secretary of State Colin Powell bestowed the Distinguished Alumnus Award on Jeffrey L. S. Koo Sr. to recognize his eminence in his field of endeavor and his leadership in the Eisenhower Fellowships' alumni network. Powell said the award was for "his long and illustrious history as an EF donor, trustee, and nominator of new Fellows and president of the EFACT's alumni association."[8]

To conclude, the family plants hedgerows around the family empire, shielding their successors by means of the institutionalizing of social capital. The pattern of the Koos to secure the transfer of social capital depends enormously on the setting up of reputable institutions that they hope can help organize their social network and allow their social capital to continue onwards.

Social alchemy – training system of social capital

> [M]embers of the second and third generations have typically studied overseas and often hold degrees in business administration; they follow a more Western management style and maintain a more global perspective.
>
> (Lin Mie-Chun, American Chamber)[9]

Koo Chen-fu received his business training by working in Japanese corporations. Taiwanese businessmen working in Japanese corporations heralded the coming of an era and a system of entrepreneurship training that helped to prepare younger members for family succession. To preserve their business empire, the next generation was channeled into an uncompromisingly upward trajectory, which remains strictly disciplined. In a gospel TV interview released on January 10, 2013, Jeffrey Koo Jr. commented on the situation concerning their family upbringing; that is, for most of the time, the atmosphere in the family was quite tense, especially when his father was at home.[10] "Restrained" was the attitude his father manifested towards them. Jeffrey Koo Jr. was good at sports when he was young. The question his father always raised was, "When will you be the leader of the sport's team?" Leadership is one of the assets the family explicitly cultivates. To cope with the increasing challenges of a globalized era, both branches of the Koo family, indeed, carefully create a good educational environment for their children.

Tables 5.3 and 5.4 summarize the backgrounds of five of the family's principals whilst growing up. Two sons from each side hold MBAs from the elite Wharton School at the University of Pennsylvania, while Andre Koo (Jeffery L. S. Koo's youngest son) earned his MBA from his father's alma mater, New York University. All the sons and sons-in-law have either economics or business-related majors and have earned MBAs.

The Koo family has strong, longstanding ties to the Wharton Business School. Koo Chen-fu was awarded the school's Dean's Medal in 1991. These honorary

Table 5.3 Koo Chen-fu's Branch (The Taiwan Cement Corporation)

	Generation Order	Education and Background	Training and Experience
Koo Chen-fu	2nd	• Taihoku Teikoku University (Taiwan Empire university, in Japanese colonial period) • Further studies on finance and BA, Tokyo University (self-exile period as he described himself)	Dainippon Seito Kabushiki Kaisha in Japan (Great Japan Sugar Corporation, 3 years)
Chester Koo	3rd	• Economics major, Tung-hai University, Taiwan • MBA, Wharton Business School, University of Pennsylvania (1979)	• Planning section, Chinatrust • America Continental Bank Financial Service Department, Mitsubishi Trust Planning section, Chinatrust America Continental Bank; Financial Service Department, Mitsubishi Trust
Leslie Koo	3rd	• Accounting major, University of Washington, Seattle • MBA, Wharton Business School, University of Pennsylvania (1981)	• Auditor, T N Soong & Co./ Arthur Anderson & Co. • A specialist in the Electronic Data Processing Center, Taiwan Cement
Nelson Chang	Son-in-law	• Economics major, Princeton University • MBA and Financial Management, Stern Business School, New York University (1976)	• Financial Management System, Project Chief Director, New York City Government • Vice Chairman, Chia Hsin Cement

Source: Revised from Ho and Kao (2010, 345)

Table 5.4 Jeffrey Koo Sr.'s Branch (The Chinatrust Group)

	Generation Order	Education and Background	Training and Experience
Jeffrey Koo Sr.	3rd	• Born in the Japanese colonial period • Accounting major, Soochow University, Taiwan • MBA, Stern Business School, New York University (1961)	• Citibank, USA • Financial security analyst, USA • ICBC, Taiwan
Jeffrey Koo Jr.	4th	• Juvenile period in American School in Japan • Japanese major, in Soochow University, Taiwan • MBA, Wharton Business School, University of Pennsylvania (1991)	• Morgan Stanley • New York Bank • Mitsubishi Trust • Yashuda Trust
Angelo Koo	4th	• Juvenile period in American School in Japan • Economics major and Education major, Northwest University • MBA, Wharton Business School, University of Pennsylvania (1993)	• Merrill Lynch Japan Securities (Foreign Exchange Trader) • Long-Term Credit Bank of Japan
Andre Koo	4th	• Juvenile period in American School in Japan • Junior Reserve Officer Training Corps program at New York Military Academy near the United States Military Academy at West Point • BA/MBA, Stern School of Business, New York University (SCPS '93, MBA '94)	• Managing six Chinatrust-owned hotels in the USA
Steven Cheng	Son-in-law	• Young overseas student in USA • BA, Science of Information engineering, Northwest University • MBA, Wharton Business School, University of Pennsylvania	• Bonds Trading Department, Merrill Lynch in Japan • Vice President of Credit Department, UBS • Executive Director, UBS

Source: Revised from Ho and Kao (2010, 346)

titles are repeatedly part of the social alchemy that distinguish the family and bring eminent status in relation to others. The Koo family is, in a very substantial way, one of the major benefactors to the Wharton Business School. The family once gave US$10 million to help support planning and construction at Wharton.[11]

The school even named one part of the campus the Koo plaza. The family has endowed two professorships at the school, and each year provides three scholarships of US$25,000 each for Taiwanese students to attend Wharton.

"If life is about choices, then mine ended the day I left Wharton,"[12] said one of the heirs, Chester Koo. This quote is quite realistic, albeit melancholy. It reflects the tendency among large, powerful families to train their succeeding generations – or better yet – to predestine them to become successors. In fact, the "end-of-choices day" for many of the succeeding generations does not always come on the day the young person leaves school, but in many cases, it comes much earlier.

Without a doubt, the quality of education is important to the family. More significantly, what lies behind the formal educational system – the hidden curriculum, including the aspect of social capital – is the family's major concern. Putting children into the educational system is mainly for "habitus" cultivation rather than for acquiring knowledge, particularly in kindergarten, elementary schools, and high schools. Habitus, according to Bourdieu (1984), discloses the relationship between individual agents and the contextual environment. The place to cultivate habitus refers to a field of forces, in which any prospective alliance is to be nurtured. A prospective alliance can be obtained through the activities and experiences of everyday life, taste, lifestyle, values, and the disposition of particular social groups.

The two branches of the Koo family have adopted different ways – but with the same purpose – to nurture their successors. They both stress the formative process called habitus. To prevent their children from being spoiled in Taiwan, Jeffrey L. S. Koo Sr. sent his boys to Japan where his wife was born and grew up: He also had them study in an American school. According to Jeffrey Koo Jr. his father demanded that he shoulder the responsibility of taking care of his younger two brothers, Angelo and Andre (Koo Chung-Li 辜仲立). In an attempt to train himself, Andre Koo, Jeffrey L. S. Koo Sr.'s third son, even attended the Junior Reserve Officer Training Corps program at the New York Military Academy near the U.S. Military Academy at West Point. Since childhood, the heirs have been intentionally exposed to various cultures, as much to strengthen their global vision as to help them advance their adaptability.

The Koos have enduring and strong affinities, not only to the Wharton School, but also to the Tsai Hsing School. Koo Chen-Fu's three daughters and two sons attended the Tsai Hsing School, which was established by Dr. Helen Chu Hsiu-jung (朱秀柔) with a strong Catholic ethos in 1949 – incidentally, the same year that Chiang Kai-shek's ROC government retreated to Taiwan from mainland China. Tsai Hsing has developed to become the first private, comprehensive secondary school with a fifteen-year curriculum from kindergarten through high school. The first preparatory meeting for setting up the junior high school was held in Koo Chen-fu's house (Song 2006, 42). In the eyes of ordinary Taiwanese people, Tsai Hsing is a school for the aristocracy, a place to which many renowned families send their children. Koo Chen-fu's wife, Cecilia Koo, was Tsai Hsing's executive director for more than thirty years. The fourth generation of Koos, Leslie's and Chester's children, were educated there. Leslie has now taken over his mother's post of director. Altogether, about fifteen Koo family members spanning at least two generations have studied or are presently studying at Tsai Hsing. Not only are the descendants of enterprise owners educated at this school, but also children of politicians, celebrities, cultural intellectuals, and social elites. Cecilia Koo's brother-in-law Yeh Ming-Shun, who helped Koo Chen-fu gain connections with the KMT, was once the director, and his descendants also studied in Tsai Hsing. Another example of perceived aristocracy is the present first lady, Christine Chow Mei-ching (周美青, wife of President Ma Ying-jeou), who was educated in this system, as were her two daughters. Before he studied in the US, Nelson Chang (張安平) was a classmate of Chester Koo in Tsai Hsing. Several years later, he became Koo Chen-fu's son-in-law. As Nelson Chang has expressed,

> Tsai Hsing is certainly an educational institution. In my eyes, it is more like a big family. That many alumni like to send their children to Tsai Hsing becomes a family tradition. Our trust in school comes from our own deep understanding about Tsai Hsing during our student period.
>
> (Song 2006, 320)

Leslie mentioned the influence Tsai Hsing has had on him: "The 15-year long education in Tsai Hsing has coached me how to try my very best, and to get myself ready to compete with the strongest, and to win them over" (Song 2006, 316). Students are encouraged, not only to participate in competitions, but also to triumph. Team morale is often boosted during competitions.

Mediated by the exclusive form of their educational system, social elites of the top rank are apt to avail themselves of the economic, cultural, and social capital they inherited from their predecessors; simultaneously, other social classes are edged out. It has been pinpointed that Tsai Hsing is characterized by a "life and moral education" rather than a "rate of entering higher school" (Song 2006, 55).

Conclusion

Family businesses can slip into a downward spiral for many reasons, including family conflicts over wealth distribution, poor management, and infighting over the succession of power from one generation to the next. It is the entrepreneurship of each generation that preserves the family business and enables it to thrive over time. Training of the heirs in entrepreneurship comes as early as the childhood years. Through skillful intervention, patriarchs of the family carefully select schools for the next generation. Taking it one step further, they will even serve on the school board of directors in order to secure the school's policy.

By means of the process of social alchemy, succeeding generations develop into entrepreneurs. They gain, not only intangible social capital, but also have already been rooted in a set of social relationships. The destiny to become the next generation of entrepreneurs, armed with qualities including an emotional attachment and a strong commitment to the company or business group, has been, as much as possible, planned. All this is intended to serve as a driving force to run the business to the best of their ability and to preserve the reputation enjoyed by the family over the long term.

Power transition is risky, so keeping in close contact with political figures is important since information about business opportunities might be transmitted and received via these social ties, especially if the opportunity is related to policy changes. Next, it is insufficient to explain the enduring prosperity of the family by only relying on the thesis of political connectivity. The case of the Koo family implies that marriage ties can play an important role in shoring up any structural holes; they do this by leading the family towards other elitist groups of social networks. This helps overcome some of the deficits in social capital that the family needs in order to ensure the survival of the family business.

As people come and go, social ties become unstable. To cope with such uncertainty, the Koos are good at binding, bridging, and organizing their social ties. The Koo family discloses the patterns of transferring and managing social capital by 1) forming social relationships via marriages, 2) embedding their heirs into associations, 3) converting personal relationships into institutions and structuring social capital for the assurance of their reproduction, and 4) putting their children into a process of social alchemy that cultivates them in every aspect. In so doing, the family's increase in social capital can be structuralized and secured. Consequently, their personal and social networks are extended and expanded among interorganizations; all of this has a direct effect on their social capital. Organized contacts will help the offspring inherit the social capital their predecessors have meticulously cultivated. Social capital is hence reproduced, and so is entrepreneurship.

Notes

1 The author would like to thank the Ministry of Science and Technology for financially supporting the "Business Dynasties—Comparing the Koo and Li Families in Taiwan and Hong Kong" project
2 *Taiwan Nichinichi Shinpōsha* (Taiwan Daily Newspaper in Japanese), Oct. 30, 1940, Taihoku, p. 3.
3 Itō Kinjiro, *Taiwan bu ke shi chi*. (Taiwan Cannot be Bullied). Taipei: Wen Yiing Tang Chu Ban She, 1948.2000, p. 177.
4 Michelle S. Chaing, "Six Influential Local Business Groups," American Chamber of Commerce, *Topics Archive 2008*, 38 (12), www.amcham.com.tw/content/view/2618/413/.
5 ROC-USA Business Council. 2012. *In Memoriam: Jeffrey Koo*, March 8, 2013. Accessed June 24, 2013. www.rocusabc.org.tw/menu/detail?menu_id=96
6 *San San Fe* (Third Wednesday Club), http://sansanfe.org.tw/index.php?target=about.php&sn=1.
7 Wang Jun, "Zong Tong Xian Shen de Tong Xue Hui: 36 ge Taiwan Aisenhao de Gu Shi in Chinese" (Mr. President's Alumni: 36 Stories of Taiwanese Eisenhower Fellows). Taipei: Shin Shin Wen Publishers, 2001.
8 See the News Archive, Eisenhower Fellowship website, May 23, 2011, www.efworld.org/news/newsarchive/11/0511.php.
9 Lin Mei-chun, "Special Report: Time of Transition for Many Business Families," American Chamber, *Topics Archive 2006* 36 (9). www.amcham.com.tw/content/view/901.

10 Exclusive interview, shown on Good TV, Monday 14, 21:00 January 14. www.iptv. com.tw/goodtv/?class=witness&m=lCh_MbIvN9I. On this show, Jeffrey Koo Jr. shared his conversion to Christ.
11 Wharton Magazine, "Koo Family Gives $10 Million for New Educational Facility," School Update, posted June 1, 1998. http://whartonmagazine.com/issues/summer-1998/school-update/.
12 Jesse Wong and Jason Dean. "A Favoured Son Builds His Career—At a Cost," *The Wall Street Journal Online*, August 31, 2001.

References

Bourdieu, Pierre. 1973. Cultural Reproduction and Social Reproduction. In *Knowledge, Education and Cultural Change: Papers in the Sociology of Education*, edited by R. Brown, 71–112. London: Tavistock.

Bourdieu, Pierre. 1984. *Distinction: A Social Critique of the Judgment of Taste*, translated by Richard Nice. Cambridge, MA: Harvard University Press.

Bourdieu, Pierre. 1986. The Forms of Capital. In *Handbook of Theory and Research in the Sociology of Education*, edited by J.G. Richardson, 241–258. New York: Greenwald Press.

Bourdieu, Pierre. 1996. *The State Nobility: Elite Schools in the Field of Power*, translated by Lauretta C. Clough. Cambridge, UK: Polity Press.

Burt, Ronald. 1992. *Structural Holes: The Social Structure of Competition*. Cambridge, MA: Harvard University Press.

Coleman, James. 1988. "Social Capital in the Creation of Human Capital." *In American Journal of Sociology* 94: S95–S120.

Eisenhower Fellowships. 2011. "News: May 2011." Accessed June 24, 2013. www.efworld.org/news/newsarchive/11/0511.php

Eisenhower Fellowships. 2013. *"EF History."* Accessed June 24, 2013. www.efworld.org/about/eisenhower_fellowships_history.php

Fan, Joseph P.H., Ming (Jane) Jian, and Yin-Hua Yeh. 2007. "Succession: The Roles of Specialized Assets and Transfer Costs" (December 6, 2007). (Second Singapore International Conference on Finance, 2008) Available at SSRN. http://ssrn.com/abstract=1088287 or http://dx.doi.org/10.2139/ssrn.1088287

Granovetter, Mark. 1985. "Economic Action and Social Structure: The Problem of Embeddedness." *American Journal of Sociology* 91 (November): 481–510.

Ho, Tsai-man, and Cheng-shu Kao. 2010. "The Era of Professionalism and the Development of the Family Business: The Story of the Koo's Group." In *Economic Dynamism in the Sinospheres and Anglospheres: Identities, Integration and Competition*, edited by Tsai-man C. Ho and Louella Cheng, 333–367. HK: The University of Hong Kong

Inkpen, A.C., and E.W.K. Tsang,. 2005. Social Capital, Networks, and Knowledge Transfer. *Academy of Management Review*, 30 (1): 146–165.

Itō, Kinjiro. 1948/2000. *Taiwan bu ke shi chi.* (Taiwan Cannot Be Bullied). Taipei: Wen Ying Tang Chu Ban She (in Chinese).

Lin, Mei-Chun. 2008. "Special Report: Time for Transition for Many Business Families." *The American Chamber of Commerce in Taipei* 36 (9). www.amcham.com.tw/topics-archive/topics-archive-2006/vol-36-no-9/901-special-reporttime-of-transition-for-many-business-families

Lin, Nan. 2002. *Social Capital: A Theory of Social Structure and Action*. London and New York: Cambridge University Press.

Lin, Shan-Zuo, 2006. "Wai zi: xiao ti da zuo, jin rong gu quan zao yang" (Foreign Investment: Making a Big Deal out of the Little Things Leading to a Disaster in Financial Stocks). *China Times*. July 21.

ROC-USA Business Council. 2012. *In Memoriam: Jeffrey Koo*. Accessed June 24, 2013. www.rocusabc.org.tw/menu/detail?menu_id=96

Shane, S. 2000. "Prior Knowledge and the Discovery of Entrepreneurial Opportunities." *Organization Science* 11 (4): 448–469.

Shane, S., and D. M. Cable. 2002. "Network Ties, Reputation, and the Financing of New Ventures." *Management Science* 48 (3): 364–381.

Song, Yazi. 2006. *Teaching for Excellence: The Principal, Helen Chu Hsiu-jung and the Legend of Tsai Hsing*. Taipei: Taiwan Commercial Press.

Wang Jun. 2001. *Mr. President's Alumni: 36 Stories of Taiwanese Eisenhower Fellows* (in Chinese). Taipei: Shin Shin Wen Publishers.

Wharton Magazine. 1998. "Koo Family Gives $10 Million for New Educational Facility." Accessed July 19. http://whartonmagazine.com/issues/summer-1998/school-update

Wong, Jesse and Dean, Jason. 2001. "A Favoured Son Builds His Career – At a Cost." *The Wall Street Journal Online*, 31 August.

Yanaihara, Tadao. 1956/2003. *Taiwan under the Japanese Imperialism* (in Japanese). Translated by Chou Xian-wen. Taipei: Hai Hxia Academic Publisher (in Chinese).

6 Network capital and the Li & Fung Group in Hong Kong

Four generations of inculcation and inheritance

Victor Zheng and Siu-Lun Wong[1]

Introduction

On 3 September 2000, about 1,000 guests assembled at the Hong Kong Exhibition Centre for a lavish wedding banquet. As the bride (Sabrina Fung, daughter of Victor Fung, chairman of Li & Fung Group) and the bridegroom (Kevin Lam, grandson of the late key founder of Hang Sang Bank, Lam Ping-yim) were from local dynastic families, invited guests were mostly celebrities in Hong Kong, Macao, Mainland China and all over the world. The wedding setting was well designed; the programme, well-planned; and the food and drink, high quality. Against this background, the Exhibition Centre was full of joy and happiness. Both hosts and guests seemed to be enjoying the banquet and saw the gathering an occasion for social interaction and exchange (*The Sun* 2000; Leung and Lee 2003).

On 21 September 2012, over 3,000 people flocked to the small northern Dutch town of Haren to attend a teenage girl's 16th birthday party. The invitation was posted by the girl on Facebook, who sent it to her friend but "then sent it to other friends and soon it spread like wildfire across the Internet." Worried that the celebration would get out of control, the girl cancelled the party, which turned the frustrated party-goers into rioters. Not were only shops vandalised and a car set on fire, but a number of people were injured, and some were even arrested by the police (Cavaliere 2012).

Although a wedding banquet and a birthday party are common social gatherings and are regarded as two important ways of networking, they can end up with diverse results because of different ways of management and organisation. The wedding banquet demonstrates how a well-planned social gathering turned into social investment that can forge stronger ties. The birthday party shows how social consumption does not add value but chaos and frustration because of a lack of planning and management. This chapter uses the case of Li & Fung Group, a family-controlled and highly globalised firm based in Hong Kong, for closer study. There is no dearth of academic research on Li & Fung (Hutcheon 1992;Clemetson and Ernsberger 1996; O'Connell 1996; Magretta 1998; Feng 2006; Fung et al. 2008), but they focus on management, especially on management reformation, organisational restructuring and supply chain theory. Little research looks from the perspective of network capital even though the current chairman describes the company as a "network orchestrator" (Fung et al. 2008, 13). Therefore, in this chapter, our research explores how socio-economic and political connections are deployed as an indispensable strategy for sustaining business control, expansion and enhancing competitiveness.

Cultivating network capital for enterprise building and control

Social networks form part of our social life, and social networking is ubiquitous in human society. But whether it is cultivated as a kind of investment or is simply treated as an ordinary form of consumption determines the propensity or capacity for the next round of development but reflects different points of view. Unlike economic capital or human capital, which is relatively visible and can be measured more objectively, network capital (largely similar to the concept of social capital or *guanxi* but not exactly the same) is invisible and cannot be quantified easily or clearly (see below for definition). More importantly, because the cultivation of social networks (accumulation of network capital) takes time, and positive feedback is less instant, indirect and not easily observed, few people realize its importance, let alone be willing to spend too much effort, time or resources cultivating it.

Notwithstanding the far from clear and direct benefit network capital can bring, the fact that, once it is established, it can "facilitate certain actions of individuals who are within the structure" is beyond question (Coleman 1990, 302). In some situations or cases, whether it is thin or thick, network capital can be the most decisive factor that can change the balance and make the distinction among competitors or options. In fact, there is no lack of research and discussion on the matter of social capital and social networking directly or indirectly. To fill the lacunae in social and economic theory, which offers little convincing explanation to address social attributes such as social position, status, and personal connections and how they shape economic behaviour and business decisions, a significant number of interpretations have been suggested since the 1980s. Theories such as social capital, cultural capital and social exchange are frequently quoted (Smelser and Swedberg 1994).

Of the theorists, Pierre Bourdieu emphasises social and cultural capital in equal importance to economic capital. By using these concepts, Bourdieu tries to explain that varying degrees or predispositions of social and cultural capital reflected in aesthetic criteria, dress code, living style, and so forth, not only determine one's social relations, life chances and career preferences, but enforce one's distinction from people in other social classes. The implicit meaning is that, because social and cultural capital are transmitted from generation to generation, one also inherits social class and social status from one's parents (Bourdieu 1984; 1986; Bourdieu and Wacquant 1992).

By addressing the same theoretical gap between society and economy, James Coleman uses similar concepts of social capital and cultural capital but in a dynamic way. He sees social capital as a kind of potential resource that one can use alongside human capital and economic capital although the availability varies among social groups. Unlike Bourdieu, Coleman points out that the way of establishing social capital is based on rational choice and calculation, which any social class can do. He goes a step further to explain that the accumulation of social capital is based on trust and shared values that are enforced through repeated social exchanges. Nevertheless, Coleman comes to the conclusion that social capital can affect the creation of human capital in succeeding generations, which is similar to Bourdieu's argument of social class and social status reproduction (Coleman 1988; 1990; 1994).

Following the line of thought of rational choice and social trust, Mark Granovetter sociometrically proves that small-scale interpersonal ties (weak ties) could be translated into large-scale patterns, which in turn will generate positive results (strength) to the actors, and states that economic rationality is "embedded" within social relationships. He therefore argues that maintaining good social connections not only can enhance social trust but can reduce malfeasance in transactions. In short, Granovetter suggests that economic relations between actors in fact are embedded in social networks, which implies economic action or decisions are not interpreted only from one side but multidimensionally (Granovetter 1973; 1985; 1994).

There are also many researchers who have paid much attention to the innovative idea of social capital and cultural capital (Williamson 1975; 1979; Lin 1990; Putnam 2000). Although their approaches to these concepts are different and their focuses are on various aspects, they come to almost the same conclusion. On the whole, they consider social capital and cultural capital as powerful factors or valuable elements that not only have far-reaching and fundamental effects on daily life, interpersonal interaction, business operations, economic development, and so forth but will be transmitted from generation to generation. Therefore, not only have people from different walks of life tried to invest in their social capital to enhance their competiveness, but the World Bank has also recently set the promotion of social capital around the globe, especially in developing societies, as one of their key social development missions (World Bank 2013).

Although social capital and cultural capital are forceful concepts for better understanding socio-economic behaviour, they are undoubtedly generic/brief ideas that mostly deal with social actors who come from the same social class, social group or have a similar cultural background. Also, interpersonal relation may not be purely social in nature. Some may be political connections while some may be religious attachments. We further argue that common social connections, such as attending social gatherings or being member of social clubs, and so forth, could not generate sufficient/significant useful effect to the actor if these kinds of activities are usually taken in the form of consumption. Only socio-economic-political relations that are highly embedded in the social actor could be turned to capital and could be used for achieving goals or, specifically speaking, could be deployable. Hence, we think the concept of social capital and cultural capital cannot offer us very sharp and precise explanatory power for distinguishing individuals who come from the same social group or even the same family, especially when family networks or socio-economic-political relations are transferred from one generation to the next and when competition for leadership or fight for family estate among succeeding generations is very tense.

In order to grasp the generic explanatory power of the idea of social capital and cultural capital, and to have a more specific focus for differentiating individual variation particularly within a single social group or family, we propose using the concept of network capital – by combining the effect of social networking and social capital, on the one hand, and extending the essences of political capital and moral capital, and so forth, on the other – but put emphases on the embeddedness of personal connection on an individual (Zheng and Wong 2010). As such, we see network capital as a kind of capital that not merely includes social contact or acquaintance but is blended with various essences like business connections, political affiliation, as well as religious association, and so forth. And more importantly, this kind of capital is highly embedded in a particular person, that is, the social actor.

Admittedly, social networks are usually seen as "webs of relationships that link the individual directly to other people, and through these others, indirectly to even more people" (Robertson 1987, 174). Social capital is defined as "the sum of the resources, actual or virtual, that accrue to an individual or a group by virtue of possessing a durable network of more or less institutionalised relationships of mutual acquaintance and recognition" (Bourdieu and Wacquant 1992, 119). By bringing together these two concepts, we mean those human behaviours that are featured by taking the initiative for cultivating interpersonal, socio-economic-political connections of each individual for a definitive aim or with a specific intention.

To be precise, we consider the spending of effort, time and resources to establish certain particularistic relations with a specific person or institution for an individual (person, family or institution) to be like a kind of "idiosyncratic investment," in Oliver Williamson's (1979, 242) words, which aims at generating benefit to the "investor" or with a specific purpose. So, it is not a form of social consumption but a typical form of investment. Of course, we have to bear in mind that such capital is built on the foundation of mutual benefit and mutual trust. It also follows the internal logic that positive feedback enhances social relations, whereas negative feedback does the opposite.

In the subsequent paragraphs, we use this concept to explain how Li & Fung was founded, developed and restructured. Then, the research focus shifts to examine mechanisms for establishing or enhancing network capital, such as sending children to noble schools, organizing high-end social activities, undertaking political position/role and even "arranging" marriages for enhancing wealthy families "alliance," and so forth. Also, this chapter assesses to what extent inculcated network capital can complement other kinds of capital to substantiate business expansion and especially to exercise certain family (or certain family members') control. Internal conflict between partners of the company and among members of a single family is duly addressed. After that, discussion is given to exploring the dynamism of Li & Fung in particular and the stock market as well as Chinese family business in general. Also, the pervasiveness and indispensability of network capital for different generations' socio-economic endeavours is closely examined.

A brief history of Li & Fung: house divided, house united

Like many multinational corporations with a modest beginning, the Li & Fung Group, an internationally well-known conglomerate, came into being as a small trading house. It was cofounded by two partners, Li To-ming and Fung Pak-liu, in Guangzhou in 1906.[2] The major business at the beginning was porcelain and earthenware exporting, especially to the United States. Later, as the company gradually established trade connections in the US and other Western countries, their business grew. The variety of products exported increased, and Fung Pak-liu's role in the trading house becoming increasingly dominant. Fireworks and firecrackers, jade and stone, Chinese handicrafts, and bamboo and rattan products became key commodities that mostly American purchasers ordered (Woo 1937; Hutcheon 1992; Feng 2006).

As a result of the strong commitment and endeavours of the two partners, Li & Fung's exporting business made remarkable progress. By the end of the 1910s, the firm had made the following significant achievements: (1) A multistory building was erected in Shamian, a bustling business hub in Guangzhou, and its headquarters were moved there. (2) A self-run factory was set up in the self-owned building to produce Chinese handicrafts directly, for better profit. (3) A large-scale warehouse was rented near Shamian for storing goods waiting for shipment. (4) A trading branch in Hong Kong was established to facilitate the growing trade (Hutcheon 1992; Feng 2006).

In the late 1920s, as the business became more prosperous and the Western-educated second-generation Fungs, such as Fung Mo-ying, Fung Hon-chu and Fung Lai-wah, grew up, they joined the firm to make their contribution. Some of the second-generation Li family members probably joined the company about that time, but very few records were found. Although the 1920s to 1930s marked a tumultuous period of socio-political strife in China (for example, the Guangdong and Hong Kong General Strike and warlordism), Li & Fung kept thriving and soon emerged as one of the leading export houses in China in the early 1930s (Hutcheon 1992; Feng 2006).

In July 1937, the Anti-Japanese War broke out. Realising the conflict could cause heavy loss of lives and property, the Lis and the Fungs made two critical decisions. They incorporated their Hong Kong branch business into Li & Fung Limited, so it was the centre for their export business, and they relocated most of their business to Hong Kong. In addition, they moved their families from Guangzhou to Hong Kong. Therefore, from 1937 to 1941, although the Chinese mainland was tormented by war and society was in serious chaos, Li & Fung's Hong Kong business remained vibrant.

In spite of the farsighted decision to move their business and families to Hong Kong at the beginning of war, neither could escape the war as the Japanese guns and bayonets finally pointed at Hong Kong. The Japanese occupation in Hong Kong from December 1941 to August 1945 not only resulted in tremendous loss of lives and mass social destruction but almost completely stopped business activity. Inevitably, Li & Fung Limited also suffered heavy loss. On a trip back home in

1943 to visit relatives and check on family property, Fung Pak-liu died of a stroke (at the age of 63) when he saw the serious war destruction there (Feng 2006).

Like many firms and families that started the process of rebuilding after the surrender of the Japanese troops, Li & Fung Limited quickly reactivated their business connections and production. However, an internal dispute erupted at that time between the Lis and the Fungs, as the former accused the latter of ill management and dominance. After negotiations, in 1946 (forty years after its establishment), the Lis chose to sell all their shares, which made the Fung family "the sole owner" of Li & Fung.[3] Notwithstanding the probably unhappy separation of the two families, the Fungs resolved to keep the firm's name unchanged (Hutcheon 1992; Feng 2006).

As the firm became solely owned, the second-generation Fungs could work more smoothly and with greater incentive. Thanks to the joint effort of the energetic siblings, Li & Fung's business picked up remarkably in the early postwar period. However, in 1950, as the United Nations, under the influence of the US, imposed a trade embargo on the newly established People's Republic of China because of the Korean War, Hong Kong's economy fell into the doldrums because of the sudden drop of the re-export trade. As a trading firm that mainly relied on re-export trading, the embargo was deadly for Li & Fung Limited.

Although many investors were pessimistic about the Hong Kong economy, the Fungs saw the challenge positively. Instead of sourcing out the work when the firm received orders, the Fungs established their own assembly lines for producing goods for export. Because of their solid experience in running a factory in Guangzhou before the Anti-Japanese War, their shift from trading to manufacturing was very successful. In less than five years, the firm had founded not only manufacturing arms in Hong Kong but in neighbouring areas like Macao and Taiwan and became one of the driving forces for Hong Kong's industrialisation (Hutcheon 1992; Feng 2006).

As the Hong Kong economy took off in the late 1950s, Li & Fung reconsolidated and soon entered another stage of rapid development. After two decades of maneuvering and making impressive growth, in 1973, the second-generation Fungs decided to turn Li & Fung Limited into a publicly listed company when the Hong Kong stock market was booming. Although absorbing public capital through the stock market for further development was regarded as a key consideration, other critical goals such as having a transparent and publicly accountable management, having an objective mechanism for transferring shares, and having an open corporate culture in attracting nonfamily professionals were equally emphasised (Hutcheon 1992; Feng 2006).

About that time, the well-educated third-generation Fungs, such as Kwok-hong and Kowk-chor (sons of Fung Mo-ying), Victor and William (sons of Fung Hon-chu) and Li Wing-hong (son of Fung Lai-wah) joined the management. They not only brought in new concepts of Western management but social connections around the globe. As a result of better financial and human capital backup, Li & Fung Limited first expanded to toys and retail shops and later to shipping, insurance and property investment. In no more than a decade of development, the

firm had emerged as a multinational corporation not only with diversified investment but with widespread business networks (Hutcheon 1992; Fung 2006). If we
look at annual sales, we see that the figures rose from HK$83.7 million in 1974
to HK$283.4 million in 1980, and then to HK$1,453.1 million in 1987. Profits
after tax increased from HK$1.8 million to HK$11.5 million in 1980 and then to
HK$45.0 million in 1987 (Figure 6.1).

In 1989, due to political turmoil in the Chinese mainland, the Hang Seng Index,
a measurement to track the performance of the stock market in Hong Kong, plum-
meted. Like many listed companies whose share prices experienced prolonged
falling, Li & Fung Limited saw the price of their shares fall. About that time, red
tape and serious family conflict among the third-generation members reportedly
intensified (Leung and Lee 2003). In order to avoid conflict becoming malicious
and to save Li & Fung Limited from declining, Victor and William Fung proposed
privatising the company through a "leverage buy-out," which was ultimately
accepted by other Fungs and the public shareholders. In other words, about forty
years after its first split, Li & Fung underwent another division, which made the
line of Fung Hon-chu the sole managing team of the business.

In 1992, as the Hong Kong economy picked up and the stock market recovered,
Victor and William Fung restructured Li & Fung Limited by making the core
business into Li & Fung (1937) Limited and going public again. As a result of a
streamlined management team and more focused investment (mainly trade and
retail), Li & Fung (1937) Limited experienced another stage of impressive growth
from annual sales of HK$2,855 million in 1991 to HK$24,993 million in 2000,
and then to HK$124,115.1 million in 2010. In the same period, annual profits after
taxes rose from HK$86.9 million in 1991 to HK$860.0 million in 2000 and then
to HK$4,280.3 million in 2010 (Figure 6.1). In about twenty years, the annual

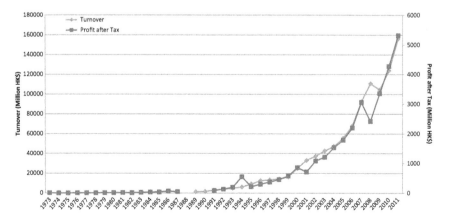

Figure 6.1 Li & Fung's sales and profits, 1973–2011

Source: Li & Fung Limited, various years

sales recorded an increase of forty-two times and the annual profits increased forty-eight times.

In addition to stable internal growth that relied on reinvestment and management enhancement, Li & Fung (1937) Limited's drastic expansion was brought on by a series of acquisitions and mergers. Some even attracted international attention. For instance, the takeover of Inchape Buying Services in 1995, the acquisition of Swire & Maclaine and Camberley Enterprises in 1999 and the purchase of Colby Group Holdings 2000, as well as the purchase of Janco Overseas in 2002, made headlines in the global business news (Feng 2006).

Li & Fung (1937) Limited kept expanding and evolving. Fourth-generation family members, particularly Sabrina, Spencer and Joseph Fung (daughter and sons of Victor Fung) and Terence Fung (the only son of William Fung), joined the group at different management levels and in various capacities at the beginning of the new millennium. As Victor and William Fung entered their sixties, they started to plan for their succession, like their predecessors did, to ensure that the family business could successfully be passed on to the next generation.

In 2001, the group spun off into the retail business into Convenience Retail Asia Limited (CRA) and made it publicly listed on the Hong Kong Growth Enterprise Market, which was transferred to the main board of the Hong Kong Stock Exchange in 2011. About that time, the group also branched out into the distribution business to form Integrated Distribution Services Group Limited (IDS Group), which was listed on the Hong Kong Stock Exchange in 2004. Five years later, the group also publicly listed its "high-end luxury menswear retailing business, Trinity Limited (Figure 6.2).

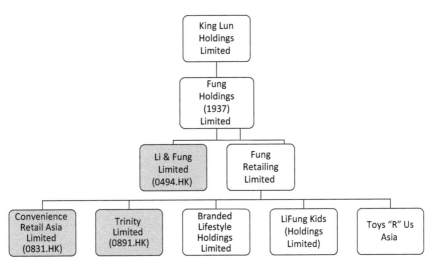

Figure 6.2 Organisational chart of Li & Fung

Sources: Fung Group 2013; Li & Fung Limited, various years

Note: Companies highlighted are listed in the Hong Kong Stock Exchange

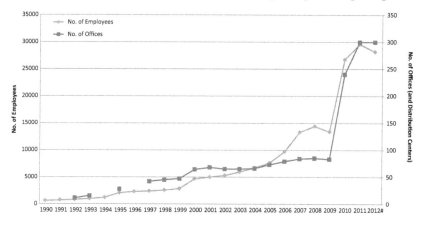

Figure 6.3 Li & Fung's staff and offices, 1990–2012

Source: Li & Fung Limited, various years

In sum, in about twenty years of development, Li & Fung became a multinational conglomerate that controlled several dozen subsidiaries and four publicly listed companies[4] and employed "a total staff of more than 24,000 across 40 countries worldwide, and with revenues of more than US$8.7 billion in 2006" (Fung et al. 2008, 215). Solid longitudinal statistics show that, in 1992, the Li & Fung Group employed approximately 800 staff and established 11 offices in 8 economies. In 2000, the total number of staff employed by the group jumped to 4,668, and in 2012, it jumped to 28,198. In the same period, the total number of offices established by the group went up to 64 offices in 37 economies in 2000 and then 300 offices in 40 economies in 2012 (Figure 6.3). Such impressive figures explain why, in a recent report, Victor and William Fung ranked ninth on a list of the wealthiest people in Hong Kong (*Forbes* 2013).

The cultivation and transmission of the first generation's network capital

From Li & Fung's more than a hundred years of extraordinary development, we can see that network capital complements economic capital and human capital in encouraging the firm's growth as well as in exercising control. To some extent or at some critical junctures, network capital seemed to be one of the critical factors that determined frequently asked questions like who gets what and in what proportion. Therefore, in this section, research attention is given to unravelling how network capital was cultivated "to make the difference" among members who had the same background.

To begin, we talk about Li To-ming and Fung Pak-liu's "rags to riches" story and their split, which turned Li & Fung into a solely owned enterprise of the

Fung Pak-liu family. According to a local scholar, before joining to start their own store in equal share, Li To-ming and Fung Pak-liu were employees of Po Hing Company, a porcelain exporting house in Guangzhou (Woo 1937). Some indirect information revealed that Li To-ming was older than Fung Pak-liu (which implies seniority in old China) and had solid experience in trading porcelain and had certain business networks (Hutcheon 1992; Feng 2006). As such, we can infer that Li To-ming might have thick human and economic capital.

In-depth archival research data show that Li To-ming in fact came from an affluent family and had a good education. In a business directory published in 1915, we found a record relating to Li To-ming, who had opened a porcelain exporting firm called Yee Chan in sole proprietorship at the heart of Hong Kong's bustling business centre, Central, and assigned an "accountant" named Lau Kung-tong to help him manage all accounts and daily business. The shop was at 10 Chiu Lung Street, where the Melbourne Plaza and Queen's Theatre are now (Zheng 1915, 549). Because this information was published in 1915, it is reasonable to suggest that, before that year, Li To-ming had conducted business in Hong Kong. Judging from the location of the shop, it is equally reasonable to argue that the business was not small scale. In another business directory published in 1922, Yee Chan was still in the porcelain and china exporting business at 10 Chiu Lung Street, Central (The Publicity Bureau for South China 1922, 190). This record further confirmed that Li To-ming's business in Hong Kong was substantial, especially in porcelain exporting.

Other obvious circumstantial evidence further demonstrates that the Li To-ming family could not be in a disadvantaged or inferior position to the Fung Pak-liu family, as the company put "Li" before "Fung." Moreover, Li To-ming took up a higher post (chairman) than Fung Pak-liu (general manager) in the trading house (Feng 2006). Even in Li & Fung Limited's company record maintained in Hong Kong,[5] we can see that Li To-ming took higher posts (chairman and managing director) than Fung Pak-liu (general manager and managing director). Although a number of shareholders from the second generation of the two families were different (seven from the Fung family, five from the Li family; Fung Lai-wah marrying a Li could be seen as a "mixture" of the families), the proportion of shares allotted the families was equal when it was first registered on 24 December 1937 ("Li & Fung Limited," Companies Registry File No.: 122–5–16; Hutcheon 1992). In other words, we can see that, until the mid-1940s, the Li To-ming family human capital and economic capital could not be less, but may have been more, than that of the Fung Pak-liu family. Their loss of control over Li & Fung seems to be affected by other factors that the family overlooked or that there is insufficient information about. Less network capital appeared to be the most salient one.

There are more records on Fung Pak-liu than on Li To-ming. However, most seem to come from the Fung family and are quoted repeatedly without double-checking. It appears that Fung Pak-liu also came from an affluent family (at least, not from poverty). The most critical decision in his life seems to be his education in Hong Kong. Born in 1880 in Heshan (a small town near Guangzhou), he was sent to Hong Kong as an adolescent for education. He entered the government-funded

Queen's College (QC), the so-called "cradle of elites in Hong Kong" (Zheng and Wong 2007), in the late 1890s. From that westernised education, Fung Pak-liu not only acquired modern knowledge and learned to speak fluent English but also activated an important mechanism, the old boy's network, for establishing his network capital. Upon graduation in 1900, he received a Junior Morrison Scholarship for one year of further study in the US. He then served his alma mater as a teaching assistant (also called junior teacher) for about a year when he returned to Hong Kong (Queen's College Hong Kong 1891–1901; Stokes and Stokes 1987). After that, he went back to Guangzhou and found a job in Po Hing Company, which started his lifelong relationship with Li To-ming (Feng 2006).

As Li & Fung grew, Fung Pak-liu's network capital, especially his QC old boys' connections, came into play. His role as a "company representative" and in handling "external affairs" seemed also gave him more chances forging a personal socio-economic-political network than Li To-ming whose role was to manage the company's "internal affairs." An irrefutable fact was that, as the accumulation of network capital got thicker, it not only brought Li & Fung greater business opportunities but more political affiliation, business credit and social status to Fung Pak-liu. Some indirect, less visible, but critical, evidence can be cited for illustration. The first piece of evidence is a porcelain plate – "a blue-and-white willow-pattern plate of the kind popular as exportware in the early years of this century; It was specially ordered by Mr. Fung Pak-liu for a valued friend, Dr. G.H.B. Wright" (Hutcheon 1992, 4; see Figure 6.4). This "valued friend" in fact was the headmaster of QC from 1881 to 1906.

Because Dr. Wright had retired in 1906 and Li & Fung had been founded that year, it seems to us that the specially designed delicate porcelain plate might have been presented after 1906. If so, some implications could be drawn, one related to another. As indicated by Stokes and Stokes (1987), many QC old boys entered the upper echelons of government, commerce, the professions, and so forth, not only in Hong Kong, but also in Mainland China and Southeast Asia. Sun Yat-sen (founding father of the Republic of China, ROC), Tong Shao-yee (the first Prime Minister of ROC), Ho Tung (the wealthiest tycoon in Hong Kong) and Lai Man-wai ("the father of Hong Kong cinema") are some of the frequently mentioned, famous QC old boys in different socio-economic-political echelons (Stokes and Stokes 1987). Through the QC old boys' ties, members could get connected and offer mutual assistance if needed. Like many other old boys, Fung Pak-liu maintained good relationships with his alma mater, the headmaster and the other old boys. Hence, we argue that the presentation of the porcelain plate after 1906 probably related to other issues that we might not be aware of.

Gross speculation may involve the Panama-Pacific International Exposition that was held in San Francisco in 1915, which Fung Pak-liu "was asked to join" when the Chinese government chose a delegation to attend (Hutcheon 1992, 9). Further information revealed that the official chief representative of the Chinese delegation was Chan Kam-tao, a QC old boy who earned a doctoral degree from Yale University and was appointed Minister of Finance when the ROC was founded (The History of the Ministry of Finance, ROC. 2013). Because the major

Figure 6.4 A porcelain plate presented to G.H.B. Wright, headmaster of Queen's College,
        by Fung Pak-liu in the early twentieth century

Source: Hutcheon 1992, 12

business of Li & Fung was exporting porcelain and Chinese handicrafts, products
with Chinese features, to the US, Fung Pak-liu took the initiative to maneuver his
QC old boys' network for help, so having the chance of being "asked to join it"
seemed logical and understandable. Dr. Wright offered some help in matching up
some QC old boys, but it was not possible. Whatever the real reason was, records
show that, after the Panama exhibition, Li & Fung got more access to the lucrative
American market, which marked the company's rapid take-off (Hutcheon 1992;
Feng 2006).

As the company grew, although the amount of wealth brought to both families
was more or less the same, the network capital accumulated between them seemed
to diverge. Later, as Sino-Japanese hostilities became more severe in the early
1930s, the company put more reliance on its Hong Kong branch, which made
Fung Pak-liu's Hong Kong-based QC old boys' network capital more valuable.
More importantly, Fung Pak-liu seemed paid particular attention to his children's
education in Hong Kong. This might be due to his personal experience that Western education in Hong Kong ensured him better chances for upward social mobilization. As such, most of his children were also brought up and educated in Hong
Kong, which implied that they had stronger social connections in the colony (see

the next section). Therefore, in spite of the fact that registration of Li & Fung Limited in Hong Kong in 1937 followed the principle of equal sharing between them, the real controlling power had fallen into the hands of Fungs.

As a result, in 1946, shortly after the end of the Japanese occupation in Hong Kong, many residents were busy rebuilding their homes. Li To-ming decided to put nearly forty years of relationship with the Fung family to an end by selling all the controlling shares of Li & Fung Limited, after a dispute "alleging that the new management was unable to run the business satisfactorily" (Hutcheon 1992, 25). The departure of Li To-ming was mysterious, as he was chairman and managing director of the company and one generation more senior than the second-generation Fungs (Fung Pak-liu had passed away earlier), so the general public might expect the reverse outcome.[6] Given that both families were equipped with similar thickness of economic capital and human capital, different levels of network capital seemed to be a reasonable explanation for the change in the situation the company.

The cultivation and transmission of the second generation's network capital

The split of the two cofounding families in 1946 marked another stage of development for Li & Fung. As the company became a solely owned business of the Fungs, concerted effort was made and commitment devoted to foster business growth and to overcome crisis in time of difficulty. As a result, although the business environment from the late 1940s to the early 1960s was not favourable, the second-generation Fungs could navigate the storms and turbulence to make Li & Fung a leading trading firm in Hong Kong (Hutcheon 1992; Feng 2006).

Although the economic capital and human capital of the second-generation Fungs were more or less the same (as they were from the same family), the network capital they invested and cultivated varied when they became older. Therefore, network capital could become a crucial factor for determining "who gets what and in what proportion" when decisions had to be made to solve problems or conflicts.

Briefly, most traditional family businesses could assign siblings to different departments and put older members in a higher position. Some of the members might lack interest in the business and chose to become professionals, academics or civil servants. Nevertheless, they mostly were the shareholders of the family business with more or less equal shares among brothers although some families also allotted a certain proportion of shares to be equally shared among sisters (Zheng 2009). To some extent, the structure and functioning of Li & Fung Limited also followed this pattern and mentality (Hutcheon 1992; Feng 2006).

If we look at the management team of the company, we see that the oldest brother, Fung Mo-ying, held the position of chairman; Fung Hon-chu served as general manager; Fung Lai-wah was appointed administrative manager and Fung Hong-hing was the company's division manager (woodware). Like many other family businesses, the Fungs had conflicts and disagreements in managing and planning the company. However, as they once faced the threat of the company splitting and disintegrating, they seemed able to put aside different opinions to find ways of working harmoniously. Run by siblings, Li & Fung enjoyed resilient, double-digit growth for nearly twenty years, from the early 1950s to the early 1970s (Hutcheon 1992; Feng 2006).

Although the amount of economic capital and human capital enjoyed by the second-generation Fungs did not change much as the company grew, the "balance of power/control" among them at that time, the level of network capital, varied since Fung Hon-chu's appointment to a political position: first, as Urban Councillor for the Colonial Government in 1960 (a post he held until 1966) and then as Legislative Councillor (until 1970), a position with great honour and high socio-political status in Hong Kong. After years of these public/political services tendered, Fung Hon-chu received a DBE (Dame Commander of the Most Excellent Order of the British Empire) from the British Royal Family as a token to acknowledge his contribution to Hong Kong society (Hutcheon 1992). Because of all his public service and political contribution, Fung Hon-chu gradually established personal connections across commerce and politics. Hence, he could accumulate far more network capital than his brothers and sisters could, which turned out to be the most important factor that determined "who gets what and in what proportion" (Table 6.1).

As the family business grew, more well-educated, third-generation family members were absorbed, which inevitably made the management structure swollen and bred more disagreement and conflict. In order to better handle internal family disputes and the lack of efficiency in management, the family came to a big decision in the early 1970s by publicly listing Li & Fung Limited when the Hong Kong stock market flourished (Hutcheon 1992; Feng 2006).

After going public, the company not only got more capital for expansion but brought to the board some nonfamily professionals with good qualifications and connections, which created greater synergy as expected. Therefore, the company got greater impetus for expansion to new heights. Its competitiveness in core businesses like manufacturing and exporting could be enhanced, and its diversification strategy to other business such as convenience stores and toys could be substantially backed up.

In 1975, the company's chairman, Fung Mo-ying, died. The board restructured and made some personnel rearrangements, which not only paved solid ground for further development but set in centrifugal force in the next split. Under the new management team – the board of directors[7] – new business ideas and management philosophy were brought in, which generated greater developmental momentum that drove the company forward and with more impressive growth. According to Robin Hutcheon (1992, 69), from 1973 to 1988, "the firm's turnover had grown from HK$84 million to HK$1,500 million in that period of 15 years."

However, the breathtaking business growth did not reduce internal family conflict but made it worse. Therefore, when the third-generation family members were autonomous or not interested in compromising, breaking up appeared to be inevitable (Leung and Lee 2003). Like the first-generation division, as they were

Table 6.1 Education, occupations and public service records of second-generation Fungs

Name	Position at Company	Education	Public Services
Fung Mo-ying	Chairman and Managing Director (Li & Fung, 1973–75)	Ellis Kadoorie School	N.A.
Fung Hon-chu	Managing Director (Li & Fung, 1973–81) Chairman (Li & Fung, 1975–89)	King's College	Certificate of Honour (1958), OBE (1965) Member of the Urban and Legislative Council Chairman of Tung Wah Group of Hospitals Director of Hong Kong Tuberculosis Association Member of Ruttonjee Hospital President of the Heshan Townsmen Association Vice-President of the Fung Clansmen Association Executive Director of the Hong Kong Industrial Association Chairman of the Hong Kong Cotton Spinners' Association Councillor of the Urban Council Councillor of the Legislative Council
Li Fung Lai-wah	Director (Li & Fung, 1973–1989)	Sacred Heart Canossian College	N.A.
Fung Hon-hing	Director (Li & Fung, 1975–1989)	BA Horticulture (Lingnan)	N.A.
Fung Hon-pong	Shareholder (Li & Fung, 1973–1989)	BS (Lingnan), PhD (Iowa State)	N.A.
Fung Lai-sheung	Shareholder (Li & Fung, 1973–1989)	N.A.	N.A.
Fung Hon-yin	Shareholder (Li & Fung, 1973–1989)	MBBS (HKU)	
Fung Lai-ngoi	Shareholder (Li & Fung, 1973–1989)	N.A.	N.A.

Source: Feng 2006; Li & Fung Limited, various years

from the same family, supposedly having similar economic capital and human capital, network capital seemed to be the critical factor that determined "who gets what and in what proportion" when final decisions had to be made.

The cultivation and transmission of the third generation's network capital

Although some of the third-generation family members like Fung Kwok-hong, Fung Kwok-chor and Li Wing-hong had joined the family business in the late 1960s, they were assigned to the subdivision level for solid training and learning in hopes that they would be involved in daily operations. Even when they were later promoted to division managers, none of them joined the group's board of directors. Many other family members in fact chose to keep a distance from the family business, as if they were sleeping shareholders. In other words, although Fung Pak-liu had eleven children and the number of third-generation family members totalled thirty-seven, few chose to work in the family business without making a contribution (Figure 6.5).

In an interview, Fung Hon-chu made the following comment:

> We are sons from the same father but why do the opinions of some sons weigh more? This is very difficult to deal with. Like us, Li & Fung, few family members are willing to stay in the company to manage it. There are only several of us. My nephews chose professional careers. Some are lawyers. Some are professors in the States. They see family business as troublesome and do not want to get involved.
>
> (*Capital* 1992, 71)

His eldest son, Victor Fung, on another occasion gave the following opinion:

> [T]he family members controlled the key posts and the shareholders were spread among the eight surviving members of the second generation of the founder. . . . But when the third generation came in, you couldn't benefit from the shareholding; you had to get involved. Some of my cousins came into the business but didn't like it.
>
> (Hutcheon 1992, 53)

Although father and son have some contradictory views in certain aspects, both said that the family members that made a great contribution to cultivating the business did not get most or all the profits, but profits were shared by members who did not make any contribution. In order to "cut the Gordian knot in this family situation," in Victor Fung's words (Hutcheon 1992, 53) and to bring in more advantages, the family decided to list the company publicly in 1973. These advantages, as suggested by Victor Fung,

> [w]ould provide an element of public scrutiny which would be of benefit for shareholders, institute a consistent dividend policy, and create value for the

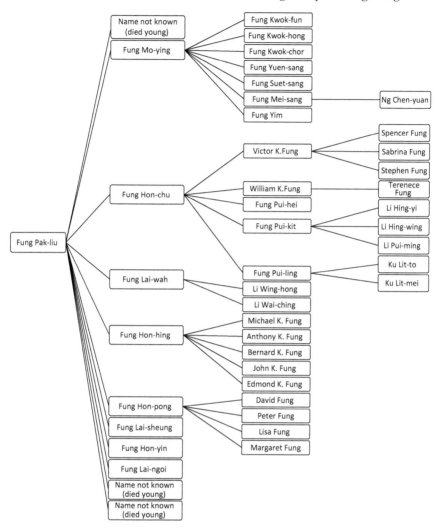

Figure 6.5 Family tree of the Fung Pak-liu family

Source: Feng 2006; Li & Fung Limited, various years

Note: Only identified members are listed, but some names are unknown.

shareholders and give them liquidity. The least of our concerns was getting money from the market because we were cash rich at the time.

(Hutcheon 1992, 53)

Few people object to a family business being conflict free or even that there is no rivalry. Equally, few disagree that going public could bring many positive effects to family business, including those advantages mentioned by Victor Fung. In fact, after going public, Li & Fung undertook a series of reforms in streamlining

the organisation to improve efficiency. Therefore, the company became successful and brought impressive growth from 1973 to 1988, as indicated earlier. When
commenting on various areas the company had achieved success in after going
public, Fung Hon-chu said: "It would take some time before they became successful and a lot of consolidation had to be done. . . . It would be easier for the
management if it had control of the company" (Hutcheon 1992, 69). An interesting question to ask is: did management lack control over the business?

If we look at the composition of the board of directors, we can see that, after
1975, three second-generation members were on the board (Fung Hon-chu, Fung
Lai-wah and Fung Hon-hing). Fung Hon-chu even concurrently held the positions
of chairman and managing director until 1981. In 1981, Victor Fung joined the
board and was appointed managing director. Five years later, William Fung also
joined the board as managing director. No other third-generation family member
joined the board. Given that the father was chairman and two sons were managing
directors, the argument that management lacked control over the business seems
weak.

In evaluating the achievement the company had made after going public, Robin
Hutcheon (1992, 69) unintentionally revealed a striking figure, "[w]ith about
70–75 per cent of the shares still in family hands, . . . " which appeared to be
the most critical point that led to the plan of privatisation. This figure echoes
Victor Fung's early comment that "you couldn't benefit from the shareholding"
and reflects the fact that many family members regarded themselves as sleeping
shareholders and saw the shares as a long-term investment.

Regardless of the real reasons, in 1989, as China and Hong Kong's socio-
political atmosphere was at its lowest ebb, the company share price was low, and
Fung Hon-chu was approaching eighty (he was not in good health), Victor and
William Fung proposed privatising the company. Such action not only reflected
serious family conflict but the breaking up of family and business relationships.
Of course, the proposal was not without disagreements and opposition. The following brief description is a frequently cited version of events.

> Amidst these economic shockwaves, the Fungs convened a full-scale fam-
> ily meeting in Boston to discuss the future of Li & Fung and particularly its
> shareholding. It is understood that there were serious disputes at the meeting.
> As Li-Fung Lai-wah recalled, "Different views were raised during the meet-
> ing." Fung Hon-hing, one of the board members, was said to have objected
> violently to the privatization of Li & Fung.[8] After thorough discussion, how-
> ever, most of the family members agreed to sell their shares to the manage-
> ment of the company, i.e., Victor and William, so that the two could proceed
> to privatize the company.
>
> (Feng 2007, 147)

Almost twenty years later, when reporters from a tabloid-like magazine interviewed Fung Mo-ying's two daughters, who lived like ordinary citizens in Hong
Kong, they gave the following response:

We don't have any relationship with the Victor Fung family. In a word, [we] are never in contact with each other even as we become older or until death. In case we meet on the street, we regard each other as strangers. . . . At that time, we and other family members who lived in the States knew little about Li & Fung's operation. Our uncle told us to sell all the shares, so we did.

(Leung and Lee 2003, 47–48)

Apparently, the process of privatisation seemed less than simple. Looking back, one could argue that, given the company had made remarkable progress after going public, the short-term setback seemingly affected by political factors in China should not be judged as ill performance. Equally unconvincing logic is that the proposal of privatisation in fact contradicted the reasons put forward when the company advocated for public listing fifteen years earlier. It seems a stretch to jump to the conclusion that "privatization has become Li & Fung's key to modernization" (Feng 2007, 95). In short, the action of privatising Li & Fung Limited in 1989 was mysterious.

Agreed or not, through the process of privatisation, controlling shares changed hands. Victor and William Fung became co-owners of Li & Fung Limited through King Lun Limited, in which two brothers have equal shares. Even though Victor and William Fung had got the approval for privatisation, getting sufficient financial backup to activate the "leverage buy-out" was challenging. The network capital that they and their father built seemed critical.

It was reported that, in order to raise capital for financing the "leverage buy-out," Victor and William Fung originally approached Citibank, a US-based bank that was described by Fung Hon-chu as a bank that "has helped us in many ways . . . in trade finance, for deposits, foreign exchange, credit checking and collections" (Hutcheon 1992, 57) for financial backup. However, the request was mysteriously declined (William Fung said it was that their "lending procedure was very complicated"; see Feng 2007, 88). At such a critical juncture, Victor and William Fung approached William Purves, the chief manager (chairman in 1991) of the Hong Kong and Shanghai Banking Corporation (HSBC), "sending in all the information by fax" for assistance. It was accepted after "half an hour" meeting the next day.[9] The major reason that they could get HSBC's blessing was "they look at who they are dealing with first" (Feng 2007, 89).

Although the process of Victor and William Fung getting Purves's endorsement might be dramatised, that Fung Hon-chu and his two sons had accumulated sufficient thickness of network capital and thus could win Purves's trust, confidence and therefore assistance should not be neglected. There is indirect evidence that Purves was a personal friend of Fung Hon-chu and his two sons. When Fung Hon-chu was appointed Legislative Councillor from 1964 to 1970, he had regular contact with Purves. So, one can see that there was socio-political contact and relationship. There were also business relation between Li & Fung Limited and HSBC, although the level of business interaction was probably less substantial than with Citibank.

In addition to Fung Hon-chu's strong connection with Purves, Victor and William Fung's equally solid relations with HSBC should not be overlooked.

Although we cannot find documents that demonstrate their ties, a remark made by John Bond, who succeeded William Purves as chairman of HSBC in 1998, can be cited for illustration. He said: "I have had contacts with Victor and William Fung for nearly thirty years [i.e., he knew them over ten years before 1989] and have seen in these years Li & Fung's impressive growth" (Feng 2006: back cover). Clearly, in doing business, Victor and William Fung tried to establish their network capital on top of economic capital and human capital.

No more than two years after finishing all procedures for privatisation, Victor and William Fung repackaged Li & Fung Limited by putting the core business as Li & Fung (1937) Limited and returned to the stock market in 1 July 1992 (Feng 2006). Although public investors' initial response was not as good as expected because of the feebleness of the overall market performance, striking progress was seen three years later when Li & Fung (1937) Limited announced a take-over of Inchape Buying Services (IBS), an internationally well-known trading group that has been in business for 200 years. After fully "digesting" IBS, Li & Fung took further action to acquire Swire & Maclaine and Camberley Enterprise in 1999, Colby Group Holding in 2000 and then Janco Overseas in 2002 (Feng 2006). From a series of expansionary policies, not only was tremendous financial support solicited in which HSBC appeared in almost every big deal, but network capital that had been accumulated seemed to be "operated" directly or less directly in different aspects.

Table 6.2 shows some of the public services rendered (and socio-economic-political positions held) by Victor and William Fung in the past decades. If we

Table 6.2 Education, occupations and public service records of third-generation Fungs

Year	Organisation	Post
Victor Fung, OBE (1988), CBE (1992), BSc, MSc (MIT), PhD (Harvard)		
1981–1986	Li & Fung Limited	Managing Director
1986–1989		Deputy Chairman
1992–2012		Nonexecutive Chairman
Present		Honorary Chairman
Present	Fung Group	Group Chairman
Present	Convenience Retail Asia Limited	Nonexecutive Chairman
Present	Trinity Limited	Nonexecutive Chairman
Present	Fung Global Institute	Founding Chairman
As of 1981	Public Service Commission	Member
As of 1981	Trade Advisory Board	Member

Year	Organisation	Post
As of 1981	Hong Kong Export Credit Insurance Corporation	Member
As of 1992	Securities and Futures Commission	Member
1991–2000	Hong Kong Trade Development Council	Chairman
1996–2003	APEC Business Advisory Council	Hong Kong representative
1997–2006	HKSAR Judicial Officers Recommendation Commission	Member
1999–2008	Airport Authority Hong Kong	Chairman
2001–2009	Council of The University of Hong Kong	Chairman
2003	HKSAR Economic Relaunch Strategy Group	Member
2004–2010	HKSAR Standing Committee on Judicial Salaries and Conditions of Service	Member
2005–2007	HKSAR Commission on Strategic Development Executive Committee	Member
2008–2009	HKSAR Task Force on Economic Challenges	Member
Present	Asia Advisory Board of Prudential Financial, Inc (USA)	Chairman
Present	Greater Pearl River Delta Business Council	Chairman
Present	People's Government of Nanjing	Economic advisor
Present	International Chamber of Commerce	Honorary Chairman
Present	Hong Kong Federal of Journalists	Honorary Chairman
Present	Renmin University	Honorary Professor
Present	Peking University	Honorary Trustee
Present	Chinese People's Political Consultative Conference	Member
Present	International Business Leaders Advisory Council for the Mayor of Beijing	Member
Present	Advisory Board of the School of Economics and Management of Tsinghua University	Member
Present	WTO Panel on Defining the Future of Trade	Member
Present	Commission on Strategic Development of the Hong Kong Government	Member
Present	China Centre for International Economic Exchanges	Vice Chairman
Present	China–United States Exchange Foundation	Vice-Chairman

(*Continued*)

Table 6.2 (Continued)

Year	Organisation	Post
Past (1992-date unknown)	PCCW-HKT Limited	Nonexecutive Director
1996–2003	Kerry Properties Limited	Independent Nonexecutive Director
1996–2009	Orient Overseas (International) Limited	Independent Nonexecutive Director
1998–2003	Hysan Development Company Limited	Independent Nonexecutive Director
1999–2007	Sun Hung Kai Properties Ltd.	Independent Nonexecutive Director
2000–2007	PCCW Limited	Independent Nonexecutive Director
Present	Baosteel Group Corporation	Independent Nonexecutive Director
Present	China Petrochemical Corporation (People's Republic of China)	Independent Nonexecutive Director
Present	Bank of China (Hong Kong) Limited	Independent Nonexecutive Director
Present	Chow Tai Fook Jewellery Group Limited (Hong Kong)	Independent Nonexecutive Director
Present	Koc Holding A. S. (Turkey)	Independent Nonexecutive Director
William Fung, JP (1989), BSE (Princeton), MBA (Harvard)		
1986–1989 1992–2011	Li & Fung Limited	Managing Director
2011–2012		Executive Deputy Chairman
Present		Group Chairman
Present	Fung Holdings (1937) Limited	Group Deputy Chairman
Present	Convenience Retail Asia Limited	Nonexecutive Director

Year	Organisation	Post
Present	Trinity Limited	Nonexecutive Director
Present	Fung Global Institute	Director
As of 1992	Economic Advisory Committee	Member
As of 1992	Textiles Advisory Board	Member
As of 1992	Hong Kong Tourist Association	Member
As of 1992	Hong Kong Exporters' Association	Member
As of 1992	Hong Kong General Chamber of Commerce	Member
As of 1992	Consultative Committee on the Basic Law	Member
As of 1992	Trade Development Council	Member
Past (date unknown)	Hong Kong General Chamber of Commerce	Chairman
Past (date unknown)	Hong Kong Exporters' Association	Chairman
Past (date unknown)	Hong Kong Committee for Pacific Economic Cooperation Council	Chairman
Present	The Chinese University of Hong Kong	Councillor
Present	The Hong Kong University of Science & Technology	Honorary Courtier
Present	HKSAR Justices of the Peace (nongovernment)	Member
Present	HKSAR Competition Policy Review Committee	Member
Present	VTech Holdings Limited	Independent Nonexecutive Director
Present	Shui On Land Limited	Independent Nonexecutive Director
Present	Sun Hung Kai Properties Ltd	Independent Nonexecutive Director
Present	The Hongkong and Shanghai Hotels, Limited	Independent Nonexecutive Director
Present	Singapore Airlines Limited	Independent director
Present	The Hongkong and Shanghai Banking Corporation Limited	Deputy Chairman and Nonexecutive Director

(*Continued*)

Table 6.2 (Continued)

Year	Organisation	Post
Fung Kwok-hong, educational background unknown		
As of 1981	Sundries Division, Li & Fung (Trading) Limited	Divisional Manager
As of 1981	Li & Fung (Trading) Limited	Director
As of 1981	Li & Fung (Finance & Investment) Limited	Director
As of 1981	Li & Fung (Properties) Limited	Director
As of 1981	Li & Fung (Development) Limited	Director
As of 1981	Dansville Investments Limited	Director
As of 1981	World Trade Merchandise Limited	Director
As of 1981	Kwok Yue Limited	Director
As of 1981	Check Out International Limited	Director
Fung Kwok-chor, Studied Biochemistry at Johns Hopkins University		
Date unknown	Manufacturing	Divisional Manager
1990	Barrister in practice	Divisional Manager
Li Wing-hong		
As of 1981	Li & Fung (Properties) Limited	Director
As of 1981	Li & Fung (Development) Limited	Director
As of 1981	Dansville Investments Limited	Director

Source: Leung and Lee 2003; Feng 2006; Li & Fung Limited, various years

look at Victor Fung, we can see that some of positions were held before 1989, but many of them were after. We can infer that Victor Fung spent large portion of his valuable time doing nonprofit work, which is unimaginable for a meticulous businessperson if we interpret the behaviour from an ordinary and simple perspective. However, if we look through the lens of network capital, we can have a fuller picture.

Unlike economic capital such as investment in shares, for which we can count the return clearly and easily, investment in network capital tells us a different story. Nevertheless, we can see that public service rendered brings social prestige and social recognition but increases the thickness of network capital. From the process through which Victor and William Fung built their dynastic enterprise, although we cannot see or quantify how network capital helped, especially at critical junctures, we cannot have a satisfactory explanation if network capital is not brought into play.

The cultivation and transmission of the fourth generation's network capital

Education is generally perceived as key human capital that not only maintains family status but also fuels family business expansion. It is also regarded as an important indicator of professional status and earning power. Like their father who sent them to top universities in the US for education when they were young, Victor and William Fung sent their children, Sabrina, Spencer, Stephen and Terence, to the US for better education when they were small. Supported by tremendous socio-economic resources, fourth-generation family members got a good education and brilliant qualifications. However, as men who were involved in various business turbulences, Victor and William Fung seemed to fully understand the importance of network capital.

Therefore, when their children returned to Hong Kong, they started to plan for their own succession. A somewhat similar path that they had walked in accumulating human capital and network capital several decades before was put forward to their children. They first sent their children to work in internationally well-known companies to gain experience and to establish some initial connections with these companies. After one or two years, they called them back to work in a family-controlled subsidiary, sometimes the holding company. At the beginning, their children were required to work at a relatively lower level (so-called "bottom-up training'). Then, they could be gradually promoted to higher-level management such as head or deputy head of a subsidiary. Only when they considered their children had gone through all-round training and testing could they be given full autonomy and independence (Zheng 2009).

Table 6.3 shows the occupations and public service records of Victor and William Fung's children and Victor Fung's son-in-law. We can see that, because the fourth generation is only in their late twenties to early forties, they are "young and green" by today's standards. Therefore, most of them have positions only in big corporations and/or in family subsidiaries, not at the senior management level. Also, although some of them have rendered public service, those public institutions are not top-tier influential bodies, and the positions they held are less influential. Such a phenomenon reflects the fact that the network capital of the fourth generation is still in the making.

As the fourth generation have undergone more training and testing, we can expect that the members will be given more responsible positions both in their family business and in the public sector. In other words, in the years to come, it is expected that the third generation will try to help the fourth generation or that the fourth generation will make their own effort/initiative to establish (or to invest) more human capital and network capital. In fact, the marriage of Sabrina Fung and Kevin Lam, cited at the beginning of the paper, can be seen as a kind of important network capital formation that can integrate the network capital of both big families, like the merger of two big corporations (Berkowitze 1976; Scott and Griff 1984).

An interesting but reasonable follow-up question to ask is: Will the fourth generation bring Li & Fung to another level of development and repeat the process of

Table 6.3 Education, occupations and public service records of fourth-generation Fungs

Year	Organisation	Post
Spencer Theodore Fung, BA (Harvard), MS, MBA (Northeastern)		
Present	Li & Fung Limited	Executive Director and Group Chief Operating Officer
Past (date unknown)	LF Europe	President
Present	Clothing Industry Training Authority	Member
Present	Swire Properties Limited	Independent Nonexecutive Director
Sabrina Fung, BA (Harvard)		
Present	Trinity Limited	Executive Director
Stephen Fung, educated at Harvard		
Date unknown	Toys Li Fung Asia Ltd	Chief Financial Offer
Terence Fung, educated at Princeton and Boston College		
Present	Li & Fung (Trading) Ltd	Executive Vice President, Corporate Services

splitting and restructuring that their predecessors did when they come to the final stage of succession and inheritance? Although it seems too early to draw such a conclusion, some phenomena are obvious and have to be included before making any projection or prediction.

1   Unlike the previous generations, which included a large number of siblings, Victor and William Fung have fewer children. Therefore, internal family conflict or centrifugal force for separation seems less serious than it was in the previous generation.
2   Notwithstanding the unpredictability, network capital will still be highly emphasised and mobilised to ensure smooth transition and control.
3   In case there is a split, the thickness of network capital will certainly be one of the crucial factors that will determine "who gets what and in what proportion."

From Ambrose King's (1991) point of view, network building is the cultural strategy used to create Chinese society. Wealthy and long-established families must agree to it, as they show us that they put great resources into building their network capital. The crucial factors are not only because it can bring in more opportunities, but it can allow the "investor" to have greater control and a bigger say, to ensure that the wealth and social influence is transmitted from generation to generation (Zheng 2009). Therefore, whether competing in a round world or flat world, putting more investment into network capital, especially in wealthy family circles, will not make any difference.

Conclusion and discussion

As a notable global sourcing corporation that describes itself as "a network orchestrator in its purest form" (Fung et al. 2008, 13), Li & Fung has gone through a trajectory that demonstrates at least two realities worth mentioning that most long-establishing family businesses experience: (1) Development usually follows the path of formation, division and recentralisation. (2) Network capital is deployed to complement economic capital and human capital, to acquire more business opportunity, to exercise family control and to maintain business vitality and sustainability.

In S.L. Wong's research examining the organisational evolution of Chinese family business, he found a four-phase pattern of establishment, centralisation, segmentation and disintegration. He also argued that these phases tend to coincide with generation shifts in the family. If it follows this developmental model, the old Chinese saying that "wealth can't pass through three generations" seems valid. Nevertheless, Wong theoretically suggested a possible route in saving the business from segmentation to disintegration by reversing to centralisation to maintain family business vitality and continuity but did not point out the concrete mechanism in his paper (Wong 1985).

The way Li & Fung chose at different critical points (in the mid-1940s, the early 1970s–late 1980s and the early 1990s) clearly shows us the solid mechanism that family business can take to avoid disintegration and to regain developmental momentum. The stock market seems to be the most important platform to help the mechanism to work most smoothly and effectively, whereas network capital appears to be the crucial element that determines "who gets what and in what proportion."

Given the family members or company partners generally come from similar backgrounds and have more or less equal amounts of economic capital and human capital, people who can accumulate thicker network capital doubtlessly can have a bigger say and the upper hand in the business. In order to better illustrate how network capital functions in the way Chinese family business-controlling power and organisational structure evolved, see Figure 6.6.

As we all know, there are inherently two forces, centrifugal and centripetal, within the family. In Chinese philosophy, these two forces are usually described as yin and yang, which are seemingly interconnected and interdependent. The structure of a company is mostly triangular, which means senior management is on top and usually fewer in number. There are more people at middle-level management, and the most at the bottom level. In a family business, family members are usually the senior management, which means they are at the top of the triangle. Network capital, although intangible (broken line), can facilitate business development, so it is usually established to encompass the family and business (Figure 6.6).

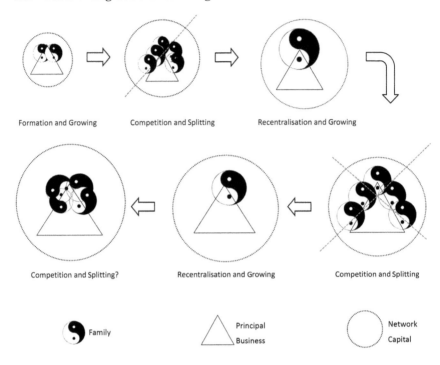

Figure 6.6 Network capital and the evolution of company ownership: Li & Fung's developmental trajectory

The way the business expands is that the second generation grows up and joins the business, initially at middle-level management but later in top management. Then, when the members of this generation get married and the founding generation ages or dies, the baton will be passed to the second generation. The split of the two cofounding families of Li & Fung reflects a less close relationship but also indicates those that have established thicker network capital can use it to gain control of the business.

Because the second-generation Fungs maintain good relationships with each other, they cooperate to make the business grow. Then, when the third generation is grown up and joins management, some subtle change first appears and later galvanises the centrifugal force that provokes another cycle of division. Again, the thickness of network capital seems to be the discriminating factor in deciding who gets control of the business as they are from the same big family, which was supposed to have similar economic and human capital. Selling the controlling shares of some family members to others through the stock market appears to be a more objective and transparent mechanism that can reduce ambiguity and subjectivity. As various branches of the family are pruned in the process and the controlling power is recentralised, the succession from the second to the third generation ends.

Having more controlling shares and management power, the third generation can bring the business to new heights. Network capital and the stock market are two important vehicles that help leadership to accomplish different goals. As time goes on, the third generation gets older and the fourth generation enters the family business. A new process of succession is activated. Whether they will resort to separation as they reach top management, or cooperate with their cousins, remains to be seen (Figure 6.6). Nevertheless, network capital will continue to be the most decisive factor for exercising control and development.

Last but not least, in studying family business development, management, strategy and succession, we frequently focus on the functioning of economic capital and human capital and leave the question or area of network capital unattended or ignored and therefore understudied. Such a research "blind spot" is partly due to the invisibility and indirectness to business decisions and partly caused by the uneasiness to obtain "insider" information as most related plans or actions were taken behind the scenes and hence mostly off the record. Notwithstanding this, from the story of Li & Fung, we can see that, if we spend time and are patient sifting through archival data from past newspapers, magazines, public registration records, annual company reports, corporate histories, minutes of meetings and memoirs of family members or relatives, we can get a fuller picture of the development of Chinese family business.

Notes

1 This paper is part of the Chinese Family Business and Stock Market project and A Quest for Business Continuity and Sustainability project. The former is funded by the Chiang Ching-kuo Foundation (Project Ref. No. RG012-P-10). The latter is supported by the Vincent and Lily Woo Foundation. Thanks are due to our assistants, Ms. Akira Zhang, Ms. Viola Cheung, Ms. Joan Chong and Mr. Chan Hing-fong, for their great help on the draft of the paper.
2 To signify the business was a coventure, they used Li & Fung, the surnames of two founders, as the company name. But, in Chinese, they cleverly changed the two surnames to two different words that have the same Cantonese pronunciation, for better connotation. The Chinese word "Li' means profit, victory or sharpness. "Fung' implies plentiful, harvest or prosperity. It was common practice to have an auspicious name in the old days.
3 It seemed clear that the Fungs not only had firm control over the company but had extensive trading networks both in Hong Kong and in Western countries.
4 In 2010, the IDS Group declared privatisation, thus reducing to three the number of groups under Li & Fung Group's control of publicly listed companies. In 2012, Li & Fung (1937) Limited was renamed Fung Holdings (1937) Limited.
5 The company was located at 1 Catchick Street, Western District. The registered addresses of the two partners, Li To-ming and Fung Pak-liu, were On Lok Village, Fanling, New Territories, Hong Kong, and No. 213 Garden Road, Kowloon, Hong Kong, respectively. Both declared themselves "merchants' ("Li & Fung Limited" Companies Registry File No.: 122–5–16).
6 According to a will maintained in Probate Court, Li To-ming died in Hong Kong in November 1951, at the age of 75 (hence he was born in 1876, four years before Fung Pak-liu). He bequeathed his estate to his surviving family members, including one wife, one concubine, one son and four daughters ("Li To-ming" Probate File No.: 96–1–4752–1).

7 The board of directors from 1973 to 1975 were Fung Mo-yin (chairman), Fung Hon-chu (managing director), Fung Lai-wah, Albert Rodrigues (leading physician, once appointed as Executive Councillor and Pro-Chancellor of the University of Hong Kong) and Oswald Cheung (Queen's Counsel, once appointed as Legislative Councillor and Executive Councillor). From 1975 to 1980 they were Fung Hon-chu (chairman and managing director), Fung Lai-wah, Fung Hon-hing, Albert Rodrigues and Oswald Cheung. From 1981 to 1988, they were Fung Hon-chu (chairman), Fung Lai-wah, Fung Hon-hing, Victor Fung (managing director), Kerry Johnston (chairman of Wilrig A.S., which operated and owned oil rigs internationally) and Anthony Hayward (president and CEO of Private Investment Co), Albert Rodrigues and Oswald Cheung; William Fung joined the board in 1986 (Hutcheon 1992; Feng 2006).

8 As the fourth eldest son was five years younger than his third brother, Fung Hon-chu, Fung Hon-hing could reasonably expect that, if Li & Fung remained publicly listed, when his elder brother died, he could become chairman. At that time, the management team might experience another drastic reshuffling of personnel, like in 1975, when his second brother, Fung Mo-yin, died. In fact, five years later, on 9 September 1994, Fung Hon-chu passed away. However, at that time, Li & Fung was in Victor and William Fung's full control and had been relisted for two years.

9 The total amount of money acquired for buying "the shareholdings of the family trust and the general public" was "$459 million" (Hutcheon 1992, 70). It seems to be a drop in the ocean if compared to the total capitalisation of today's Li & Fung (1937) Limited.

References

Berkowitze, S.D. 1976. "The Dynamics of Elite Structure." Unpublished PhD Thesis, Brandeis University.

Bourdieu, P. 1984. *Distinction: A Social Critique of the Judgment of Taste*. London: Routledge & Kegan Paul.

Bourdieu, P. 1986. "The Forms of Capital." In *Handbook of Theory and Research for the Sociology of Education*, edited by John G. Richardson, 241–258. New York: Greenwood.

Bourdieu, P., and L.J.D. Wacquant. 1992. *An Invitation to Reflexive Sociology*. Cambridge: Polity Press.

Capital. 1992. "Fung Hon-chu Plans for the Next Generations." February, 70–73 (in Chinese).

Cavaliere, V. 2012. "Dutch Teen's Sweet 16 Party Invitation Goes Viral on Facebook, Ends in 3,000 Rioting in Groningen Suburb." *New York Daily News*, September 22. Accessed July 24, 2013. www.nydailynews.com/news/world/dutch-teen-sweet-16-party-invitation-viral-facebook-ends-3–000-rioting-groningen-suburb-article-1.1165386

Clemetson, L., and R. Ernsberger. 1996. "How to Succeed in Dad's Business? Go to Harvard." *Newsweek*. October 14.

Coleman, J.S. 1988. "Social Capital in the Creation of Human Capital." *American Journal of Sociology* 94 (Supplement Organizations and Institutions: Sociological and Economic Approaches to the Analysis of Social Structure): S95–S120.

Coleman, J.S. 1990. *Foundations of Social Theory*. Cambridge, MA: Belknap Press of Harvard University Press.

Coleman, J.S. 1994. "A Rational Choice Perspective on Economic Sociology." In *The Handbook of Economic Sociology*, edited by Neil J. Smelser and Richard Swedberg, 166–182. Princeton, NJ: Princeton University Press.

Feng, B.Y. 2006. *100 Years of Li & Fung: Rise from Family Business to Multinational*. Hong Kong: Joint Publishing (Hong Kong) Limited (in Chinese).

Feng, B.Y. 2007. *100 Years of Li & Fung: Rise from Family Business to Multinational*. Singapore: Thomson Learning.

Forbes. 2013. "Hong Kong's 50 Richest People." Accessed July 24, 2013. www.forbes. com/hong-kong-billionaires/

Fung Group. 2013. "Who We Are." Accessed July 24, 2013. www.funggroup.com/eng/ about/

Fung, V.K.K., W.K. Fung, and Y. Wind. 2008. *Competing in a Flat World: Building Enterprises for a Borderless World*. Upper Saddle River, NJ: Wharton School Publishing.

Granovetter, M.S. 1973. "The Strength of Weak Ties." *American Journal of Sociology* 78 (6): 1360–1380.

Granovetter, M.S. 1985. "Economic Action and Social Structure: The Problem of Embeddedness." *American Journal of Sociology* 91 (3): 481–510.

Granovetter, M.S. 1994. "Business Groups." In *The Handbook of Economic Sociology*, edited by Neil J. Smelser and Richard Swedberg, 453–475. Princeton, NJ: Princeton University Press.

The History of the Ministry of Finance, ROC. 2013. "An Index to Financial People: Chan Kam-Tao." Accessed July 24, 2013. www.mof.gov.tw/museum/ct.asp?xItem=3063&ct Node=63&mp=1

Hutcheon, R. 1992. *A Burst of Crackers: The Li & Fung Story*. Hong Kong: Li & Fung Limited.

King, A.Y.C. 1991. "Kuan-hsi and Network Building: A Sociological Interpretation." *Daedalus* 120 (2): 63–84.

Leung, S.M., and W.T. Lee. 2003. "A Billionaire Has Paved the Road for Ten Years: Victor Fung Aims at the Position of Chief Executive (of HKSAR)." *Next Magazine* 706: 42–50 (in Chinese).

Li and Fung Limited. Various years. *Annual Report* (including *Interim Report*). Hong Kong: Li & Fung Limited.

Li and Fung Limited. Companies Registry File No.: 122–5–16. Hong Kong: Companies Registry.

Lin, N. 1990. "Social Resources and Social Mobility: A Structural Theory of Status Attainment." In *Social Mobility and Social Structure*, edited by Ronald L. Breiger, 247–271. Cambridge: Cambridge University Press.

"Li To-ming." Probate File No.: 96–1–4752–1. Hong Kong: Public Records Office.

Magretta, J. 1998. "Fast Global, and Entrepreneurial: Supply Chain Management, Hong Kong Style: An Interview with Victor Fung." *Harvard Business Review* 76 (5): 102–114.

O'Connell, J. 1996. "Li & Fung (Trading) Ltd," *Harvard Business Case Studies* 9–396–075, June 28.

The Publicity Bureau for South China. 1922. *Anglo-Chinese Directory: Hong Kong*. Hong Kong: The Publicity Bureau for South China.

Putnam, R.D. 2000. *Blowing Alone: The Collapse and Revival of American Community*. New York: Simon and Schuster.

Queen's College Hong Kong. 1891–1911. *Yellow Dragon*. Hong Kong: Queen's College.

Robertson, I. 1987. *Sociology*, Third Edition. New York: Worth Publishers, Inc.

Scott, J., and C. Griff. 1984. *Directors of Industry: The British Corporate Network, 1904–1976*. Cambridge: Polity Press.

Smelser, N.J., and R. Swedberg. Eds. 1994. *The Handbook of Economic Sociology*. Princeton, NJ: Princeton University Press.

Stokes, G., and J.P. Stokes. 1987. *Queen's College: Its History, 1862–1987*. Hong Kong: Queen's College Old Boys' Association.

The Sun. 2000. September 5 (in Chinese).

World Bank. 2013. "Overview: Social Capital." Accessed July 24, 2013. http://web. worldbank.org/WBSITE/EXTERNAL/TOPICS/EXTSOCIALDEVELOPMENT/EXT

TSOCIALCAPITAL/0,,contentMDK:20642703~menuPK:401023~pagePK:148956~pi
PK:216618~theSitePK:401015,00.html

Williamson, O.E. 1975. *Markets and Hierarchies, Analysis and Antitrust Implications: A Study in the Economics of Internal Organizations*. New York: Free Press.

Williamson, O.E. 1979. "Transaction-cost Economics: The Governance of Contractual Relations." *Journal of Law and Economics* 22 (2): 233–261.

Wong, S.L. 1985. "The Chinese Family Firm: A Model." *The British Journal of Sociology* 36 (1): 58–72.

Woo, S.L. 1937. *The Prominent Chinese in Hong Kong*. Hong Kong: Five Continents Book (in Chinese).

Zheng, V. 2009. *Chinese Family Business and the Equal Inheritance System: Unravelling the Myth*. London; New York: Routledge.

Zheng, V., and S.L. Wong. 2007. *Ho Tung: The Grand Old Man of Hong Kong*. Hong Kong: Joint Publishing (Hong Kong) Limited (in Chinese).

Zheng, V., and S.L. Wong. 2010. "The Mystery of Capital: Eurasian Entrepreneurs' Socio-cultural Strategies for Commercial Success in Early Twentieth-century Hong Kong." *Asian Studies Review* 34: 467–487.Zheng, Z.C. 1915. *Hong Kong Chinese Business and Transport Directory*. Hong Kong: Published by the Author (in Chinese).

7 Changes in corporate social capital and their implications for the semiconductor industry in Taiwan

Ray-May Hsung and Yi-Jr Lin

Introduction

Sociologists and management scientists have noted the importance of corporate social capital. Global competition and uncertainty in the semiconductor industry are strong, so the corporations in this industry have built up a variety of inter-organizational and intraorganizational networks to deal with market uncertainties. These interorganizational networks include joint ventures, technological alliances, and interlocked directors among corporations. Firms' competence in innovation or patent inventions has become the most important competition strategy, and networking with firms with high status in the semiconductor industry and networking with different social circles of firms provide advantageous social capital in the high-tech competition of the market.

Previous research on interlocked networks of board directors in Taiwan focuses primarily on governance by family directors or state directors (Lee 2007; 2009). In Taiwan's financial sector, the dominant pattern is interlocked networks of board directors that cross-share holding stocks between state and financial directors (Hsung and Hu 2011). The importance of financial and state board directors changed over time. Hsung and Lin (2012) show that the financial director, such as an investment company, increased and cross-seated many companies, but the number of state directors decreased. Guan et al. (2013) indicate that the importance of professional training, such as a PhD degree and work experience abroad in the semiconductor industry, was extremely important during the period of inventing the $0.13\,\mu m$ copper manufacturing process at the beginning of twenty-first century. A kin relationship with the chair of the board is not as important as most literature found. None of these abovementioned findings specifically use social capital theory and network analyses to analyze the data on the interlocked networks of board directors.

Interlocked networks among firms through overlapped board directors are a fundamental way of constructing corporate social capital. Firms learn more information or gain more resources from other firms through sharing common board directors. Family board directors and business group directors have played important roles in corporate governance in Taiwan. We assume that interlocked networks through sharing common family board directors are more highly connected within smaller social circles; however, through sharing common business group directors, those networks tend to be loose and connected to a larger social circle. As a consequence, the performance of the firms by means of different networking strategies differs.

This chapter focuses on the following research problems:

1   This work examines the changing patterns of the ownership composition of board directors in the firms of Taiwan's semiconductor industry from 1995 to 2010. The ownership composition of board directors is measured by the share of family directors and that of business group directors on the board.
2   We then use different measures of interlocked networks among firms in this industry by sharing common directors to indicate corporate social capital.

This chapter analyzes two network structural characteristics: structural holes and status signals. We conceive the characteristics of an interlocked network structure as the firm's investment in social capital and different network characteristics that produce different performances for the firm. This work first describes changing ownership composition and then examines the changing characteristics of interlocked networks among firms by type of ownership and by sector of industry. Finally, we use eight company cases to illustrate the implications of the plausible relations among changing ownership combinations, changing network structural characteristics, and performance of firms in Taiwan's semiconductor industry.

Theories on corporate social capital

Interlocked networks of board directors have been used in the study of corporate governance. Management scientists use these data to indicate the allocation of power and resource control among members of power elites in the firm. Sociological work in organization theory disagrees with this functionalist view and provides alternative interpretations based on networks, power, and culture (Mizruchi 1996; Davis 2005). Corporate social capital has been conceptualized as the function of structural characteristics of interlocked networks of board directors (Mintz and Schwartz 1981; Mizruchi and Bunting 1981; Kang and Sørensen 1999; Keister 2002). The interlocked linkage between two firms is defined as two firms sharing the same board director. Management science often uses corporate interlocks to study interorganizational networks or alliances. Two major recent theories on the structural characteristics of interorganizational networks are structural holes and status signal theories.

Structural holes

Since the 1980s, the concept of social capital has been developed and applied widely in different fields. James Coleman, Nan Lin, and Ronald Burt are three key figures who created the theories and influenced empirical research. James Coleman (1988; 1990) comprehensively conceptualizes social capital theories and focuses on the social system and structural closure of social networks. Coleman (1988) defines social capital as the function of social networks and illustrates how social capital functions as the collective assets in the performance of schoolchildren. The degree of social capital is conceptualized as the density of intergenerational (parents and children) networks. The greater density of the ego's network implies that there is higher structural closure. If the members of the ego's networks are densely structured, then the social obligation, trust, and social control among the members of ego's networks are strong as well. Consequently, the behavior performance of children in Catholic schools are better than in other schools. To some extent, Granovetter's (1985) embeddedness theory on economic action theory and Uzzi's (1996; 1997; 1999) empirical research on the New York garment industry and social capital with bank networks for manufacturing firms support such arguments on the function of trust in closured networks in firms' economic outcomes.

In a plural and competitive context, the function of structural closure can be challenged. When the network structure of individuals or organizations becomes loose, then more structural holes occur in this network. Lin et al. (1981), Lin and Dumin (1986), Lin (2001), and Burt (1992) stress the function of loosely linked ties or diversified social networks. Lin conceives the assets of the maximum accessed social resources through weak ties as a better form of social capital. This better accessed social capital facilitates the attainment of instrumental actions, such as better job searches or better business deals. Burt (1992) conceives the strategic position, network brokerage, as an advantage in competition. Structural hole theory suggests that individuals, organizations, and even industries that occupy brokerage positions in networks are more likely to exhibit entrepreneurial behaviors because of access to nonredundant information in a network. A person or firm located in a position with more structural holes tends to be promoted in the workplace or perform better in the competitive market.

Previously interlocked networks found it difficult to measure structural holes. Network researchers recently created some proxy measures for structural holes in two-mode networks. This density in the local network surrounding focal nodes (Burt 1992) indicates the structural constraints for an ego. The high density implies that the ego has strong and dense linkages with his/her other personal network members, and these closured personal networks often has a function of social control and constrains the members linking with alters outside personal networks. Therefore, an ego with high-density personal networks tends to have fewer structural holes linking with other nonredundant social circles. In the past, two-mode networks were often transformed into one-mode affiliation networks. These transformed one-mode affiliation networks often contained more triangles and thus overestimated the level of density of the ego's personal network (Watts and Strogatz 1998). The new measure of density in the ego's networks was often measured by clustering coefficients (Newman 2001). Clustering coefficients are often defined as whether triplets (three nodes with at least two ties among all pairs of personal networks) are closed. The higher number of pairs among alters in personal affiliation networks and high clustering coefficients indicate more structural holes to link with other social clusters in the global networks.

Status signals

The market is socially constructed by interorganizational networks with hierarchical order through interorganizational exchanges in terms of interlocked directors, technological collaboration, and joint venture and venture capital networks (White 1981; Granovetter 1985; Podolny 2005). Especially for those firms in highly uncertain environments, the fast-changing and globally competitive market forces these firms to judge all kinds of market information about potential collaborators or competitors according to the degree of centrality in terms of all kinds of interorganizational networks. The higher the centrality of a firm, the more significant the signal of market status. Firms tend to exchange social resources with firms that have greater centrality (or status signal) in interorganizational networks, especially under the environment of highly uncertain market information.

A producer's status in the market is the perceived quality of its products compared to those of its competitors (Podolny 1993, 830). A central board is composed of directors who sit on many other boards. A board's centrality is a proxy for its quality as a monitor. Stock investors have a higher degree of trust in those firms with a greater number of central board directors (Shivdasani 1993). For shareholders, board centrality is a proxy of status under the unobservable quality of corporate governance.

The centrality of interlocked networks among firms was traditionally conceived as the power or influence of a firm in the industrial field. Different combinations of firm ownership, such as the share of family directors or business group directors, affect the position of the firm. Organizational sociologists have recently brought the perspective of the status signal into studies of interlocked networks of board directors (Davis and Greve 1997). Firms in the central position of interorganizational networks tend to respond to environmental uncertainty efficiently and effectively. In terms of political environmental uncertainty, those firms in central positions generally have better political relations, which helps firms learn how to respond to new regulations while considering the benefits for their own firms. For example, large family-run financial firms restructured their interlocked networks and business groups more efficiently and have increased their benefits faster after the release of new merger and acquisition laws for financial firms (Hsung and Hu 2011).

Research methods

This study uses four years (1995, 2000, 2005, and 2010) of data from the *Taiwan Economic Journal Data Bank* on directors and supervisors in Taiwan's semiconductor companies. The following are the measures of type of ownership, sector of semiconductor industry, network characteristics, and firm performance variables.

Type of ownership

The definition of family members on a board is that the director has a kin relationship with the chairman of the board. The definition of a business group member is that the director works for the company in the same business group, and the director is often a delegate in a related investment company in the same business group. We created two variables on the composition of ownership types for board directors of firms: (a) *percentage of ownership by family directors* and (b) *percentage of ownership by business group directors.*

Sectors of the semiconductor industry

Because of the characteristic of vertical disintegration in Taiwan's semiconductor industry, we classified sectors into four categories: upstream, midstream, downstream, and other sectors. The firms in the upstream sector are IC (integrated circuit) design firms, those in the midstream sector are IC manufacturing foundry firms, and those in the downstream sector are IC packaging firms.

Network characteristics

This chapter uses recently developed two-mode network measures on structural holes and status signals (Borgatti and Everett 1997; Opsahl 2013). Network analysis examines the characteristics of structure of dyadic ties. The two-mode data include two sets of data: directors and companies. The assignment of directors to boards of companies can be seen as a relation between the set of directors and the set of company boards. Similarly, the membership of individuals in voluntary organizations can be seen as a relation between two equally interesting sets. The two-mode approach develops new metrics and algorithms to measure structural holes and centrality (Bonacich 1987). We use this new approach to calculate the network indicators on status signal.

Measures of Centrality in Two-Mode Networks: (a) The two-mode degree centrality of a node (firm) is defined as the number of edges incident on that node. The degree of a company board is the number of directors who attend this board (Borgatti 2009). The two-mode degree centrality in this study includes director degree centrality and firm degree centrality. For a director in $V1$, the maximum number of possible ties is $n2$, whereas for a firm in $V2$ the maximum number of ties is $n1$. Hence, the formulas of director degree centrality and firm degree centrality are as follows:

$$d_i^* = \frac{d_i}{n_2}, for\ i \in V_1$$

$$d_j^* = \frac{d_j}{n_1}, for\ j \in V_2$$

However, we only use firm-degree centrality in this study.

(b) Eigenvector centrality: Bonacich (1972) created the eigenvector centrality and Borgatti and Everett (1997) modified this measure by using two-mode matrices and graphs. This two-mode eigenvector centrality was measured by the most recent version of the UCINET program.

(c) Number of interlocked companies: We first transformed the two-mode, director-firm matrix into a one-mode, firm-firm affiliation network and then deleted the diagonal figures. We recoded the cells of this matrix into 1 and 0. Those overlapped directors over and equal to two were recoded as one. Finally, we calculated the degree centrality for this 1 and 0 firm-firm affiliation network for each firm. The centrality for each firm is the number of interlocked companies.

Structural Holes Measures: Network researchers have recently been using the clustering coefficient as the index of structural holes. This variable was created by Newman (2001) to indicate one component of the small world phenomena. The global clustering coefficient is based on triplets of nodes. A triplet is defined as three nodes that are connected by either two (open triplet) or three (closed triplet) undirected ties. The global clustering coefficient is the number of closed triplets over the total number of triplets (both open and closed). The number of triplets can be measured as the pairs among alters of an ego's affiliation. The formula of clustering coefficient (CC) is as follows:

$$CC = \frac{3 \times no \ of \ triangles \ on \ the \ graph}{no. of \ connected \ triplets \ of \ vertices}$$

Firm performance variables

(a) Patent number

We use the number of patents registered in the United States Patent and Trademark Office (USPTO) as an indicator to measure a company's innovation level.

(b) Return on Assets (ROA) and Return on Equity (ROE)

Two indicators of profitability measure the performance of a company: ROA and ROE. ROA indicates how efficient a company is at exploiting its assets to create earnings. It is expressed as:

ROA (%) = Net income / Total assets

ROE indicates the degree of profit that a company creates with the money that shareholders have invested. The formula of ROE is as follows:

ROE (%) = Net income / Shareholders Equity

(c) Percentage of R&D expenditure

This variable indicates R&D expenditure divided by revenue. The higher the proportion of R&D expenditure, the greater the importance of innovation for this firm.

(d) Revenue

Revenue is an indicator of firm scale. With a natural logarithm of revenue in models, a greater value means a larger organization, and vice versa.

The steps of analyses in this chapter are discussed in two parts. The first part describes the changing ownership composition and the changing characteristics of interlocked networks among firms by type of ownership and by sector of industry. In the second part of the analysis, we choose eight important companies in three sectors of the semiconductor industry to illustrate all the related indexes on type of ownership, indexes on network characteristics, and performance. The upstream sector includes MediaTek (聯發科), VIA Technology (VIA, 威盛), and Silicon Integration System (SiS, 矽統). The midstream sector includes Taiwan Semiconductor Manufacturing (TSMC, 台積電), United Microelectronics (UMC, 聯電), and Macronix International (Macronix, 旺宏). The downstream sector includes Advanced Semiconductor Engineering (ASE, 日月光) and Siliconware Precision Industries (SPIL, 矽品).

General description of different sectors of firms

The interlocked networks of board directors in Taiwan's semiconductor industry have changed dramatically since 1995. The semiconductor industry has increased continuously and has upgraded to the leading position in the world. The number of firms and board directors and the percentage of directors crossing two or more firms have increased as well. We created affiliation networks among board directors in 1995, 2000, 2005, and 2010 and examined the network characteristics of large components each year. In the early period of Taiwan's semiconductor industry, very few cohesive elite directors coming from the same state-sponsored research institute governed the network field with high local network closure and fewer bridges. However, after a series of global economic depressions and strong industrial competition, the networks of interlocked directorates are now characterized by a moderate degree of local clustering. Most of the old elites with state backgrounds have retired, and newly emerging elites with backgrounds in investment banking and as industrial executives now govern the networks, have more cross-firm ties, and have become the brokers of multiple components. The business community of Taiwan's semiconductor industry appears to be transforming into robust networks that are open to innovation. We further examine these indexes by the sector of the semiconductor industry in Table 7.1.

Table 7.1 demonstrates that firms in upstream and other sectors of the semiconductor industry have increased faster than those in midstream and downstream sectors because the founding and maintenance of mid- and downstream firms require intensive capital and high technology. However, the fast growth of IC design houses and firms in other sectors became the engine for consumers of foundry manufacturing and IC packaging firms. The interdependent leverage between IC foundry and IC design maintains the growing capacity of Taiwan's semiconductor industry.

The average size of a board in an upstream or downstream firm is smaller than that in the midstream sector, and midstream firms are mainly large manufacturing foundry and dynamic random access memory (DRAM) firms with high technology that require a large amount of financial capital and a greater number of board directors. In 1995, the percentage of family directors on firms' boards in upstream and downstream sectors was higher than that in midstream sector; however, that percentage has continuously declined from 1995 to 2010. In 2010, the percentage of family directors on the board was at a low level for all sectors of the semiconductor industry. The market for the semiconductor industry is globally competitive, and a high number of family board directors is disadvantageous

Table 7.1 Interlocked networks of board directors and performance indicators of public semiconductor companies

		1995	2000	2005	2010
Number of firms	Upstream[1]	4	38	57	79
	Midstream	7	10	10	11
	Downstream	5	18	25	28
	Others	2	20	26	41
	Total	18	86	118	159
Total of board members	Recurring members included	184	743	1108	1476
	Overlapping in 2 or more companies/Total	4.55%	7.01%	7.47%	9.73%
Average of board members	Upstream	21	277	494	741
	Midstream	98	132	135	138
	Downstream	38	175	248	264
	Others	27	159	231	333
Family board members (%)	Upstream	25.00 (.180)	19.83 (.189)	12.43 (.142)	6.76 (.104)
	Midstream	8.95 (.117)	8.82 (.129)	6.59 (.097)	9.15 (.099)
	Downstream	26.29 (.151)	16.23 (.137)	13.38 (.159)	8.40 (.117)
	Others	.00 (.000)	17.95 (.259)	12.53 (.175)	11.79 (.156)
Group board members (%)	Upstream	.00 (.000)[2]	15.04 (.165)	14.74 (.197)	12.82 (.150)
	Midstream	.00 (.000)	29.57 (.199)	30.17 (.195)	21.02 (.166)
	Downstream	.00 (.000)	23.42 (.306)	20.76 (.287)	21.20 (.256)
	Others	.00 (.000)	31.71 (.279)	31.03 (.226)	20.74 (.212)

External financial related board members (%)	Upstream	.15 (.137)	.13 (.168)	.13 (.163)	.15 (.136)
	Midstream	.27 (.107)	.24 (.129)	.23 (.199)	.14 (.14)
	Downstream	.26 (.422)	.18 (.212)	.14 (.195)	.12 (.148)
	Others	.41 (.056)	.30 (.263)	.27 (.218)	.21 (.205)
Scale (number of employees)	Upstream	275.00 (–)	104.95 (88.617)	404.88 (827.268)	445.52 (776.087)
	Midstream	1441.25 (1481.988)	1626.75 (1585.096)	5739.30 (6754.552)	6802.45 (10230.395)
	Downstream	1437.00 (999.998)	834.08 (771.555)	2893.44 (6049.750)	4108.57 (9498.146)
	Others	81.00 (–)	227.00 (103.352)	824.38 (772.410)	1152.27 (1748.524)
R&D (%)	Upstream	10.07 (.086)	509.40 (29.865)[3]	14.55 (.127)	18.46 (.134)
	Midstream	4.42 (.039)	5.50 (.044)	8.03 (.063)	6.33 (.035)
	Downstream	0.63 (.007)	3.63 (.060)	2.32 (.025)	2.67 (.027)
	Others	1.65 (.023)	57.13 (2.328)	2.83 (.036)	3.67 (.071)

[1] Upstream: IC design houses and design service companies; midstream: foundry and DRAM companies; downstream: packaging and testing companies; others: equipment providers, IC distributors, optoelectronics devices manufacturers, etc.

[2] There is no data on business group directors in 1995.

[3] The major cause of high percentage of expenditure on research and development is few newly founded firms with low net revenue and high expenditures on research and development.

for extending interorganizational alliances globally. The trend toward a declining number of family and business groups' directors on the board implies that incorporating board directors from the global market becomes an even more important strategy of competition for high-tech firms.

Beginning in 2000, the percentage of business group directors on boards increased, then declined after 2005. In 1995, the percentage of business group directors on boards was zero in all sectors. When semiconductor firms were first listed on the stock market in 1995, there were no business groups at all. Upstream firms have had a lower percentage of business group directors on boards compared to those in midstream and downstream sectors. The percentage of business group directors on the boards of midstream and upstream sectors increased until 2005, and then declined in 2010. The number of employees in companies in the midstream sector has been the largest, and the percentage of research and development expenditure in upstream companies has been the highest compared to other sectors.

The changing composition of ownership types

We classified firms into four types of business groups: 1) high proportion of board directors belonging to business groups and high proportion of board directors being kin relations, 2) high proportion of board directors belonging to business groups and low proportion of board directors being kin relations, 3) low proportion of board directors belonging to business groups and high proportion of board directors being kin relations, and 4) low proportion of board directors belonging to business groups and low proportion of board directors being kin relations. From 1990 to 2010, the percentages of firms with a high proportion of business group directors and a high proportion of kin members declined rapidly, and those of firms with a low proportion of business group directors and a low proportion of kin members increased greatly. This changing trend in the composition of board directors implies that board directors' arrangements in this industry are strongly driven by market forces. More financial companies and foreign investors invest in semiconductor firms and become board directors.

Table 7.2 presents the ownership percentage of family directors and business group directors in the four types of firms. In 1995, the total number of listed firms

Table 7.2 Percentages of four types of family-and-group combinations – ownership structure (%)

	1995	2000	2005	2010
High family & high group	0.0 (0)	5.8 (5)	3.4 (4)	1.3 (2)
High family & low group	33.3 (6)	34.9 (30)	23.7 (28)	22.6 (36)
Low family & high group	0.0 (0)	33.7 (29)	33.9 (40)	28.9 (46)
Low family & low group	66.7 (12)	25.6 (22)	39.0 (46)	47.2 (75)
Total	100.0 (18)	100.0 (86)	100.0 (118)	100.0 (159)

was very few, so it is better to examine the changing patterns of ownership types from 2000. Up to 2000, the number of firms in this industry increased rapidly to eighty-six firms. Firms with business group directors increased as well. In other words, the mutually shared directors among different firms within the same business group increased. In 2005, the number of firms in this industry had increased to 118 firms, and firms with a low number of family and business group directors increased faster than other types of firms. In 2010, the number of firms in this industry had increased to 159 firms, and firms with a low number of family and business group directors increased from 39.0 percent in 2005 to 47.2 percent in 2010. Evidently, the most common form of ownership combination tends toward a low number of family and business group directors on the board. In sum, the ownership percentage of family directors has declined in all four types of firms. The ownership percentage for the three types of family and business group directors have all declined since 2000, except for those firms with the ownership type of a low number of family and business group directors. From 2000 to 2005, many firms adopted the ownership type of low family directors and high business group directors, and there was a trend toward virtual vertical integration during this period.

In 1995, the percentage of shares was high for family directors in companies with high family and low business group directors; however, this percentage has since declined. Since 2000, the percentage of the shares of business group directors of companies with high business group directors has increased (Table 7.3).

Table 7.3 Corporate governance of four types of family-and-group combinations – ownership structure (%)

	1995	2000	2005	2010
High family & high group				
Shareholding (%)				
within family	0.00	7.58	8.18	7.13
within group	0.00	18.15	21.72	26.64
High family & low group				
Shareholding (%)				
within family	25.67	16.11	11.35	10.33
within group	0.00	1.43	1.57	1.04
Low family & high group				
Shareholding (%)				
within family	0.00	0.75	0.74	0.31
within group	0.00	32.99	30.67	32.34
Low family & low group				
Shareholding (%)				
within family	0.99	0.76	1.02	0.53
within group	0.00	1.85	2.58	2.34

Table 7.4 Percentages of shares by family and group directors in different sectors

		1995	2000	2005	2010
Share (%) by family board members	Upstream	23.73 (16.300)	7.19 (8.244)	4.53 (6.328)	2.35 (3.865)
	Midstream	1.53 (2.178)	1.35 (2.094)	.87 (1.490)	1.84 (3.635)
	Downstream	12.06 (19.366)	6.04 (8.548)	3.26 (6.068)	2.30 (4.722)
	Others	.00 (.000)	8.23 (20.060)	3.00 (4.586)	4.14 (6.832)
Share (%) by group board members	Upstream	.00 (.000)	8.46 (11.853)	7.36 (11.000)	7.12 (13.589)
	Midstream	.00 (.000)	20.60 (22.950)	17.70 (18.998)	13.67 (15.435)
	Downstream	.00 (.000)	15.44 (22.588)	16.69 (23.893)	15.82 (22.262)
	Others	.00 (.000)	16.28 (18.249)	17.78 (16.618)	14.58 (17.391)
Share (%) by external financial-related board members	Upstream	1.25 (2.500)	3.58 (7.496)	4.33 (8.034)	3.51 (4.546)
	Midstream	14.29 (6.897)	7.90 (9.061)	4.70 (8.097)	3.64 (5.065)
	Downstream	4.40 (7.701)	6.83 (8.860)	4.96 (8.147)	3.64 (5.472)
	Others	24.00 (33.941)	11.40 (10.995)	10.08 (11.074)	8.46 (10.235)

Furthermore, Table 7.4 presents the percentage of the share of family directors or business group directors on boards by different sectors of Taiwan's semiconductor industry. The declining trend in the percentage of family directors on
boards mainly occurs in the upstream and downstream sectors. The declining
trend of the percentage of business group directors on boards occurs only in the
midstream sector. This trend implies that the rigid competition in the midstream
sector forces these firms to search for directors in the global capital market with a
strong capacity for interlocking networks, linking with more diversified and long-
distance directors.

The percentage of external financial directors on boards has increased in the
IC design sector, but that trend did not occur in foundry and packing sector firms.
The major reason is that the firms in midstream and downstream sectors have
long-term development theories and no longer gain financial capital from external
venture capitalists. Small and medium-sized IC design firms have continuously
grown, and incorporating financial directors is a good strategy for expanding their
financial capital mobilization.

Structural holes in four types of ownership and different sectors

A company with more structural holes or fewer constraints in personal affiliation networks has the advantage of playing a brokerage role. Table 7.6 provides statistics on the clustering coefficients and number of pairs among the
personal network members of affiliation networks in firms with the four types
of ownership.

Firms with high family and high business groups tend to have little interlocking or overlapping with other firms' directors; therefore, the clustering coefficients and pairs among ego network members are all zero. From 1995 to 2010, there were zero pairs of ego's affiliated networks for those firms with high family and high business group directors on the boards, so the average clustering coefficients were as well. Zero clustering coefficients indicate that the firm is isolated and does not mean low density with a better chance for structural holes to link with other social clusters. In order to link with other nonredundant social clusters, it is necessary to have some linkages within and between social clusters (Table 7.5).

Firms with a low proportion of family directors facilitate the brokerage power of networking capability. Table 7.5 indicates that the number of pairs among

Table 7.5 Indexes of structural holes for firms by type of ownership and sector

	1995	*2000*	*2005*	*2010*
Type of ownership				
High family & high group				
Clustering coefficient	0.0000	0.0000	0.0000	0.0000
Number of pairs	0.0000	0.0000	0.0000	0.0000
High family & low group				
Clustering coefficient	0.0000	0.1111	0.0476	0.0861
Number of pairs	0.1667	0.3667	0.3214	0.8611
Low family & high group				
Clustering coefficient	0.0000	0.2149	0.1451	0.2877
Number of pairs	0.0000	4.3793	2.6500	3.9783
Low family & low group				
Clustering coefficient	0.0000	0.2121	0.1978	0.2421
Number of pairs	0.5000	1.1364	1.9348	4.2533
Type of sector				
Upstream				
Clustering coefficient	0.0000	0.1864	0.1550	0.2221
Number of pairs	0.2500	2.3700	2.1200	3.7500
Midstream				
Clustering coefficient	0.0000	0.4981	0.0800	0.2939
Number of pairs	0.0000	5.1000	3.8000	4.9100
Downstream				
Clustering coefficient	0.0000	0.0278	0.1706	0.1766
Number of pairs	0.0000	0.3900	1.3600	4.5700
Others				
Clustering coefficient	0.0000	0.0834	0.0897	0.2138
Number of pairs	3.0000	0.7500	0.4200	1.3400

interlocked directors of the firm is higher for those firms with low family and high business group directors and those firms with low family and low business group directors on their board. If we examine the local clustering coefficients in detail, we find that those firms with low family and high business groups tended to have higher structural holes in 2000 and 2005 instead of in 2010. In 2010, the firms with low family and low business group directors built more structural holes and had a strong capability of playing the brokerage role.

In 2005, the structural constraints, or average local clustering coefficients, of firms with low family and high business group directors declined. In other words, there were more structural holes in their ego's affiliated networks. The major reason is that business group directors played more brokerage roles. The firms with a higher proportion of family directors tended to have relatively iso-lated personal networks with low pairs and low density among alters of their own affiliated networks. The ego's networks with few alters implies that there was a low chance of linking with other social circles and that it was harder to play the brokerage role.

In 2010, the structural holes in those firms with low family and low business group directors on the board seem to be greater than in firms with low family and high business group directors on the board. On average, firms with low family and low business group directors connected with more alter companies, and these firms also contained more pairs of alters (4.25) and low clustering coefficients (low density). Evidently, firms with low family and low business group directors tended to have more structural autonomy in 2010.

In terms of changing indexes on structural holes for the firms in different sec-tors, the firms in the upstream and midstream sectors tended to have equivalently higher structural holes compared to those in the other sectors. The exception is that of downstream firms in 2010. There was a group of small packaging and testing firms that were interlocked with one another to compete for new niches. This is a good example of smaller firms' advantageous strategy for overcoming current structural constraints through an increasing number of nonredundant pairs of ties and low density of local networks or local clustering coefficients (Table 7.5).

Status signals of firms in four types of ownership and different sectors

Table 7.6 provides three types of measures to indicate the centrality of two-mode networks: eigenvector centrality, number of interlocked companies, and two-mode degree centrality. In 1995, business groups in this industry were not yet established, so family director ties made some firms become the center in inter-locked networks. The average number of interlocked companies in firms with high family and low business group directors was greater than firms with low family and low business group directors.

Since 2000, the centrality has been higher for those firms with a low percent-age of family directors regardless of having a high or low percentage of business

Table 7.6 Indexes of status signal for firms by type of ownership and sector

	1995	2000	2005	2010
Type of ownership				
High family & high group				
Eigenvector centrality	0.0000	0.0000	0.0000	0.0000
Number of interlocked companies	0.0000	0.0000	0.0000	0.5000
Two-mode degree centrality	0.0000	0.0108	0.0085	0.0065
High family & low group				
Eigenvector centrality	0.0170	0.0018	0.0023	0.0016
Number of interlocked companies	0.8333	0.7333	0.8571	0.9444
Two-mode degree centrality	0.0485	0.0116	0.0085	0.0065
Low family & high group				
Eigenvector centrality	0.0000	0.0551	0.0389	0.0389
Number of interlocked companies	0.0000	2.3103	1.9250	2.4783
Two-mode degree centrality	0.0000	0.0138	0.0100	0.0073
Low family & low group				
Eigenvector centrality	0.0830	0.0235	0.0022	0.0003
Number of interlocked companies	0.7500	1.3182	1.7609	2.5733
Two-mode degree centrality	0.0630	0.0133	0.0095	0.0073
Type of sector				
Upstream				
Eigenvector centrality	0.0213	0.0042	0.0027	0.0007
Number of interlocked companies	0.7500	1.4700	1.6500	2.2900
Two-mode degree centrality	0.0428	0.0110	0.0087	0.0069
Midstream				
Eigenvector centrality	0.1423	0.1514	0.1365	0.1204
Number of interlocked companies	0.5700	3.0000	2.9000	3.2700
Two-mode degree centrality	0.0723	0.0175	0.0118	0.0084
Downstream				
Eigenvector centrality	0.0034	0.0274	0.0076	0.0083
Number of interlocked companies	0.6000	0.8300	1.4800	2.4300
Two-mode degree centrality	0.0432	0.0144	0.0102	0.0074
Others				
Eigenvector centrality	0.0000	0.0001	0.0004	0.0062
Number of interlocked companies	2.0000	0.8500	0.8500	1.3900
Two-mode degree centrality	0.0770	0.0121	0.0092	0.0070

group directors. In 2000, firms with low family and high business group directors on the board tended to have a high degree of eigenvector centrality (.0551) and a greater number of interlocked companies (2.3103). Firms with low family and low business group directors on the board had greater centrality than those with high family and low business group directors. On the whole, the centrality of firms with a high proportion of family directors was low. This result implies that family businesses tend to build up their own inner circle through kin ties and exclude crossing to other firms; they thus have fewer chances to be affiliated with other firms in this industrial field. However, until 2000 business groups in this industrial field increased, and these business groups tended to use the strategy of interlocking with other firms by sharing common directors.

In 2005, the contribution of increasing affiliated ties with other firms in semiconductor industry for the firms was due to the increasing proportion of business group directors on the board. Firms with a low proportion of family directors and a high proportion of business groups on the board kept the highest centrality, but the centrality measure was close to those firms with low family and low business group directors on the board. Similarly, in 2010, the advantage of a low proportion of family directors in firms seemed to be more significant for increasing the degree of centrality. The number of interlocked companies in firms with a low proportion of family directors was high, regardless of whether firms had a high (2.4783) or low (2.5733) proportion of business group directors.

In terms of changing indexes on status signals for firms in different sectors, the indexes of centrality for firms in the midstream sector were the highest in the industry in general. On the whole, the centrality of firms in the downstream sector was higher than those in the upstream sector.

Social capital and the performance of eight firms

In order to understand the meaning of structural constraints and the status of interlocked networks through sharing common directors in different sectors of the semiconductor industry, we use eight important firm cases in the upstream, midstream, and downstream sectors. This clarifies the characteristics of social capital in terms of interlocked networks of board directors and performance (profits and patents) from 1995 to 2010 (Table 7.7).

Firms in the upstream sector

MediaTek (聯發科)

The MediaTek company was founded in 1997 and listed on the stock market in 2001. This firm has experienced the fastest growth in the upstream sector. The major characteristic of interlocked networks of board directors is that United Microelectronics (UMC, 聯電) board directors held the major shares of ownership even in 2000. This is the reason why the percentage of share of MediaTek's business groups was 18.98 percent at the beginning stage of firm's development. However, this firm was independent from the UMC Business Group, so the share of business group directors later declined to 0.71 percent. The ownership type

Table 7.7 Summary of eight cases of semiconductor firms: 1995, 2000, 2005, 2010

Firm	Year	Shares (%) by Family Directors	Shares (%) by Business Group Directors	Shares (%) by External Financial-Related Directors	% of Number of Family Directors	% of Number of Business Group Directors	% of Number of External Financial-Related Directors
MediaTek	2000	0	18.98	0.15	0	0.29	0.14
MediaTek	2005	4.01	6.24	0.04	0.13	0.13	0.13
MediaTek	2010	3.71	0.71	0.71	0.13	0.13	0.13
VIA	2000	13.77	10.91	12.52	0.38	0.25	0.50
VIA	2005	13.02	4.66	4.66	0.25	0.25	0.13
VIA	2010	8.52	2.55	2.55	0.25	0.25	0.13
SiS	1995	37.17	0	0.07	0.29	0	0.14
SiS	2000	17.17	0	0.17	0.22	0	0.11
SiS	2005	0	16.13	0.04	0	0.5	0.13
SiS	2010	0	16.94	0.14	0	0.11	0.11
TSMC	1995	0	0	23.65	0	0	0.38
TSMC	2000	0	0.03	12.13	0	0.2	0.4
TSMC	2005	0	0	6.40	0	0	0.17
TSMC	2010	0	0	6.38	0	0	0.14
UMC	1995	0	0	11.09	0	0	0.33
UMC	2000	0	4.18	7.10	0	0.33	0.4
UMC	2005	0	6.14	3.98	0	0.55	0.45
UMC	2010	0	5.83	3.40	0	0.33	0.22
Macronix	1995	0	0	5.98	0	0	0.16
Macronix	2000	0	0	2.76	0	0	0.19
Macronix	2005	0	0.12	2.62	0	0.07	0.36
Macronix	2010	0	0.11	2.05	0	0.07	0.27
ASE	1995	3.41	0	0.00	0.38	0	0
ASE	2000	3.62	20.38	0.00	0.25	0.75	0
ASE	2005	3.78	17.61	0.00	0.25	0.67	0
ASE	2010	1.34	18.34	0.00	0.21	0.64	0
SPIL	1995	7.02	0	0.00	0.27	0	0
SPIL	2000	8.05	0	0.00	0.36	0	0
SPIL	2005	3.83	1.38	1.38	0.25	0.08	0.08
SPIL	2010	2.49	0	0.00	0.18	0	0

(*Continued*)

Table 7.7 (Continued)

Firm	Year	Degree	Eigenvector	Number of Interlocked Companies	Number of Interlocked Companies (Normalized)	N-Pairs	Clustering Coefficient
MediaTek	2000	0.01	0	2	2.353	1	1
MediaTek	2005	0.008	0	6	5.128	15	0.133
MediaTek	2010	0.006	0	7	4.43	21	0.286
VIA	2000	0.012	0.052	1	1.176	0	0
VIA	2005	0.008	0	0	0	0	0
VIA	2010	0.006	0	0	0	0	0
SiS	1995	0.04	0.085	2	11.765	1	0
SiS	2000	0.013	0	3	3.529	3	0.333
SiS	2005	0.008	0	6	5.128	15	0.133
SiS	2010	0.007	0	7	4.43	21	0.333
TSMC	1995	0.074	0	0	0	0	0
TSMC	2000	0.015	0.381	3	3.529	3	1
TSMC	2005	0.012	0	1	0.855	0	0
TSMC	2010	0.005	0	1	0.633	0	0
UMC	1995	0.085	0	1	5.882	0	0
UMC	2000	0.022	0	1	1.176	0	0
UMC	2005	0.011	0	4	3.419	6	0.333
UMC	2010	0.007	0	4	2.532	6	0.5
Macronix	1995	0.108	0.996	1	5.882	0	0
Macronix	2000	0.023	0.027	3	3.529	3	1
Macronix	2005	0.014	0	5	4.274	10	0.1
Macronix	2010	0.011	0	5	3.165	10	0.3
ASE	1995	0.045	0	0	0	0	0
ASE	2000	0.018	0	0	0	0	0
ASE	2005	0.012	0	0	0	0	0
ASE	2010	0.011	0	0	0	0	0
SPIL	1995	0.063	0	1	5.882	0	0
SPIL	2000	0.016	0	2	2.353	1	0
SPIL	2005	0.012	0.009	3	2.564	3	0.333
SPIL	2010	0.008	0	0	0	0	0

Firm	Year	ROA	ROE	Net profit (After Tax)	Gross Profit	Scale (Employees)	% of R&D Expenditure	Number of Patents Granted by USPTO
MediaTek	2000	46.19	67.13	25.86	41.7	218	0.04	3
MediaTek	2005	32.59	38.4	35.72	51.66	1171	0.13	32
MediaTek	2010	22.37	28.05	27.25	53.65	5381	0.24	241
VIA	2000	26.58	36.55	21.19	41.78	1234	0.06	31
VIA	2005	0.48	0.41	0.3	23.54	1543	0.13	149
VIA	2010	−5.95	−10.67	−13.89	41.65	861	0.21	144
SiS	1995	24.33	31.32	19.57	28.94	275	0.06	0
SiS	2000	−0.43	−1.21	−2.89	4.07	1448	0.15	6
SiS	2005	4.87	5.81	8.28	34.16	657	0.10	25
SiS	2010	1.07	1.11	5.39	40.31	612	0.30	0
TSMC	1995	41.06	57.55	52.43	55.95	3412	0.03	25
TSMC	2000	22.14	30.83	39.15	47.29	14636	0.03	445
TSMC	2005	18.77	22.15	35.13	44.34	19642	0.05	444
TSMC	2010	24.76	30.11	38.68	49.35	33232	0.07	434
UMC	1995	35.91	52.77	54.66	64.52	2982	0.06	152
UMC	2000	23.66	30.69	45.34	50.64	9373	0.06	571
UMC	2005	1.76	2.05	5.41	9.61	12068	0.10	101
UMC	2010	8.9	10.83	18.86	29.16	13671	0.07	156
Macronix	1995	26.33	39.16	34.82	48.29	1754	0.09	6
Macronix	2000	19.09	29.91	32.92	54.47	3758	0.10	33
Macronix	2005	−14.38	−23.24	−38.73	1.26	3529	0.16	101
Macronix	2010	14.16	17.66	27.36	52.89	4154	0.10	192
ASE	1995	17.84	31.71	14.94	23.08	3387	0.01	0
ASE	2000	9.59	16.18	14.42	30.11	18121	0.02	8
ASE	2005	−3.3	−9.69	−6.19	17.28	17811	0.03	45
ASE	2010	10.99	23.05	10.17	21.48	16338	0.04	69
SPIL	1995	18.37	21.07	30.77	37.15	1720	0.01	0
SPIL	2000	10.91	15.38	17.09	20.9	6394	0.01	2
SPIL	2005	12.33	20.43	18.96	21.91	12316	0.02	26
SPIL	2010	7.01	9.05	8.81	15.37	16411	0.03	20

also changed from a low proportion of family and a high proportion of business group directors into a low family and low business group directors type. This firm has attracted state and global financial investors, so the board is globally linked to diversified directors and the interlocked networking characteristics tend to have more structural holes. The number of pairs increased rapidly from 15 to 21 pairs, and the local clustering coefficients also increased from .133 to .286. Since 2005, the networking strategy of increasing more structural holes by means of independence from the UMC business group and the high degree of interlocking with diversified firms seemed to show some association with high profit indexes (ROA, ROE, net profit, gross profit) and high innovation indexes (R&D expenditure and number of patents). Between 2005 and 2010, the gross profit increased from 51.66 to 53.65, and the number of patents increased from 32 to 241.

VIA Technology (VIA, 威盛)

VIA was founded in Silicon Valley in the United States by Wen-chi Chen (陳文崎), the husband of Xue-hong Wang (王雪紅), in 1987; the headquarters were then moved back to Taiwan in 1992. The composition of board directors has been the ownership type of a high proportion of family directors and a low proportion of business group directors. The high share of family directors resulted in few interlocked ties with other firms. Table 7.7 indicates that there were no overlapped ties with other firms through sharing common directors. This firm thus has a low degree of centrality and no structural holes or capability to link with diversified social circles. Evidently, this firm lacks corporate social capital. This firm has not performed well in terms of profit indexes, even though it continues to invest in research and development and holds a considerable number of patents.

Silicon Integrated System (SiS, 矽統)

SiS was founded in 1987. It invested in its own foundry firm, which caused a financial crisis. By 1995, most firms were interlocked with one other firm through overlapped directors, but Silicon Integrated System (SIS, 矽統) was interlocked with two firms. Along with the change of ownership type from a high proportion of family directors in 1995 and 2000 to a high proportion of business group directors in 2005 and 2010, the number of interlocked companies increased from two in 1995 to seven in 2010. In 2004, Jun-yuan Du (杜俊元), the founder of SiS, left the board, and the UMC business group directors played major roles in merging with SiS.

The family ownership of SiS was quite high in 1995 and 2000, but the ownership composition rapidly changed to being mainly owned by business group directors after UMC (聯電) merged with this company in 2004. The company's profit in 2000 was negative, and UMC's investment in this firm created an increase in structural holes of interlocked networks of board directors. The number of interlocked companies and pairs among alters of personal affiliation networks increased, and clustering coefficients also increased. This position is even more advantageous for linking with global nodes in interlocked networks of an industrial field. The indexes on profit also show that the profit changed from negative to positive since the firm's transformation from family ownership to business group ownership. The firm invested more in research and development but produced fewer patents. One alternative interpretation is that the interlocked networks tended to be less linked with a highly centralized firm or the local network structure tended to have stronger constraints, which are not advantageous for patent innovations.

On the whole, the dynamic change of board directors in these three important IC design firms indicates two changing mechanisms. One is strong control by family directors, such as control of VIA by the couple Xieu-hong Wang and Wen-chi Chen. This continuing family control made its interlocked networks change less, but low interlocked ties with other firms made profit and patent innovation performance relatively low. In contrast, UMC played an important role in the dynamic change of board directors of MediaTek and SiS. MediaTek used this strategy to get out of UMC's control and merge with more diversified but related firms. Its market and innovation capability dramatically increased, and it became the most successful IC design firm. The major dynamic mechanism shaping the structure of board directors and its interlocked linkages and position of interlocked networks was the decision to invest in its own foundry firm and integrate IC design and IC foundry manufacturing. In fact, this decision created conflict with previous customers of the IC foundry, such as UMC. Therefore, conflict regarding patents and orders led to negative profit. Finally, the board members were replaced by UMC, which has kept this firm in UMC business groups since 2004.

Firms in the midstream sector

United Microelectronics Company (UMC, 聯電)

UMC was founded by state capital in 1980 and technologically supported by the Industrial Technological Research Institute (ITRI, 工研院). From the beginning, UMC's founder, Xin-cheng Chao (曹興誠), stressed that this firm would not allow relatives to sit on their board of directors. In addition, this firm encouraged the managers of the business group firms to sit on each other's boards. Therefore, this firm had the ownership type of a low proportion of family and a low proportion of business group directors from 1995 until 2010. UMC has long competed with TSMC in the foundry field, but these two firms used different strategies of competition. UMC used financial leverage strategies and built up more pseudonetworks of business groups, also called the UMC Family Army (聯家軍). UMC has thus had the highest proportion of external financial directors on its board. UMC has a high proportion of business group directors, but their share has been low. Since 2000, UMC has lagged behind TSMC because its technological innovation capability did not catch up with TSMC's new copper manufacturing technology after 2000. The difference in the number of patents between these two firms also increased in 2005 and 2010. Profit and financial indexes also show UMC to be far behind TSMC in 2005 and 2010.

Taiwan Semiconductor Manufacturing Company (TSMC, 台積電)

TSMC was founded in 1987 by Morris Chang (張忠謀) and became the first and the largest global, specialized foundry manufacturing firm. TSMC has long recruited directors with strong, specialized management experience in the fields of engineering, finance, and business management from global market. The independent directors (獨立董事) often include global executives of high-tech companies and deans or distinguished professors from elite US universities. In short, these directors did not cross-seat on the boards of other semiconductor firms in Taiwan. The percentage of directors in terms of numbers and overlapping directors among firms was almost zero. The Development Foundation of Executive Yuan (行政院開發基金) holds the largest share of stocks. This company has the highest proportion of foreign directors. Although this company interlocked with very few directors of domestic semiconductor companies by sharing common directors, it has the highest profit and greatest number of patents. In contrast to UMC, this firm's strategy of competition puts more emphasis on technological innovation and upgrading instead a strategy of financial leverage. The network characteristic of interlocked networks by sharing common directors is not associated with performance and patent innovation. Technological collaboration with these global semiconductor firms is the major strategy for TSMC to keep its competitive advantage.

Macronix International Company (MIC, 旺宏)

Macronix was founded by Ming-qiu Wu (吳敏求), who mobilized a group of elite engineers in the semiconductor industry from Silicon Valley. Instead of being an original equipment manufacturing (OEM) or own-design manufacturing (ODM) firm, Macronix insisted on having its own patents and technology. Therefore, MIC holds a large number of patents. This firm has had zero percentage of family directors and a very low percentage of business group directors. There is a relatively large proportion of external financial directors. The networking pattern in MIC is quite similar to that of UMC. The proportion of seating the boards of other companies through financial directors has increased. Centrality was high in 1995 and 2000, but there was no centrality influence after 2000. This firm recently used more of a structural holes strategy with more pairs among alters and a moderate degree of clustering coefficients. MIC has generally performed well, except in 2005 when the CEO of this firm was in a US hospital.

The networking strategies of these three firms in the midstream sector are different. UMC (聯華電子) and MIC (旺宏) have increased their interlocked networks with other semiconductor firms through shared board directors. However, TSMC changed their networking strategies by reducing their networking with domestic semiconductor firms and bringing in more international board directors. The networking strategies of reducing family and business groups and bringing top global CEOs or internationally well-known scholars from engineering schools continued to upgrade TSMC's technological level. The most important characteristic of the board directors is that there are no family board members. This ownership type has become a dominant concept of control in midstream semiconductor firms.

Firms in the downstream sector

Advanced Semiconductor Engineering (ASE, 日月光)

ASE was founded in 1984 by the brothers Qian-Sheng Chang (張虔生) and Hong-Ben Chang (張洪本). This firm has a very high proportion of family directors but a low percentage of share of these family directors for such a large-scale firm. If we use the percentage of family directors as the index, ASE can be counted as being strongly controlled by family directors. Both indexes on shares of stocks by business group directors and percentages of business group directors indicate that this firm is also controlled by the ASE business group. Therefore, external financial directors cannot get on the board. There is no interlocked networking with other firms in the semiconductor industry. The ownership type of board directors has changed from a low share of family directors and a low share of business group directors in 1995 to a low share of family directors and a high share of business group directors from 2000 to 2010.

ASE's power control tends to be restricted to its own family business group directors and has high structural constraints. Therefore, ASE has had a low degree of centrality and zero interlocking with other firms since 1995. Compared to the other case firms mentioned above, ASE has had a moderate level of performance though it has had isolated interlocked networks. This fact may indicate that a networking strategy of interlocked networks of board directors may not work as well in a well-established, large-scale, high-tech firm such as ASE. The ROE and ROI was negative in 2005, and they increased again. The Chinese investment may make some contribution to the firm's revival of growth. During 2005 to 2010, a private fund expected to acquire ASE. Compared to sales or capital, the patent contribution index is not very high. The relatively low connections with domestic firms in interlocked networks did not constrain performance or innovation capability.

Siliconware Precision Industries (SPIL, 矽品)

SPIL was founded by Zhong-li Lin (林鐘隸) in 1973. His son, Wen-bo Lin (林文伯), inherited ownership of this firm. The structure of the board directors maintained a high degree of family and low degree of business group directors from 1995 to 2010. However, in keeping with the general trend, the share of family directors also declined in 2010. The number of patents has declined, and ROE and ROI have also declined. On the whole, there have been few interlocking ties with other companies except in 2005. The high proportion of family board members resulted in a low innovation capability. However, the innovation ability in packaging firms was not expected to be as high as that in foundry firms. Compared to the technology of IC design and IC foundry, the technology of packaging and testing is relatively low. The percentage of research and development in the total expenditures and the number of patents are also low in these eight cases. Although the innovation capability of this firm is not that high, the ownership type and corporate governance has been quite unique and stable. Keeping a firm in an appropriate technological niche and governance structure can also make a firm survive with a moderate level of revenue.

SPIL has maintained a unique, stable ownership by combining family directors and key members of the management team on the board. Since a new regulation on the independent board directors of corporations was issued in 2006, the firm made a minor change in the composition of board directors by inviting the former directors of UMC and the wife of the board director of the Premier Company. The new independent directors became the bridge between UMC and SPIL, then SPIL and UMC built up a stronger strategic alliance.

Conclusion and discussion

Previous research on interlocked networks of company boards in Taiwan indicate that state and financial actors were important in these networks, but most of this work does not use corporate social capital theory and network analyses to specifically show how different types of ownership composition for the firms created different network structures and changed their position in the interlocked networks. These changes of network positions may be associated with their financial performance and innovation capability.

Generally speaking, there are two types of these changing patterns in the semiconductor industry: one oriented toward technology leverage and one oriented toward financial leverage. For those firms with strong technological innovation capability such as TSMC (台積電), the intensification and extensiveness of technological capability and capacity has become the dominant strategy for competing in the global market. Therefore, the choices of independent board directors are mainly based on the demand for linking with all diversified elites in global semiconductor firms or professionals. These independent board directors seldom cross-seat with other Taiwanese companies, so the interlocked number of crossing board seats with other domestic firms is quite low. TSMC board directors did not want to share their own tacit knowledge, so they did not cross seats with the boards of other firms. TSMC has had a low proportion of family and business group directors and lacked interlocking ties with domestic companies but has still performed well. TSMC's directors are mainly foreign investors and globally well-known CEOs or scholars. These directors can serve as brokers between Taiwan and global companies; update information, resources, and technology; and continuously upgrade TSMC's technology.

The other type of interlocked networking pattern tends to have a mixed ownership of family directors and business group directors and often reacts to the environment and changes their composition of ownership. Structural hole strategies can make the position in the industrial field more advantageous. For example, MIC (旺宏) had a negative performance in 2005, but the increasing number of interlocked ties with other companies created more structural holes with greater pairs among alters of ego's affiliation networks and high clustering coefficient. In 2010, MIC's performance regained a high level of performance and produced a number of patents that exceeded even that of UMC (聯電). Although there was a temporary crisis of leadership in 2005 (the CEO's illness), the restructuring of MIC's interlocked networks has restored the firm's innovation ability and competitiveness.

A social circle has occurred with a virtual vertical integration group in the interlocked networks of board directors of Taiwan's semiconductor firms. UMC (聯電) began to use merging, acquisition, and division strategies to build up the interlocked networks of business groups. This mother company sent its colleagues to related firms and built up virtually integrated business groups with vertical integration characteristics. This networking strategy of crossing different board seats from the same business groups (化整為零) is advantageous for investing in China. The decentralized but loosely coupled business group had the advantage of avoiding the rigid supervision of the government, especially before 2008. The disadvantage was that the UMC gradually lost its competitiveness with TSMC in its capability for technology and innovation.

There has been a significant declining trend from a high degree of family board members to a high degree of members of business groups in Taiwan's semiconductor industry. The typical case is ASE (日月光). The board directors included a high degree of family members and a high degree of business group members until 2005. However, this composition changed along with the market expansion in China and deregulation of restrictions on investing in China beginning in 2008. A dramatic decrease of the share of family ownership is due to the inclusion of global private capital and funds. Even though SPIL (矽品) has had the ownership type of a high degree of family and a low degree of business group directors, the percentage share of family directors has declined greatly. Maintaining a moderate level of technology and capturing a moderate number of technology niches may be SPIL's survival strategy. Therefore, we foresee some stability in terms of financial performance but a low level of innovation capability for SPIL.

The most unique composition of board members is that of MediaTek (聯發科). The composition changed from a low degree of high family members and a high degree of members from business groups, such as UMC business groups (interlocked with the NOVATEK Microelectronic Corporation [聯詠] and the LITE-ON Semiconductor Corporation [敦南]). The key CEOs were all connected with UMC. Since 2005, Tsai Ming-jie has controlled the largest share and strengthened the firm's family power and links with other non-UMC members, especially the networking strategies in China since 2004. The firm integrates CEO and high-level managers with previous working experience in China. The gross profit increased, but the ROE and ROI declined. Through merging with and acquiring vertical companies and collaborating with companies in China, the innovation capability has increased dramatically.

References

Bonacich, Phillip. 1972. "Technique for Analyzing Overlapping Memberships." *Sociological Methodology* 4: 176–185.

Bonacich, Phillip. 1987. "Power and Centrality: A Family of Measures." *American Journal of Sociology* 92 (5): 1170–1182.

Borgatti, Stephen P. 2009. "Two-Mode Concepts in Social Network Analysis." In *Encyclopedia of Complexity and System Science*, edited by Robert A. Meyers, 279–291. New York: Springer.

Borgatti, Stephen P., and Martin G. Everett. 1997. "Network Analysis of 2-Mode Data." *Social Networks* 19: 243–269.

Burt, Ronald S. 1992. *Structural Holes: The Social Structure of Competition*. Cambridge: Harvard University Press.

Coleman, James S. 1988. "Social Capital in the Creation of Human Capital." *American Journal of Sociology* 94 (Special Supplement): 95–120.

Coleman, James S. 1990. *Foundations of Social Theory*. Cambridge: The Belknap Press of Harvard University Press.

Davis, Gerald F. 2005. "New Directions in Corporate Governance." *Annual Review of Sociology* 31: 143–162.

Davis, Gerald F., and Henrich R. Greve. 1997. "Corporate Elite Networks and Governance Changes in the 1980s." *American Journal of Sociology* 103 (1): 1–37.

Granovetter, Mark. 1985. "Economic Action and Social Structure: The Problem of Embeddedness." *American Journal of Sociology* 91 (3): 481–510.

Guan, Yi-Ren, Ray-May Hsung, and Yi-Jr Lin. 2013. "Mechanisms of Shaping Professionalization of Board Structure: The Case of Taiwan IC Listed Companies in 2003." *Industry and Management Forum* 15 (2): 4–29.

Hsung, Ray-May, and Li-Chung Hu. 2011. "Institutional Transition and the Changing of Family Financial Networks: The Case of Interlocking Directorates in 1996, 2002, and 2006." In *Does Family Enterprises Still Matter*, edited by Jenn-hwan Wang and Chao-Tung Wen, 357–396. Taipei: CHILUI Publisher.

Hsung, Ray-May, and Yi-Jr Lin. 2012. "Embeddedness of Innovations: The Mechanisms of Industrial Upgrading of IC Industry in Taiwan." Paper Presented at The 1st World Congress of Taiwan Studies, Academia Sinica, April 26–28, 2012.

Kang, David L., and Aage B. Sørensen. 1999. "Ownership Organization and Firm Performance." *Annual Review of Sociology* 25: 121–144.

Keister, Lisa A. 2002. "Financial Markets, Money, and Banking." *Annual Review of Sociology* 28: 39–61.

Lee, Zong-Rong. 2007. "Between the State Power and Chinese Familism: Corporate Control and Intercorporate Networks in Taiwan Revisited." *Taiwan Sociology* 13: 173–242.

Lee, Zong-Rong. 2009. "Institutional Transition and Market Networks: An Historical Investigation of Interlocking Directorates of Big Businesses in Taiwan, 1962–2003." *Taiwan Sociology* 17: 101–160.

Lin, Nan. 2001. *Social Capital: A Theory of Structure and Action*. New York: Cambridge University Press.

Lin, Nan, and Mary Dumin. 1986. "Access to Occupations through Social Ties." *Social Networks* 8: 365–385.

Lin, Nan, Walter M. Ensel, and John C. Vaughn. 1981. "Social Resources and Strength of Ties: Structural Factors in Occupational Status Attainment." *American Sociological Review* 46: 393–405.

Mintz, Beth, and Michael Schwartz. 1981. "The Structure of Intercorporate Unity in American Business." *Social Problems* 29 (2): 87–103.

Mizruchi, Mark S. 1996. "What Do Interlocks Do? An Analysis, Critique, and Assessment of Research on Interlocking Directorates." *Annual Review of Sociology* 22: 271–298.

Mizruchi, Mark S., and David Bunting. 1981. "Influence in Corporate Networks: An Examination of Four Measures." *Administrative Science Quarterly* 26 (3): 475–489.

Newman, M.E.J. 2001. "Scientific Collaboration Networks. II. Shortest Paths, Weighted Networks, and Centrality." *Physical Review E* 64: 016132–1–7.

Opsahl, Tore. 2013. "Triadic Closure in Two-Mode Networks: Redefining the Global and Local Clustering Coefficients." *Social Networks* 35: 159–167.

Podolny, Joel M. 1993. "A Status-Based Model of Market Competition." *American Journal of Sociology* 98 (4): 829–872.

Podolny, Joel M. 2005. *Status Signals: A Sociological Study of Market Competition.* Princeton, NJ: Princeton University Press.

Shivdasani, Anil. 1993. "Board Composition, Ownership Structure, and Hostile Takeovers." *Journal of Accounting and Economics* 16: 167–198.

Uzzi, Brian. 1996. "The Sources and Consequences of Embeddedness for the Economic Performance of Organizations: The Network Effect." *American Sociological Review* 61 (4): 674–698.

Uzzi, Brian. 1997. "Social Structure and Competition in Interfirm Networks: The Paradox of Embeddedness." *Administrative Science Quarterly* 42: 35–67.

Uzzi, Brian. 1999. "Embeddedness in the Making of Financial Capital: How Social Relations and Networks Benefit Firms Seeking Financing." *American Sociological Review* 64 (4): 481–505.

Watts, Duncan J., and Steven H. Strogatz. 1998. "Collective Dynamics of 'Small-World' Networks." *Nature* 393: 440–442.

White, Harrison C. 1981. "Where Do Markets Come From?" *American Journal of Sociology* 87 (3): 517–547.

8 Social capital and the development of Taiwan's pharmaceutical industry

Comparing conventional and biomedical firms

Jenn-Hwan Wang, Han-yo Wu, and Tsung-Yuan Chen

Introduction

Taiwan's economic development has been widely described as being based on the small and medium-sized enterprises (SMEs) model that is inundated with entrepreneurship (Amsden 1989; Wade 1990; Weiss and Hobson 1995), indicating the spirit to create a new firm (Schumpeter 1950; Aldrich 2005). This entrepreneurship also shows clearly in the formation of the pharmaceutical industry. Currently, the pharmaceutical industry in Taiwan can be roughly divided into two sectors: the conventional pharmaceutical sector that is mainly producing and marketing chemical generic drugs and newly formed biopharmaceutical firms that are targeting, developing, and producing new drugs by using biologics methods. Both types of firms in Taiwan are very small in terms of revenue and capacity (Wang 2010; Wong 2011). In the conventional pharmaceutical sector, for example, in 2013, the total revenue of Taiwan's pharma was approximately NT$74.6 billion (about US$2.5 billion, US$1 = NT$30) Biotechnology Industry Study Centre, 2013). The revenue of the biggest pharmaceutical firm in Taiwan, YungShin Pharm (永信藥品), in 2013, was only NT$5.1 billion (about US$170 million).

Since the mid-1990s, Taiwan has promoted biotechnology as one of its pillars of strategic industries in order to further upgrade the economy into an innovative-driven one (Wang 2014). Together with the transformation of the value chain in the biopharmaceutical industry in the world in which the R&D and manufacturing activities[1] can be outsourced, many new biotech firms have been created by domestic and overseas scientists to take advantage of the state's financial support for promoting this industry (Wong 2005; 2011; Chen and Wang 2009; Wang et al. 2012). In 2010, the average number of employees of these biotech firms in Taiwan was 68.4, whereas the average revenue was only NT$65.7 million. In addition, investments from venture capital to those science firms were also very small.

The purpose of this chapter is aimed to compare and analyze the role in which social capital – bonding and bridging – has played in the formation and development of the two sectors of Taiwan's pharmaceutical industry. Bonding social capital refers to resources in social relations derived from close social ties, such as family, relatives, and close friends; whereas bridging social capital indicates resources in social relations generated from voluntary associations, working groups, or organizational colleagues. (This will be discussed in detail later.) Since bio-pharmas are at the frontier of the value chain that involves a high degree of R&D, whereas conventional pharmas mainly engage in producing generic drugs to the market and engage, to a lesser degree, in R&D activities, we thus expect that these two types of firms will have different sources of social capital in terms of capital formation and knowledge learning. However, to our surprise, as will be shown later, although bio-pharmas depend on bridging social capital more than conventional pharmas do in terms of knowledge learning, they nonetheless show a similar pattern in terms of capital formation at the initial stage. We will argue that this may be related to institutional inefficiency in supporting the newly emerging science firms in Taiwan.

The chapter will be divided into six sections. After the introduction, the theoretical part will discuss the relationship between social capital and entrepreneurship. The third section will discuss the emergence and transformation of the pharmaceutical industry. The fourth section will investigate the conventional pharmas, focusing on two representative cases, YungShin Pharm（永信藥品） and U.C. Pharma（五洲製藥）. The fifth section will discuss the new biopharmas, focusing on two representative cases, TaiMed Biologics（中裕新藥） and ScinoPharm（台灣神隆）. The final section will contain discussion and conclusion.

Social capital and entrepreneurship

Entrepreneurship refers to the creation of new organizations, and the people who create these organizations are called entrepreneurs (Aldrich 2005, 452). These nascent entrepreneurs confront various problems in creating their organizations, including gathering and analyzing information, collecting necessary capital, and recruiting essential personnel, as well as forming the business organization to compete and survive in the marketplace. In essence, they have to confront two major problems: One is to discover effective routines in order to reduce uncertainty; the other is to build ties within the business environment in order to gain recognition from the market (Thornton 1999; Aldrich 2005, 467). Among the existing resources that these entrepreneurs can acquire in order to create their business, social capital is the most effective channel that an entrepreneur can mobilize.

The concept of social capital has been widely used in social sciences, which may indicate various conceptual levels and explain totally different phenomena such as economic development (Evans 1996; Fine 1999; Bebbington et al. 2004), political development (Coleman 1988; Putnam 1993; Woolock 1998), or entrepreneurship (Nahapiet and Ghoshal 1998; Knorringa and van Staveren 2006; Gedajlovic et al. 2013). However, as many have argued, social capital does not have a clear, undisputed meaning, and there is no commonly agreed upon definition. Therefore, as most scholars agree, it is better to take a multidimensional approach to study the impact of social capital to the specific phenomenon that the research is targeting.

As Knorringa and von Staveren suggest (2006, 46), social capital can be defined as "the set of social relations that enables entrepreneurs to gain, maintain or expand access to economic resources, which are used by entrepreneurs to reinforce the productivity of these economic resources." Therefore, social capital indicates relationships, and the innate resources within the relationships, rather than the property of individuals (Lin 1999), with the latter being described as human capital. Although the concept of social capital does not exclude that individual property is important in generating an economic effect, it nonetheless still stresses the relationships, which can effectively reduce transaction costs, enable knowledge learning, enhance financial capital collection, and reinforce collective action, and so forth.

There are two forms of social capital in the conventional sense: bonding and bridging (Putnam 1993; Woolock 1998; Storper 2005; Knorringa and van Staveren 2006). Bonding social capital emerges from strong social ties (Granovetter 1985), which are based on similar backgrounds or types of persons, for example, on a similar basis of family, kinship, gender, ethnicity, community, and religion. Sometimes, this type of social capital can be referred to as an ascribed group, which has a strong social cohesion that can generate a strong trust among individuals (Knorringa and van Staveren 2006, 19).

Although bonding social capital provides a low transaction cost for the enterprise, it nonetheless has limitations. First of all, bonding social capital that is too strong will create a lock-in effect that is not beneficial for an enterprise to grow and to attain new information or to learn new knowledge. Second, a strong bonding social capital will also generate an opportunist behavior that is based on high trust. As a result, the bonding social capital will lead to its own fatal destiny if there is no proper sanction system.

In contrast, a bridging social capital emerges from weak social ties across society, or "people unlike ourselves" (Storper 2005, 33), which nevertheless are held together through the sharing of some minimum common values and interests. By bringing a broad mix of people together, bridging social capital characterizes networks, associations, or organizations that involve diverse people, or as Putnam (2000, 22), claims, this type of social capital tends to be outward looking and to "encompass people across diverse social cleavages," which is different from "bonding" social capital in that it tends to be inward looking by encouraging in-group solidarity and to "reinforce exclusive identities and homogeneous groups." Since weak ties exist among people who are heterogeneous, having different identifications and belonging to different groups, bridging social capital can thus generate social contacts that are not redundant, and in the end, it can create new values. Hence, scholars tend to regard bridging social capital as having a higher economic value than does bonding social capital.

Nevertheless, we have to note that bridging and bonding are not "either-or" but rather "more-or-less" categories into which social networks can be neatly divided. Indeed, as Knorringa and van Staveren (2006, 22), maintain,

> Without bonding social capital there is no fertile ground for bridging social capital to develop. Bridging social capital requires that economic actors are

familiar with the strong ties of bonding social capital, which provide them with the necessary social capabilities, particularly interpersonal capabilities of trust, sociability, organization, responsibility and loyalty, to connect to other people.

In addition, as Burt's (2004), concept of a structural hole describes, bonding social capital within the group provides people with the social basis to extend their relationships to others outside their group, while the benefits of the bridging social capital is built upon the bridging function that links together two or more separate and isolated clusters.

Given the above "more-or-less" feature of these two types of social capital, it is still interesting to note to what degree bonding social capital is more important than bridging social capital, or vice versa, in the development of an enterprise and whether they are different in high-tech and low-tech industries (sectors).

It is argued by many scholars that bonding and bridging social capital play different roles in technology and low-tech-technology types of firms (Liao and Welsch 2003; Storper 2005; Knorringa and van Staveren 2006). In general, bonding social capital, characterized by high-density relationships, plays a more important role in the emergence of non-technology firms. The nascent entrepreneur is able to mobilize resources from his family, relatives, and close friends, to create the firm. However, as the firm moves upward in the value chain and engages in new market competition, the existing bonding social capital may not be enough to provide the entrepreneur with sufficient information and resources. Entrepreneurs have to find new resources to fund their new adventures, for example, in the stock market or via joint ventures where resources and information are not based on close social relationships. Thus, a successful transformation of the enterprise demands a transition from bonding to bridging social capital (Knorringa and van Staveren 2006, 41).

As to technology firms, bridging social capital plays a more important role to the emergence of a nascent enterprise. This is because an entrepreneur needs more information that is beyond their personal networks to create a technology-related firm. Indeed, as Liao and Welsch (2003) found, "sparse, disconnected social networks coupled with strong social ties lead to greater growth aspiration for technology-related entrepreneurs." By contrast, "extensive network ties with strong social ties are positively related to the growth aspiration of non-technology-based entrepreneurs" (166).

What are the roles of bonding and bridging social capital in creating and developing the business of conventional and biotech pharmas in Taiwan? Do conventional pharmaceutical and biotech firms show similar types of social capital in the creation and development of the firms? Following the above description of bonding and bridging social capital, it can be hypothesized that nascent entrepreneurs tend to mobilize resources by way of bonding social capital in the conventional pharmaceutical industry; in contrast, entrepreneurs in the biotech industry tend to use bridging social capital to nurture and expand their enterprises. We, however, will show that the story is not that simple.

Table 8.1 Entrepreneur's social capital in conventional and biotech pharmaceutical industries in Taiwan

Firm Type	Initial Capital	Information and Knowledge	Form of Social Capital
Conventional	Family and friends, neighbors	Personal network, learning by doing	Bonding
Biotech	Bank, venture capital, stock market, state funding	Scientific community, association, professional exhibition	Bridging

In this chapter, we will use two dimensions of the development of a firm to show the similarities and differences between these two types of pharma. The first one is how nascent entrepreneurs collect their initial capital, which will show how they mobilize social relations (family, friends, or venture capital). The second one is how the entrepreneur gains and learns the necessary knowledge to start and develop the firm. This proposition is shown in Table 8.1.

We will use four cases, two conventional and two new biotech firms, to investigate our proposition. However, our study is not confined to the four cases but investigates the development of both sectors of the pharmaceutical industry as a whole. The data of this chapter, including the four firms, were collected mainly by field studies in Taiwan between July 2011 and July 2012. A total of thirty-four informants were asked by semi-organized questionnaires and through face-to-face or telephone interviews. Each interview was done by the authors within one or two hours. Our informants were mainly composed of high-ranking executive managers of enterprises, industrial researchers, and university professors.

The development of Taiwan's pharmaceutical industry

Taiwan's modern pharmaceutical industry started during the Japanese colonial period 1895–1945, when a Western medical system was first introduced to the island. During that period, most modern-day pharmas were Japanese owned, whereas Taiwanese working in this industry were mainly engaged in distribution and marketing. After 1945, when the Kuomintang regime took over the island, the existing thirteen Japanese pharmas were reorganized into one state-owned company. In addition, many privately owned pharmas emerged afterward, producing cod liver oil, vitamins, and other medicines (Fan 2001).

From the 1950s onwards, the state began to encourage the establishment of new pharmas in order to fill the increasing domestic demand. Therefore, many new companies were established and began to produce generic drugs by collaborating with foreign companies, especially the Japanese (Yu 1972; Han 1999; Fan 2001). Until the early 1960s, there were over 600 small pharmas in Taiwan. However, in 1960, the state took a more liberal export-oriented industrialization policy, through which many foreign firms began to invest in Taiwan to take advantage of the tax incentives. In 1961, the state invited the American Cyanimide Company to establish a joint venture firm with the Taiwan Sugar Company to produce antibiotics, and this was the first Taiwan-US joint venture in the pharmaceutical industry. Later, many Japanese pharmas, such as Takeda (1962), Tanabe (1962), Yamanouchi (1963), and Shionogi (1964) and Pfizer (1964) from the United States, also followed suit. Taiwan's pharmas began to separate into domestic-owned and foreign-owned firms, and by the early 1970s, there were as many as 750 in Taiwan. In 1982, the state launched the Good Manufacturing Practice (GMP) policy in order to regulate the chaotic pharmaceutical industry and to standardize the manufacturing procedures in drug production. This measurement had ousted many whose manufacturing capabilities were not able to conform with the state's regulations. Since then, the state has continued to regulate the pharmaceutical industries by requiring the firms to follow GMP, cGMP, and PIC/s,[2] standards in order to safeguard the drug production and links to the international market.

Taiwan began to promote the development of biotechnology in the early 1980s. But it achieved only a very small degree of success (Wong 2005; Chen and Wang 2009). It was only in the mid-1990s, when the state legislated the Promotion Program for Biotechnology, known simply as the Biotech Action Plan (1995), that the biotechnology industry began to proliferate. The main strategies taken by the state were to invite prominent overseas scientists to return and to create new firms, subsidize firms' R&D expenses, provide tax incentives and low interest rates for lending, induce venture capital to support the biotech industry, and so forth. In 2006, Taiwan's emerging biotech sector had 253 companies, with a total revenue of US$1.21 billion, of which many were created by overseas returnees from the US, and almost all of them were small to medium-sized companies (Wang et al. 2012). Also, among the newly emerged biotech firms, of which many were created after the late 1990s, were in the field of the biopharmaceutical industry (Wang 2014).

These two sectors of the pharmaceutical industry, however, have very different development paths in Taiwan (Table 8.2). The conventional pharmas emerged in the 1950s when Taiwan began to industrialize. Many emerging businessmen started their own companies simply by copying the drugs on the market even without a knowledgeable background in medicine. However, the biotech firms are essentially based on scientific frontier knowledge that originated from the biological revolution that occurred in the late 1970s in the US (Pisano 2006).

In addition, these two types of firms had very large differences in the degree of state support. In the early 1950s and 1960s, the Taiwanese government did not have any specific policies to support the pharmaceutical industry. The nascent entrepreneurs had to depend upon themselves to create their own firms. In contrast, the biotech firms that have emerged since the 1990s have been one of the targeted pillars of industry that the state has wanted to promote. Therefore, policy support has been put into this newly emerging biotechnology. With the different development background in mind, we now turn to the evolution of these two sectors and specific firms.

Table 8.2 Comparison of conventional and new biopharmaceutical industries in Taiwan

	Conventional Pharmaceutical	*New Biopharmaceutical*
Products	Generic drugs	New drugs or active ingredients (contract research organization [CRO], contract manufacturing organization [CMO])
Economic activity	Foreign representative, manufacturing, marketing	New drug development, clinical trials, patent transfer
Sources of knowledge	From abroad or domestic firms, low entry barrier	Scientific community, licensed from abroad, high entry barrier
Initial stage's institutional environment	1950–1960s: limited state support	1990–present: strong state support, pillar industry

The conventional pharmas

There are some common characteristics among conventional pharmas when the nascent entrepreneurs originally started and then ran their own businesses. First of all, initial capital was mainly generated from the founders' savings, or collected from relatives and friends. This feature was very similar with other SMEs and family firms that emerged in Taiwan during the same period in which bonding social capital was an essential element (Shieh 1991; Chen 1994). Second, the founders themselves did not necessary have any advanced knowledge of medicine, as this had to do with this industry's low entry barrier during Taiwan's earlier stage of industrialization. This section will use qualitative data to show the above features of Taiwan's conventional pharmas. We will use two cases – Yungshin and U.C. Pharma to illustrate the above features. The reasons that we selected these two firms are simply because they are the oldest and biggest pharmas in Taiwan, the details of which are as follows.

Initial capital formation

Yungshin Pharma

The founder of Yungshin Pharma was Mr. Tien Der Lee, born into a poor family from Dajia town in central Taiwan during the Japanese colonial period. Mr. Lee went to Osaka to work during his youth through which he learned the skill of trading. After the end of World War II, Mr. Lee worked at a trading company in Taipei and was responsible for importing medicine from Japan. Three years later, in 1952, Mr. Lee opened his own shop in his hometown called the Yungshin Drug

Store. The main business of this shop, initially, was to import foreign medicines and/or to become the local representative of the domestic pharmas (Huang et al. 2013), including some of the biggest local pharmas during that time, such as Sintong Chemical, China Chemical, Yong Fong, and so on. Because he did not have any medical knowledge, Mr. Lee came to understand what was required from mainly reading the instructions of those medicines in order to sell the drugs to the customers; as he often said, "The salesman of medicines, we have to know the medicines."[3]

Some factors had greatly encouraged Mr. Lee to transform his drug store into a pharma; one of them was shrinking profit margins. In the 1960s, many pharmas started to build their own marketing channels rather than be dependent upon drug stores to distribute their products. Under this situation, plus the severe competition among drug stores, profit margins had dropped sharply. Second, as a wholesale local representative, Mr. Lee had the opportunity to be invited by Japanese pharmas for sightseeing tours in Japan and to detour to various pharmas whilst there. After one tour in 1965, Mr. Lee decided to build his own pharma in order to avoid being evicted from the market by just running a profit-shrinking drug store, thereby transforming Yungshin Drug Store into Yungshin Pharma and beginning his new venture (Huang et al. 2013).

The initial capital of Yungshin Pharma was a typical case of a Taiwanese SME. He used his own savings and collected funds from relatives and friends. As one of the early cofounders said,

> Our initial capital was only NT$1.5 million. Most of the money was earned from the drug store, some of it borrowed from my relatives and friends. Some of my cofounders also contributed parts of the fund, about NT$100 thousands. Our company began to earn profits in the first year, later we lacked funding due to the expansion. Therefore, we began to collect capital from friends in Taipei. We earned profit almost every year, some friends from Keelung also began to invest in our company.

Yungshin Pharma expanded its scale along with Taiwan's economic growth. In 1988, it was listed on the Taiwan Stock Market and began to collect the necessary capital from the public.

U.C. Pharma

U.C. Pharma was another typical case. The founder, Mr. Shian-Wang Wu, was born into a poor family in Tainan and had only six years of primary school education. At the age of seventeen, he moved to Taipei to become an apprentice at a motorcycle shop, owned by an acquaintance from his hometown. Later, in his early twenties, Mr. Wu opened his own motorcycle shop in Taipei and began to import lubricant oil from Japan and then repacked it into small cans of oil. This business earned him a small fortune, which later became part of the initial capital of U.C. Pharma (Su 2010).

Mr. Wu was really an entrepreneur who was eager to create his own kingdom, trying every possible way to create his own business. When he earned higher profits from repackaging lubricant oil, he started to look for other opportunities in which to invest his capital. This was the occasion when Mr. Wu started to sell a kind of *Lyceum barbarum* cake (a type of Chinese medicine to increase weight), which also helped him to earn a fortune from this business. He then tried another venture with friends to sell Chinese herbal medicine; one of them was a famous medicine for athlete's foot, *Zushuang,* which in turn added to his success. He then bought a small workshop, called U.C.,[4] which made the medicine for him in Taipei. Later, Mr. Wu bought another sizeable manufacturing facility located in Taoyuan County to expand the U.C. production line.

Mr. Wu's venture was supported by two very important persons: One was a medical doctor, Dr. Wu, from his hometown and the other was, Mr. Wang, a can manufacturer for his lubricant oil. The former knew him very well from an early age and gave him financial support for every venture as well as the necessary knowledge about the medicine. The latter, whom Mr. Wu met when he started the lubricant oil business, provided him with full financial support for every other business that Mr. Wu wanted to build, including the new pharmaceutical venture.

U.C. Pharma had earned enormous profits by manufacturing over-the-counter medicines such as *Zushuang.* In the process, Mr. Wu also invested his money into the booming real estate market, which also earned him another fortune, and many of his friends in the real estate sector later invested in his pharma business. However, when the government began to issue GMP regulations in 1982, Mr. Wu was compelled to upgrade manufacturing facilities, and as the investors began to withdraw, Mr. Wu bought all the shares and became the sole owner of U.C. Pharma (Su 2010). Now, U.C. Pharma is a totally run family business. It does not want to be listed on the stock market. Currently, the company is run by Mr. Wu's son, whose business strategy has been to increase the prescription drugs and reduce the production of over-the-counter drugs.

Source of knowledge

As we have seen, most of the founders of the conventional pharmas did not have enough knowledge of modern medicine. They therefore had to ask for help from the medical community from within their personal networks, or had to buy technology from foreign firms, in order to engage in the production of medicine and shop-floor management. In the case of Yungshin Pharma, because the founder was the owner of a drug store, he had the opportunity to know of many medical doctors, some of whom were later hired by the founder to be consultants of his firm. One of the most important resources were the doctors from the National Taiwan University Hospital (NTUH).

Aside from providing medical knowledge, the doctors also became the foundation for Yungshin Pharma to upgrade their manufacturing capability. That was, in order to gain the trust for its medicine from the hospitals, Yungshin Pharma set up a special production area that collaborated with doctors from the NTUH, to produce medicines that matched the quality requirements from the previous doctors in the 1970s. Before the state's GMP regulations, it was the strategy that Yungshin had taken to first gain the trust and then the orders from the most prominent hospital in Taiwan. In the process, Yungshin learned valuable information from those doctors, who then contributed directly when Yungshin began to launch its GMP application.[5]

In the case of U.C. Pharma, the founder, Mr. Wu, depended very much upon a medical doctor from his hometown to provide the necessary knowledge in medicine. In addition, the owner also recruited a pharmacist from their competitor, China Chemical (one of the earliest pharmas founded in the early 1950s), to become his chief manager. This pharmacist, Mr. Guo Chen Ding, was a friend of the owner before he was recruited. Mr. Ding has made many contributions since, such as new knowledge on the development of drugs, passing through the state's regulation of GMP in 1986, and current R&D activities.

U.C. Pharma later turned its attention towards Japanese firms, and this was also undertaken through the owner's personal network. One of U.C. Pharma's most successful drugs is the Sisi Cold Capsule, and this drug was originally the product of the Japanese Hoyu Corporation. It was because Mr. Wu's daughter had a chance to work for Hoyu during her studies in Japan. Mr. Wu therefore used this opportunity to get to know the owner of Hoyu and so began their collaboration. U.C. Pharma thus upgraded their medical knowledge for producing new types of drugs. Because of the success of the Sisi Cold Capsule, these two companies have established a very close relationship[6] ever since.

Brief summary

The above two cases have shown that bonding social capital, established through existing personal networks, plays an important role for both firms' initial capital formation and knowledge learning. In the case of Yungshin, it was the owner's personal savings and money from relatives and friends that contributed to the initial capital formation. In addition, it was also the doctors from the pharma's hospital clients that contributed in gaining the medical and standardized manufacturing knowledge. As in the case of U.C., it was the owner's personal savings, friends and relatives who contributed to the initial capital for the firm. Moreover, his friend, and later his daughter's network, also contributed to this pharma's expansion. Bonding social capital, family, relatives, and friends played an important role in the conventional pharmas' initial stage.

The new science pharmas

The emergence of the new science pharmas in Taiwan has to do with the revolution of biotechnology worldwide. The molecular revolution of the 1970s, by which the methodology of finding new drugs could use rational design techniques by detecting the molecular structures of particular cells, has largely changed the way new drugs are created and developed (Dosi and Mazzucato 2006; Pisano

2006; Comanor 2007). As a consequence of this change, new drug development can be disintegrated and outsourced rather than in-house R&D. Along with this new global trend, new drug developments, clinical tests, and manufacturing processes have also been outsourced to newly established biotech firms that are created mainly by scientists (Danzon et al. 2005). It is against this backdrop that the Taiwanese government used this opportunity to enter the biopharmaceutical industry in the hope of linking it to the global value chain of the biopharmaceutical industry and to upgrade the economy. It is also through this state promotion that many new science firms were built to take advantage of the state's support and to link them to the global trend.

Initial capital formation

Furthermore, because of the state's support, Taiwanese biotech firms mainly emerged in the late 1990s, and most of them were established by returnees from the US (Wang et al. 2012). We will use two cases to illustrate the findings: TaiMed, which is mainly engaged in new drug development and thus is a contract research organization (CRO) and ScinoPharm Taiwan, which is mainly a contract manufacturing organization (CMO). The two firms represent different categories of Taiwan's biotech firms.

TaiMed Biologics

From the initial stage of promoting biotechnology in the 1990s, the Taiwanese government intended to copy the successful model of the semiconductor industry to biotechnology. Thus, many world-renowned Taiwanese biochemistry and biology scientists, who worked in the US, were recruited back to Taiwan and became the state's consultants. Those scientists later helped the state to shape its new industrial policy (Wang 2014). In 2006, Dr. Chi Huey Wong, who is an internationally renowned specialist in bio-organic and synthetic chemistry, became the ninth president of Academic Sinica. In a state-organized field trip to the US, Dr. Wong, together with other high-ranking state officials who were looking into the development of the biotechnology industry, visited Genentech and were informed by the then executive vice president of Genentech, Dr. Yu-Min Yang, a Taiwanese scientist, that the firm might sell the candidate HIV inhibitor TNX-355 (now, TMB-355) to the market. By discussing with other scientists such as Dr. Lian Bo Chen, an academian and Harvard professor, and Dr. David Ho, a renowned Taiwanese scientist on HIV/AIDS inhibitors at the Rockefeller University in New York, Dr. Wong decided to advise the National Science Council to establish a new company to collaborate with Genentech to develop the preventive HIV vaccine.

In 2007, the new company, TaiMed, was founded. At the same time, while Dr. Wong was negotiating with Genentech for the license fee, the National Science Council, whose director had collaborated closely with Dr. Wong in Academia Sinica, advised the Executive Yuan regarding the investment of the National

Development Fund into the new company; Dr. Lian-Bo Chen was working to collect the rest of the initial funding from private sources. Due to the difficulty of finding sufficient investment from the private sector, the team then asked then Deputy Premier Dr. Ying Wen Tsai for help to persuade private companies to invest. The final result was that the company collected the necessary funding from Dr. Samuel Yan Liang Yin the CEO of the Ruentex Financial Group. Dr. Tsai was then appointed as Director of the Board of the new company when she retired from the Deputy Premier post. Dr. Yin now owned the largest share of TaiMed, and the second largest shareholder was the National Development Fund. TaiMed still continues to develop the HIV/AIDS inhibitor licensed from Genentech, and has now passed the second phase of clinical tests in the USFDA.

ScinoPharm Taiwan

ScinoPharm Taiwan was established in November 1997 and is currently a leading R&D- and biotech-based, active pharmaceutical ingredients (APIs) manufacturing service provider to the global pharmaceutical industry. It is currently Taiwan's largest API producer and is one of the branch companies invested in by the Uni-President Group. ScinoPharm Taiwan was listed on the Taiwan Stock Market in September 2011.

One of the key founders of ScinoPharm Taiwan is the current CEO, Dr. Jo Shen, who has a PhD in Physical Chemistry. Before she returned to Taiwan, Dr. Shen was a vice president at Syntex pharmaceuticals in Silicon Valley. This company's revenue was about US$2.2 billion, and it had over 12,000 employees worldwide. However, Syntex pharmaceuticals was acquired by the Roche Group in 1994 and began a large-scale layoff action, of which, unfortunately, Dr. Shen was included in this action. Afterward, Dr. Shen and three other colleagues in Syntex pharmaceuticals, Hardy Chan, Bob Ells, and Bob Cook, decided to create a company of their own and began to search for investors, including returning to Taiwan to look for opportunities.

In the 1990s, not many people in Taiwan knew what biotechnology was all about, nor did they have any knowledge about APIs. Therefore, Dr. Shen's actions were not very successful at the initial stage. Luckily, then Director of the Chemical Engineering Institute of Taiwan Industrial Technology Research Institute Dr. Johnsee Lee, who was a former acquaintance in San Francisco, introduced her to the president of the Uni-President Group, Mr. Ching Yuan Gao. After hearing the briefing from Dr. Shen, Mr. Gao decided to invest in this company and built the facility nearby the Tainan headquarters of the group in southern Taiwan. In 1999, the manufacturing facilities were completed at the Tainan Science Park; it began to produce APIs in July 2000. Now, the Uni-President Group owned approximately half of the shares, along with other investors that included the National Development Fund, the Taiwan Sugar Corp., and the Mega Bank. In October 2001, SinoPharm Taiwan gained the certification from the U.S. Food and Drug Administration (FDA) to manufacture APIs, which was a license for it to expand its customer base from global pharmas. Currently, SinoPharm Taiwan has customers from all the major global pharmas and offers a wide portfolio of services ranging from custom synthesis for early phase pharmaceutical activities to brand companies as well as APIs for the generic industry. It has also become one of the more profitable enterprises of the Uni-President Group.

As discussed above, both cases gained funding through their personal networks, although the networks might be linked to the professional community. Compared to their counterparts in the US, where venture capital played an important role in nurturing new science firms (Lazonicka and Tulumb 2011), Taiwanese venture capital has played a very minor role in the emergence of biotech companies. Indeed, Taiwanese venture capital firms tended to invest during the taking off stage rather than at the seed stage. As a result, venture capital is of little help to the emergence of new biotech firms. One of our interviewees said,

> Taiwan's venture capital is not like its counterpart in the US where it would invest in brand new ideas and new innovations. Once there is a good idea, many venture capital firms would jump in to nurture the firm at its seed stage. But there are very few, or almost none of Taiwanese venture capitals doing the same. They would like to invest into firms that already have good products, make quick money for one of two years, then sell the stocks and then look for other profitable targets. Venture capital will not invest in you for too long, nor at its seed stage, this is the situation that Taiwanese biotech firms have faced.[7]

It might be due to this weak institutional support, as the biotech firms gained their support mainly from the state, their own savings, and friends in their professional circle for funding rather than from venture capital. As the CEO of Boston Investment, Dr. Wu Ding Kai, vividly describes, due to the high risk nature of a biotech firm, "In Taiwan, there are three Fs that will invest into a biotech firm at its seed stage: they are family, friends, and fools."[8]

Source of information and knowledge

As mentioned above, most of the Taiwanese biotech firms were created by returnees or domestic scientists who have PhD degrees and work experience in major biotech firms in the US. The science firms' CEOs, therefore, were already established in global science communities and had global networks at hand through which they were able to gain the most recent and updated information. The most famous example in our case is TaiMed Biologics. The main target that TaiMed is endeavoring to develop is an inhibitor for HIV/AIDS. In fact, TaiMed Biologics has been dedicated to develop an HIV inhibitor since its inception, by the introduction of world-renowned biotech scientists, Dr. David Ho from Genentech (TMB-355), and he has been totally involved in the process of the development of this new drug. Now, the new drug, called ibalizumab, has completed the second phase of clinical trials, and Dr. Ho has again helped the company to gain financial support from the Bill & Melinda Gates Foundation for further trials and research. Dr. Ho is, of course, an invaluable asset for TaiMed Biologics to gain new perspectives and international recognition through his high-profile networks. It is indeed the personal and professional networks that have contributed greatly to the knowledgeable education of the new science firms.

As in the case of ScinoPharm Taiwan, the current CEO, Dr. Jo Shen, of course, has her professional knowledge and community support to gain new knowledge and information. The company is heavily invested in R&D activity that is based on the scientific research teams. For example, when ScinoPharm was founded, Dr. Jo Shen hired six foreign biotech experts from Syntex to the company's management system, including GMP procedures, and to train local managers and technicians. The training program had gone through a three-year period and was called "ScinoPharm's EMBA" by Dr. Jo Shen. Before she served at Syntex for thirteen years, she had worked at another renowned biotech company, Monsanto, for eight years. Therefore, she was very clear about how a large company should run its personnel system and training programs. As she said, "The investment on talent training is more important than monetary investment to the company."[9] Thus, ScinoPharm mainly gained advanced knowledge from their internal research and the processing of new information from the global scientific community. Bridging social capital is pivotal to the firm.

Indeed, the bio-pharma is very different from the conventional pharma due to its high R&D intensity, which needs a knowledgeable community to sustain its survival. One of our typical cases, for example, PharmaEngine, that now has only seventeen employees, but most of them had worked for well-known pharmas like Novartis and Merck, before they joined PharmaEngine. Of these seventeen employees, ten of them are in the R&D department, with seven having a PhD degree and three having an MA degree.[10]

Brief summary

The above two cases have shown that bridging social capital plays an important role for both firms' knowledge learning. Both founders of TaiMed and ScinoPharm are US returnees who had working experience in the science community. They can easily access most of the up-to-date information and knowledge in the field of frontier biopharmaceuticals. In fact, their firms have been engaging in the frontline areas to develop new drugs. Moreover, on the initial capital formation issue, it is very interesting to find that both founders used personal networks, which thus combined bridging and bonding social capitals, to access key figures through the scientific community, may they be state officials or private financiers, to provide any and all necessary funds. This is very different from their counterparts in the US, where venture capital played a major role in the formation of new bio-pharmas at their initial stage.

Discussion and conclusion

This chapter asks questions regarding the role of social capital in the creation and development of the conventional pharmaceutical and biotech industries. We assume that bonding social capital plays an important role in the capital formation stage for the conventional pharmaceutical industry, while bridging social capital is more important for the biotech sector. In addition, we assume that due to the difference of knowledge types, biotech firms depend much more on professional networks than do conventional pharmas in every aspect of the firm's development.

As we have shown, the creation of a conventional pharma was similar to a normal SME during the 1950s or 1960s in Taiwan, when the founder collected the initial capital from their own savings and from friends and relatives. The founder received very little support from the state and had to collect and run the company by their own effort. In contrast, new biotech firms were the product of the state's strategic development policy; founders were able to gain initial capital investments from both the state's funding and private capital. But, interestingly, the ways in which these new biotech firms gained their financial investments from public or private sources[11] are all related to personal and professional networks, or bonding social capital.

Regarding knowledge learning of both types of firms, because the founders of conventional pharma tended to have little or no professional background, their sources of knowledge were therefore either from the founders' existing social networks or from hiring professionals to run the business at the firms' earliest stage. In contrast, most of the founders of biotech science firms came from the professional circles that have PhD degrees and have work experiences in major pharmas in the U.S. These biotech firms tend to have strong professional networks in supporting the company so as to access the most recent knowledge development in the cutting edge areas. Moreover, the firms in biotech have shown stronger features of the knowledge community in R&D activities, due to the founder's own professional networks.

As we have observed, in the highly professional new drug development area, personal relations are still very important in acquiring the source of capital. This is very different from what we had expected. Although we have not dealt with this issue in a detailed manner, we speculate that it may be due to weak institutions and high uncertainty to support the new venture of a science firm (cf. North 1990). New science entrepreneurs therefore have to mobilize resources from their own personal and professional networks, and the bonding social capital, to fund new firms. This issue deserves to be studied further in the future.

Notes

1 Contracting out of research and manufacture activities have been a salient phenomenon in today' pharmaceutical industry. A contract research organization (CRO) is an organization that provides research services for pharmaceutical firms on a contract basis. A contract manufacture organization (CMO) provides services for manufacturing, clinical testing, and other services related to manufacturing process on a contract basis.
2 GMP, cGMP, and PIC/s are labels developed by the Pharmaceutical Inspection Convention and Pharmaceutical Inspection Co-operation Scheme. PIC/s is a label founded by some EU members for pharmas that have passed inspections of the drug production process.

3 Interview data, TPID1202, Taichung, April 20, 2012.
4 Interview data, TPID1208, Taipei, June 6, 2012. The original U.C. Pharma was founded in 1956 that mainly made Chinese herbal medicines. During that time, most of the medicine was handmade, and the facilities were at the same place of a household that looked very rudimental like small workshop.
5 Interview data, TPID1202, Taichung, April 20, 2012.
6 Interview data, TPID1208, Taipei, June 6, 2012.
7 Interview data, TPID1207, Tainan, May 30, 2012.
8 Interview data, TPID1211, Taipei, November 8, 2012.
9 Chu Li-Chi, no publication year, "Dr. S leads the Syntex group (members of Syntex) making ScinoPharm to become an excellent API manufacturing service provider," from the website of Monte Jode Science & Technology Association of Taiwan, www.mjtaiwan.org.tw/pages/?Ipg=1007&showPg=1101.
10 Interview data, TPID1012, Taipei, November 2012.
11 The biggest private investor of biotechnology in Taiwan is Runtex Financial Corp., owned by Yin YanLiang. He has invested over NT$4 billion in biotech industry, almost equal to the investment of the National Development Fund's NT$4.6 billion (*Wealth Magazine*, No. 416, January 17, 2013).

References

Aldrich, Howard. 2005. "Entrepreneurship." In *The Handbook of Economic Sociology: Neil Smelser*, Second Edition, edited by Richard Swedberg, 451–477. Princeton, NJ: Princeton University Press.

Amsden, Alice H. 1989. *Asia's Next Giant: South Korea and Late Industrialization*. New York: Oxford University Press.

Bebbington, Anthony, Scott Guggenheim, Elizabeth Olson, and Michael Woolcock. 2004. "Exploring Social Capital Debates at the World Bank." *The Journal of Development Studies* 40 (5): 33–64.

Burt, Ronald S. 2004. "Structural Holes and Good Ideas." *American Journal of Sociology* 110 (2): 349–399.

Chen, Chieh-shuan. 1994. *Networks and Social Structure-The Analysis of Taiwan's Small and Medium Enterprise*. Taipei: Linking Publishing Press.

Chen, Tsung-Yuan, and Jenn-Hwan Wang. 2009. "Taiwan's Bio-pharmaceutical Industry: Development, Innovation and Limitations." *Taiwan Journal of Sociology* 43: 159–208.

Coleman, James. 1988. "Social Capital in the Creation of Human Capital." *American Journal of Sociology* 94: 95–120.

Comanor, W. S. 2007. "The Economics of Research and Development in the Pharmaceutical Industry." In *Pharmaceutical Innovation: Incentives, Competition, and Cost-benefit Analysis in International Perspective*, edited by F. Sloan, and C. Y. Hsieh, 91–106. New York: Cambridge University Press.

Danzon, P. M., S. Nicholson, and N. S. Pereira. 2005. "Productivity in Pharmaceutical-Biotechnology R&D: The Role of Experience and Alliance." *Journal of Health Economics* 24: 317–339.

DCB (Development Center for Biotechnology). 2013. *Yearbook of Pharmaceutical Industry*. Taipei: DCB.

Dosi, G., and M. Mazzucato. 2006. "Introduction." In *Knowledge Accumulation and Industry Evolution: The Case of Pharma-Biotech*, edited by G. Dosi, and M. Mazzucato, 1–18. Cambridge: Cambridge University Press.

Evans, Peter. 1996. "Government Action, Social Capital and Development: Reviewing the Evidence on Synergy." *World Development*, 24 (6): 1119–1132.

Fan, Zuo-syun. 2001. *History of Taiwan Pharmaceutics*. Taipei: Cheng's Foundation for Pharmaceutical Sciences.

Fine, Ben. 1999. "The Developmental State is Dead-Long Live Social Capital." *Development and Change* 30 (1):1–19.

Gedajlovic, Eric, Benson Hong, Curt B. Moore, G. Tyge Payne, and Mike Wright. 2013. "Social Capital and Entrepreneurship: A Schema and Research Agenda." *Entrepreneurship Theory and Practice* 37 (3): 455–478.

Granovetter, Mark. 1985. "Economic Action and Social Structure: The Problem of Embeddedness." *American Journal of Sociology* 91 (3): 481–510.

Granovetter, Mark. 1995. "The Economic Sociology of Firms and Entrepreneurs." In *The Economic Sociology of Immigration: Essays in Networks, Ethnicity, and Entrepreneurship*, edited by Alejandro Portes, 128–165. New York: Russel Sage Foundation.

Han, Chun-ci. 1999. "The Globalization of Taiwan Pharmaceutical Industry." Master's Thesis, Department of Sociology, Soochow University, Taipei.

Huang, Jing-yi, yu-ming Zeng, and Yao-mou Chang. 2013. *The Garden without Boundary: Li Tian-de's Dream*. Taipei: China Productivity Center.

Knorringa, Peter, and Irene van Staveren. 2006. *Social Capital for Industrial Development: Operationalizing the Concept*. Geneva: United Nation.

Lazonicka, William, and Öner Tulumb. 2011. "US Biopharmaceutical Finance and the Sustainability of the Biotech Business Model." *Research Policy* 40 (9): 1170–1187.

Liao, Jianwen, and Harold Welsch. 2003. "Social Capital and Entrepreneurial Growth Aspiration: A Comparison of Technology and Non-Technology-Based Nascent Entrepreneurs." *Journal of High Tech Management Research Volume* 14 (1): 149–170

Lin, Nan. 1999. "Social Networks and Status Attainment." *Annual Review of Sociology* 25: 467–488.

Nahapiet, Janine, and Sumantra Ghoshal. 1998. "Social Capital, Intellectual Capital and the Organizational Advantage." *Academy of Management Review* 23 (2): 242–266.

North, Douglass C. 1990. *Institutions, Institutional Change and Economic Performance*. Cambridge: Cambridge University.

Pisano, Gary P. 2006. *Science Business: The Promise, the Reality, and the Future of Biotech*. Boston, MA: Harvard Business School Press.

Putnam, Robert. 1993. *Making Democracy Work: Civic Traditions in Modern Italy*. Princeton: Princeton University Press.

Putnam, Robert. 2000. *Bowling Alone. The Collapse and Revival of American Community*, New York, NY: Simon & Schuster.

Schumpeter, Joseph. 1950. *Capitalism, Socialism and Democracy*. New York: Harper.

Shieh, Gwo-Shyong. 1991. "Network Labor Process: The Subcontracting Networks in the Manufacturing Industries of Taiwan." *Bulletin of Institute of Ethnology Academia Sinica* 71: 161–182.

Storper, Michael. 2005. "Society, Community, and Economic Development." *Studies in Comparative International Development* 39 (4): 30–57.

Su, Shih-ying. 2010. *The Poor Becomes A Richer*. Taipei: Business Weekly Publication.

Thornton, Patricia. 1999. "The Sociology of Entrepreneurship." *Annual Review of Sociology* 25: 19–46.

Wade, Robert. 1990. Governing the Market: Economic Theory and the Role of Government in East Asian Industrialization. Princeton, NJ: Princeton University Press.

Wang, Jenn-hwan, 2010, *The Limits of Fast Follower: Taiwan's Economic Transition and Innovation*. Taipei: Jyu-liu Books.

Wang, Jenn-hwan. 2014. "Developmental State in Transition: The State and the Development of Taiwan's Bio-pharmaceutical Industry." In *Developmental State for the 21st Century*, edited by Michelle Williams, 84–101. London: Routledge.

Wang, Jenn-hwan, Tsung-Yuan Chen, and Ching-Jung Tsai. 2012. "In Search of an Innovative State: The Development of the Biopharmaceutical Industry in Taiwan, Korea and China." *Development and Change* 43 (2): 481–503.

Wang, Yuan-wen. 2012. "PharmEngine: The Small Bio-pharm Company Earned Money." *Business Weekly* 1292: 58–59.

Weiss, Linda, and John M. Hobson. 1995. *States and Economic Development: A Comparative Historical Analysis*. Cambridge, MA: Polity Press.

Wong, Joseph. 2005. "Re-Marking the Developmental State in Taiwan: The Challenges of Biotechnology." *International Political Science Review* 26 (2): 169–191.

Wong, Joseph. 2011. *Betting on Biotech: Innovation and the limits of Asia's Developmental State*. Ithaca, NY: Cornell University Press.

Woolock, Michael. 1998. "Social Capital and Economic Development: Toward a Theoretical Synthesis and Policy Framework." *Theory and Society* 27 (1): 151–208.

Yu, Ching-jhen. 1972. "Taiwan's Pharmaceutical Industry." *Chang Hwa Bank Monthly* 21 (12): 21–32.

Part III

Social capital and cross-border linkages

9 Building industrial systems in China

The networking of Taiwanese machine tool firms in China

Liang-Chih Chen

Introduction

Rising production costs and shrinking markets have been driving global manufacturers to invest in China to exploit its abundant low-cost production resources and huge market (Zweig 2002; Ito 2009). In the case of Taiwan, since the 1980s, many export-oriented manufacturers have joined this trend by relocating a significant share of their production from Taiwan to China (Hsu and Chen 2011; Sadoi 2011). Studying Taiwan's direct investment in China shows that, compared with investors from elsewhere, Taiwanese investors are smaller in scale and are mostly involved in networks of production organization rather than vertically integrated (Hsing 1996; 1998; Brookfield and Liu 2005; Hsu and Chen 2011). Additionally, in their investment processes, Taiwanese manufacturing firms mainly employ the "hens lead chicks" strategy, in which they invite their Taiwanese suppliers to participate in their China ventures. And the ability to work with their familiar partners in remote sites enabled the smooth and successful transplantation of production systems from Taiwan to China (Hsing 1998; Cheng 1999; Wang and Lee 2007).

An extensive body of literature already exists on factors determining or influencing the establishment of offshore industrial systems by Taiwanese entrepreneurs (Hsing 1996; 1998; Cheng 1999; Brookfield and Liu 2005; Wang and Lee 2007; Yang 2009; Hsu and Chen 2011). This chapter engages in this realm of study through discussing the networking activities of one major Taiwanese industry, namely, the machine tool industry, in building its production and sales capabilities in China. Like most Taiwanese manufacturing industries, the machine tool industry in Taiwan also comprises primarily small and medium-sized enterprises (SMEs). However, the investments of Taiwanese machine tool firms in China have shown some different characteristics from those of their counterparts in other Taiwanese industries. Owing to lacking the support of their domestic suppliers, Taiwanese machine tool firms have been unable to construct production systems in China through the abovementioned "hens lead chicks" strategy. As a result, cultivating local sources of Chinese supplies has been a crucial task facing Taiwanese machine tool entrepreneurs. Furthermore, as opposed to most OEM (original equipment manufacture) or ODM (own-design manufacture) Taiwanese manufacturers, whose investments in China have been "production-driven" (Hsu and Chen 2011), investments in China by Taiwanese machine tool firms have been mostly "market-driven." In this context, besides undergoing localized production, product marketing and sales have also been great challenges for Taiwanese machine tool makers in China.

As the world's fourth largest machine tool exporter and sixth largest machine tool producer in 2012 (Gardner Publications 2013), Taiwan's machine tool industry has been renowned for attaining its global competitiveness by constructing a well-articulated subcontracting production system in central Taiwan, including Taichung, Nantou, and Changhwa (MOEA 2007). In this region, machine tool makers can outsource each step of the production process to capable local subcontractors, allowing them to maintain low overheads while achieving high flexibility in both internal and external operations (Liu 1999). Also, through exploiting various learning channels and mechanisms available in the spatialized production networks, these firms were able to overcome their latecomer disadvantages in production and technological upgrading (Chen 2009; 2011). Acknowledging that Taiwanese machine tool makers have been heavily embedding their development capability in their local industrial and relational networks in Taiwan then raises questions about the role that networking might play in their entrepreneurial ventures in China.

Scholars have emphasized the significance of networking for firms to access resources and capabilities from and with other actors and to better govern their business relationships (Pearce and Robinson Jr. 2000; Hitt et al. 2002). Studies of SMEs particularly suggest that an important condition for SMEs to maintain growth is the possession of network mobilization capability (Jarillo 1989; Hoang and Antoncic 2003; Lechner and Dowling 2003; Jack 2005; Ulhøi 2005; Cousins et al. 2006; Lechner et al. 2006; Partanen et al. 2008). Following this line of thought, by using Taiwan's machine tool industry as the study case, this chapter deals with issues related to the networking activities involved in the internationalization of SMEs. Based on more than sixty cases of in-depth interviews with decision-makers of Taiwanese machine tool firms, their suppliers, and related private and public agencies in Taiwan and China conducted in 2005–2006 and 2010–2012,[1] this study empirically investigates the roles of networking in the efforts of Taiwanese machine tool entrepreneurs to build industrial systems in China. In addition to exploring various networks critical to the firms' production and marketing activities, the chapter focuses on discussing how these networks are accessed and developed by Taiwanese machine tool makers and how these networks contribute to their production and business dealings in China. It further finds that the direct investments of Taiwanese machine tool makers in China are made effective through mobilizing their linkages with Taiwanese and Chinese partners nurtured by, on the one hand, the cultural proximity of the two parties and, on the other hand, the aggressive relation building efforts of Taiwanese machine tool firms. To present our findings, the remainder of this chapter is organized as follows. The second section provides a brief description about the investments of Taiwan's machine tool industry in China. The third section then discusses the networking of Taiwanese machine tool firms in the processes of undertaking their

China entrepreneurial ventures. The final section concludes with research findings and discusses their implications for the study of the changing relations among the networked actors in Taiwan's machine tool industry.

The investments of Taiwan's machine tool industry in China

Along with its continuing economic development, China has been the fastest growing market for machine tools over the past two decades.[2] Since the early 1990s, China has been one of the world's top four machine tool consumers and importers and has maintained double-digit growth in machine tool demand (USCS 2006). From 2002, it has even overtaken Germany and the USA to become the largest machine tool market in the world (ITIS 2005). In 2012, China's consumption of machine tools reached nearly US\$38.5 billion, accounting for about 41 percent of the world total, and 36 percent of its demand was satisfied by imports (Gardner Publications 2013).

As an export-oriented industry that sells its products globally, Taiwan's machine tool industry began to explore the emerging Chinese market in the late 1980s (MIRL 1995; Liu et al. 2001). By 1992, China has surpassed the USA to be the largest customer of Taiwan-made machine tools. Since 2002 roughly 40 percent of Taiwan's annual machine tool exports have shipped to China (TAMI 2013). Moreover, to exploit China's market and low-cost manufacturing resources, Taiwanese machine tool makers have established subsidiary plants across the strait since the early 1990s (Liu et al. 2001). Currently, there are already over one hundred Taiwanese machine tool firms conducing manufacturing operations in China (TAMI 2012).

As for the rationale behind their investments in China, according to our investigations, Taiwanese machine tool firms invest in cross-border manufacturing primarily to better access the Chinese market rather than to reduce production costs. (Of course, these two motivations are not necessarily mutually exclusive.) Although China's abundant and cheap labor force has attracted global manufacturers to locate production there, such cost advantages have not been enjoyed effectively by many Taiwanese machine tool investors. Since production of machine tools is technology-intensive, labor costs are not only less significant relative to total production cost than for other more labor-intensive industries, but worker skills and experiences are crucial to product quality. As a result of being unable to recruit suitable Chinese skilled workers for their plants, Taiwanese machine tool makers have been suffering from lower production efficiency and higher production costs in their offshore operations in China.

Furthermore, as suggested by existing studies, most Taiwanese manufacturing SMEs adopt networked production arrangements in China (Hsing 1996; 1998; Brookfield and Liu 2005; Hsu and Chen 2011). Thanks to their numerous domestic suppliers having joined their ventures, Taiwanese manufacturers encountered fewer problems in transplanting their production systems across the strait (Wang and Lee 2007; Yang and Hsia 2007). Yet, in the case of Taiwanese machine tool makers, the replication of their Taiwanese production networks in China, however, appears to be a tougher project. On the one hand, because of their smaller size,

Taiwanese machine tool firms have limited capacity to encourage and little leverage to pressure their local suppliers to invest in China. On the other hand, many of these suppliers are small metalworking shops with insufficient resources to establish geographically separated operations. In this context, Taiwanese machine tool firms have to build their production capabilities in China either through sourcing most of their supplies directly from Taiwan, enabling them to perform CKD (complete knock-down) or SKD (semi knock-down) assembly in their China plants[3] or to establish local production systems from scratch, which inevitably increases the production costs.

While Taiwanese machine tool makers acknowledge the difficulties of undertaking production in China, market forces have driven them to do so. As the CEO of one Taiwan's leading machine tool firms explained:

> China is the current global factory. Manufacturing firms around the world establishing factories in China would prefer purchasing machine tools from makers with Chinese manufacturing facilities. Our customers in China include not only Taiwanese and Chinese, but also manufacturers from Japan, the USA and Europe. If we did not have plants there, they might not consider doing business with us owing to concerns such as post-sale service.
>
> (Author interview, November 14, 2005)

In addition to accommodating the requests of their major customers, investments in China by Taiwanese machine tool firms also reflected their strategic responses to the changing policies of the Chinese government. To boost the development of its manufacturing sector, China has offered exemptions on import duties for machine tools. Nevertheless, the Chinese government has gradually raised the quality thresholds of the machine tools to which these duty exemptions apply in an effort to protect and promote its domestic machine tool industry. Recognizing the improving capabilities of Chinese machine tool manufacturers, in 2007, China cancelled duty exemptions on many lower-end and certain middle-end imported machine tools. Given their products shipped to China were mostly in this quality level, the price advantage enjoyed by Taiwanese machine tool makers was thus seriously compromised. As China is too large a market to be ignored, Taiwanese machine tool firms had little choice but to move their production facilities to China.

The networking of Taiwanese machine tool firms in relation to their China investments

One common feature in the operation of SMEs has been reliance on networking to access required external resources complementary to their limited internal resources (Jarillo 1989; Lechner and Dowling 2003; Jack 2005; Cousins et al. 2006; Lechner et al. 2006; Partanen et al. 2008). In the case of Taiwan's machine tool industry, the numerous machine tool SMEs are found to heavily embed their capabilities in their local extra-firm networks, nurtured by industrial clustering (Liu and Brookfield 2000; Chen 2009; 2011; Chen and Lin 2014). With regard to their ventures in China, it thus can be assumed that networking would play significant role in determining these machine tool entrepreneurs' investment processes. As network development and utilization is context-specific, the strategies required to govern networking relationships differ according to the problems or situations the actors face and the institutional and cultural environments in which the actors are situated (Hitt et al. 2002; Wang 2007; Theingi et al. 2008). Based on such understandings, this section investigates the critical networks utilized by and networking activities of Taiwanese machine tool firms in their ventures in China, a country with a distinctive production and institutional environment. As will be demonstrated in the following parts, two sets of networks cultivated by Taiwanese machine tool entrepreneurs, one Taiwanese and the other Chinese, are identified to be crucially important in facilitating their China investments.

The mobilization of Taiwanese networks

This part discusses how Taiwanese machine tool firms utilized their existing Taiwanese networks within and outside the industry in making their investments. Their important networked partners include machine tool firms' customers, other machine tool makers, and suppliers from Taiwan.

Supports received from Taiwanese customers

Local machine tool customers in Taiwan have been emphasized as essential agents helping Taiwanese machine tool firms upgrade their technological capabilities (Chen 2009). Since many of their domestic clients have built production bases in China, Taiwanese machine tool manufacturers were motivated to follow suit. The existing connections with Taiwanese customers further facilitated these machine tool entrepreneurs' cross-strait investments. More specifically, many respondents indicated that their early operations in China primarily involved transactions with Taiwanese industrial firms, including such as performing post-sales services or supplying local-assembled machine tools. By doing business with their familiar domestic customers in China, these ill-experienced Taiwanese machine tool makers with little or no prior experience of offshore operations were allowed to gradually accumulate relevant knowledge and capacity. And mainly for such a reason, most Taiwanese machine tool firms have chosen to establish their China branches near their Taiwanese customers to maintain closer interactions. Consequently, the Pearl River Delta and Yangtze River Delta regions, which host the majority of Taiwanese industrial firms, are also where about 90 percent of Taiwanese machine tool makers are concentrated (TAMI 2012).

Taiwanese customers have also been instrumental marketing agents for their domestic machine tool suppliers in China. In the interviews, some machine tool firm managers especially stated that the referrals of their domestic customers have been the key channels through which they were able to explore China's market. For example, as many Taiwanese machine tool products were installed in Taiwanese manufacturers' Chinese plants, these Taiwan-made machines gained greater exposure to local potential buyers. Here is a typical instance provided by the respondents: In their business dealings with Taiwanese manufacturers, Chinese industrial firms would need to pay on-site visits to their Taiwanese production partners to discuss issues related to their transactions and collaboration. During such visits, these Chinese firms would have the chance to learn the operational conditions and functions of Taiwan-made machine tools located in those plants. Moreover, with the information provided by their Taiwanese partners, the Chinese firms might gain further interest in sourcing Taiwanese equipment and get in touch with potential Taiwanese suppliers. As a result, the business opportunities of Taiwanese machine tool makers in China might therefore emerge.

Cooperation among Taiwanese machine tool firms

The dense interactions among agglomerated firms that stimulate localized co-opetition mechanisms have been suggested as a typical characteristic of industrial clusters (Saxenian 1994; Porter 2000). But in Taiwan's renowned machine tool cluster, the colocated machine tool firms were found to mostly demonstrate the dynamics of competition with little cooperation (Chen 2009). Acknowledging the apparent rivalry among Taiwanese machine tool makers should not lead to the conclusion that they would not work together. One notable case is the common phenomenon of Taiwanese machine tool firms that sell different products entering complementary supply arrangements (TAMI 2005). Actually, such collaborative arrangements were also adopted by a few Taiwanese machine tool entrepreneurs in their early marketing attempts in China. In the cases of Victor and Fair Friend, the two earliest Taiwanese machine tool investors in China, considering the fact that big Chinese buyers often like to purchase various types of machine tools, Victor (which specialized in lathes) and Fair Friend (which specialized in machining centers) offered each other complementary products to secure orders and thus gradually penetrated into the Chinese market.

Regardless of their business conflicts, Taiwanese machine tool firms would also help each other in providing information about local sources of supplies. For instance, when asked where and how they found local suppliers, most interviewees reported that they have benefited from the suggestions and references from some of their Taiwanese counterparts with more experiences in practicing localized subcontracting production in China. Nevertheless, one should note that, owing to the ability to source local capable suppliers are often being considered a critical competitive asset of Taiwanese machine tool makers, such intelligence might not flow freely among Taiwanese circles. However, many respondents stated that they managed to acquire it through their interpersonal networks.

Interdependence between Taiwanese machine tool firms and suppliers

After learning the factors underlying domestic suppliers' reluctance to join their ventures, Taiwanese machine tool makers have been attempting to help their important production partners to eliminate obstacles to invest in China. The most aggressive efforts of Taiwanese machine to firms in this course could be Fair Friend's case. This firm provided a series of incentives, ranging from providing factory space, material supplies, and employee recruitment to committing to placing stable orders, to persuade its critical Taiwanese suppliers to head for China (Author interview, June 21, 2011). With Fair Friend's encouragement, four Taiwanese machine tool suppliers then decided to venture into China by establishing workshops in Fair Friend's plant in Hangzhou in 2007. Through such an arrangement, Fair Friend's China plant could source prompt and reliable local supplies from trusted Taiwanese subcontractors. For the suppliers, Fair Friend's assistance enabled them to minimize the costs and risks associated with initiating their investments in China. Furthermore, along with their growth in China, in 2011, two of the suppliers moved out of Fair Friend's plant and established their own manufacturing bases nearby.

As machine tool makers from countries like Taiwan, Korea, Japan, and Germany began to rush into China, and as China's domestic machine tool industry rapidly grew, more Taiwanese machine tool suppliers became willing to enter this market. While it is observed that many of their investments did not receive direct assistance from Taiwanese machine tool firms, as has occurred in the case of Fair Friend, in the interviews, almost all suppliers admitted that orders from and connections to Taiwanese machine tool firms allowed them to survive through the early difficult days. Thanks also to the emergence of a growing pool of Taiwanese local suppliers, Taiwanese machine tool makers have been able to enhance their capabilities in organizing localized subcontracting networks in China.

The cultivation of Chinese networks

The significance of developing *guanxi* networks for successful business dealings in China has been repeatedly stressed (Orru et al. 1997; Hsing 1998; Carlisle and Flynn 2005; Theingi et al. 2008). By taking advantage of their linguistic and cultural affinity with China, compared to investors of other countries, Taiwanese investors have been able to more easily develop *guanxi* with their local agents in China (Hsing 1996). Yet, the shared commonality between Taiwanese and Chinese does not guarantee the smooth interaction and cooperation in their networking. Taiwanese firms still need to develop relation-specific skills and capabilities for better network governance (Asanuma 1989; Dyer and Singh 1998; Lorenzoni and Lipparini 1999; Chen 2011). In this part, besides studying three Chinese networks critical to the success of Taiwanese machine tool firms' China investments, we address the networking activities and strategies these firms adopted in the processes of developing their Chinese connections.

Cultivating Chinese suppliers

Since the establishment of their operations in China, Taiwanese machine tool firms have been striving to explore local Chinese suppliers. However, the manufacture of machine tools in China has been highly integrated by machine tool SOEs (state-owned enterprises), which produce most of their supplies internally. Even some of these SOEs have proper equipment and sufficient capacity, they still have little desire to take external subcontracting orders (Brookfield and Liu 2005). In this situation, Taiwanese machine tool firms sought to work with the emerging local metalworking shops in China. Nevertheless, they have encountered various difficulties in cooperating effectively with these Chinese suppliers.

First, due to the technological backwardness and inexperience of Chinese metalworking shops in manufacturing or processing machine tool parts, Taiwanese machine tool makers have to expend considerable effort to teach and communicate with them to ensure supply quality, which increases production costs and reduces production efficiency. Second, even if these machine tool makers can outsource work to suitable Chinese suppliers, they must still constantly monitor these suppliers to safeguard their orders. Many Taiwanese machine tool makers particularly commented that their Chinese suppliers have serious problems in activity scheduling. For example, once a Chinese supplier is receiving multiple orders simultaneously, it is quite often that this supplier later might fail to deliver supplies to its customers on time (Liu et al. 2001; Brookfield and Liu 2005).

To tackle these issues, rather than waiting passively for local supply capacity to gradually develop, Taiwanese machine tool makers have aggressively cultivated capable Chinese suppliers and nurtured their relationships by utilizing various governance skills. Through the referrals of their Taiwanese connections or screening the local yellow books, Taiwanese machine tool makers first could find some Chinese metalworking shops with the potential to be their suppliers. After on-site visits to evaluate the metalworking shop's technological capabilities and the owner's willingness to cooperate, they then placed subcontracting orders to suitable shops. Following a few rounds of transactions, the more capable and responsible local subcontractors were retained in the supplier network, while others were dropped. Moreover, to ensure the quality of supplies, these Taiwanese firms also dispatched technological staff to assist their Chinese suppliers to solve production issues. When the inferior manufacturing capabilities of their Chinese suppliers were identified as the result of poor equipment, Taiwanese machine tool makers might even provide loans to help suppliers upgrade their machinery.

While the technical issues of suppliers thus might be partially solved, Taiwanese machine tool firms also have to deal with a critical but common problem in their cooperation with Chinese suppliers, namely, that suppliers who fail to deliver quality supplies might be reluctant to take responsibility, leading to a serious conflict between the two parties. In Taiwan, the cluster's institutional environment and the long-term relationships between machine tool makers and suppliers have allowed many of the transactions among local actors in this industry to be based on oral agreements (Chen 2011). Due to the absence of such favorable environment and relationships in China, Taiwanese machine tool firms have learned the need to sign written contracts with Chinese subcontractors. But for these machine tool makers who are not used to having only arm's-length relations with their partners, signing contracts would not be the major means they use to govern their relationships with Chinese suppliers. In the words of the president of one machine tool firm,

> In dealing with Chinese suppliers, you cannot adopt only one strategy. For example, you have to develop emotional relationships with them. While signing contracts is indeed necessary, you also need to train them. . . . More importantly, signing a contract does not mean we would change the suppliers immediately once they perform poorly. We will still help them to do things right!
>
> (Author interview, August 23, 2010)

While Taiwanese machine tool makers are still working on developing closer collaborative relationships with Chinese suppliers, their efforts seem to be paying off. In the interviews conducted during 2005 and 2006, most respondents complained extensively about their bad impressions of and relationships with Chinese suppliers and stressed that they would place orders mainly with Taiwanese suppliers. Nevertheless, in our more recent interviews during 2010–2012, many Taiwanese machine tool makers expressed that their ratio of procurement from Chinese subcontractors had increased significantly and that they had cultivated a few reliable Chinese suppliers, making their ideal projects of building effective networked production systems in China more and more feasible.

Developing political networks

The necessity of interpersonal relationships with government officials to achieve business success in China has become common wisdom (Hsing 1996; Pearce and Robinson Jr 2000; Yau et al. 2000). Yet, it is also noted that the levels of difficulty in cultivating relationships with Chinese officials would differ according to investment type and scale (Yeung and Tung 1996). For instance, the larger, leading, high-tech or high-profile global firms that have been prioritized by Chinese authorities would have easier access to government officials. In contrast, smaller or low-tech investors, like Taiwanese machine tool entrepreneurs, cannot expect significant preferable policy measures or special attention from China's central or local governments. In this context, networking with Chinese officials demands more deliberate efforts on the part of these small investors.

Taiwanese machine tool firms have been mostly established and run by mechanical entrepreneurs who have had few political-business networks during their development processes in Taiwan (TAMI 2005). They are aware that in China they might need to change their practices and engage more actively in networking with Chinese officials since it is vital to their ventures. However, actually doing so is not an easy task, especially for these mechanical entrepreneurs with little experience and knowledge of dealing with officials. As many Taiwanese machine tool managers admitted in the interviews, although they know it is important, they have had not progressed far in building closer relationships with Chinese politicians. The CEO of one Taiwanese leading machine tool firm commented that the limited capability of mechanical entrepreneurs might be one cause:

> We mechanical engineers are not that kind of people. The managers of my firm are all similar to me with poor social skills in dealing with government officials. We have no political connections in China and still cannot find suitable people to help us cultivate such relationships.
>
> (Author interview, August 9, 2011)

While most Taiwanese machine tool entrepreneurs have struggled to build their Chinese political networks, we found that the two current largest Taiwanese machine tool firms in China, Victor and Fair Friend, both have made progress in networking with Chinese officials in their investment processes. Furthermore, their operations in China seem to all have benefited greatly from their government connections. In the case of Victor, according to the general manager of its China branch, this firm has received much support in the process of establishing its plant in Qingpu, Shanghai, such as loans and land provision guarantees, from Chinese local government officials, particularly the city mayor, with whom he is now a friend of many years (Author interview, August 30, 2011).

In the case of Fair Friend, this firm has even constructed extensive linkages with China's government officials of various levels. Fair Friend's CEO, Jimmy C.Y. Chu, was the former chairman of Taiwan's CICD (Council for Industrial and Commercial Development), one of Taiwan's major business organizations,[4] and thus is well-connected in Taiwanese political circles. Along with his aggressive investments in China, mainly in Zhejiang Province, Chu gradually developed interpersonal relationships with provincial and local government officials. When interviewed, Chu emphasized that Zhejiang officials would rely on his personal ties to access many Taiwan's important political figures. He even has been friends with China's current prime minister, Xi Jinping, since Xi served as the party chief of Zhejiang (Author interview, September 3, 2010). With its increased investments in Zhejiang, Fair Friend become more famous as its plant was frequently visited by important Chinese government officials, including such as former vice prime minister, Wu Yi. This firm's close connections to the Chinese government are also manifested in the example that the Zhejiang provincial government occasionally would use the conference room of Fair Friend's plant for meetings (Author interview, June 21, 2011).

Fair Friend's strong political networks are believed to provide many business advantages. These networks have facilitated and accelerated this firm's investment in China. In the government's recently established industrial parks in Hangzhou, for example, Fair Friend was even prioritized by the government over other incoming investors in allocating lands for Fair Friend's upcoming investment project (Author interview, June 21, 2011). Moreover, Fair Friend's abundant implicit and explicit connections with Chinese officials also have played vital role in helping it quickly build reputation and gain market acceptance in China (Yau et al. 2000). While the magnitude of the influence of Fair Friend's political networks on its business success of Taiwanese machine tool firms in China cannot be properly determined, most Taiwanese machine tool managers interviewed, and even Fair Friend's executives, all agreed that this firm's phenomenal achievements in China, in terms of becoming one of the largest foreign machine tool investors in China, would not have been possible without cultivating these important government connections.

Building relationships with machine tool customers

Besides establishing production sites, the investments of Taiwanese machine tool firms in China also include building extensive marketing networks. In the Chinese market, machine tool makers with a renowned brand name or of larger scale have clear marketing advantages. Given that information about imported foreign machine tools was not well circulated, Chinese machine tool users have been more reliant on sourcing equipment from leading global makers with well-established reputations. In addition, most Chinese machine tool buyers are large manufacturers whose orders are not easily accommodated by small-scale machine tool makers. In this situation, Taiwanese machine tool SMEs have employed both active and passive strategies to overcome the sales and marketing disadvantages.

Since the sale/purchase of machine tools is characterized by a lengthy procedure from design/development and installation/start-up to normal operation, producers and buyers require frequent and detailed interactions in their transaction process. Inexperienced Chinese machine tool users might encounter greater difficulties in communicating with foreign equipment suppliers with distinct cultural and institutional backgrounds (Gertler 2004). Such barriers of interaction, however, would be lower if they source their machines from Taiwan. Linguistic commonality first facilitates better interaction between Taiwanese suppliers and Chinese users in tackling both business and technical issues related to their transactions. As the general manager of a leading firm pointed out, one specific strength of Taiwanese machine tool makers vis-à-vis their foreign rivalries in China,

> Since we are all from Chinese-based societies, and share a similar language, culture, ethnic emotions, etc., we especially have advantages in negotiating deals with Chinese customers in terms of product price, education and training, and technological interactions. This is a very important factor allowing us to enter China's market.
>
> (Author interview, August 17, 2011)

Additionally, Taiwanese machine tool makers have been renowned for the high cost/performance ratio of their products and their flexibility in supplying machines that cater to customers' requirements, including delivery time or technological specifications, and so forth, serving well the demands of Chinese machine tool users. For instance, the major Chinese machine tool buyers, such as those SOEs, often imported advanced equipment from Europe.[5] Since the prices of Taiwan-made machine tools were sometimes just one-third of the prices of comparable

European products, purchasing equipment from Taiwan represented an economical option. Also, Taiwanese machine tool makers have been aware that, in China's political system, those SOEs often have critical concerns regarding if their annual budgets could be spent before the end of a fiscal year. By guaranteeing transactions would be completed according to their Chinese customers' specific procurement procedures, Taiwanese machine tool firms managed to successfully secure orders from such clients.

To penetrate the Chinese market, Taiwanese machine tool entrepreneurs also employed various strategies to build relationships with their Chinese customers. In fact, Taiwanese machine tool firms seem naturally familiar with the social skills required in the Chinese context, and many practices they adopted in dealing with Chinese customers were actually similar to those they used with Taiwanese customers. For instance, providing special favors, in monetary or non-monetary form, to the procurement staff of their buyers, have been utilized by some Taiwanese machine tool makers as one strategy in competing with their foreign rivals for orders in China. In addition to seeking to socialize with Chinese customers on business occasions or after-work banquets, a few Taiwanese machine tool managers admitted that they sometimes paid commissions to the key persons responsible for equipment procurement at potential or existing Chinese buyers. As most respondents said, since both Taiwanese and Chinese speak the same language and share the same culture, they could understand the implicit meanings behind the words of their Chinese customers in their business dealings and accordingly provided proper favors to secure their relationships.[6]

Concluding remarks

This chapter investigates the networking activities of Taiwanese machine tool firms in relation to their China investments. As small firms with limited resources and experiences in exploring China's production resources and market, Taiwanese machine tool entrepreneurs succeeded through utilizing and cultivating various Taiwanese and Chinese networks. On the one hand, by mobilizing their existing Taiwanese relational and business networks within and without the industry, these machine tool SMEs have obtained critical support, ranging from orders, referrals of business, and information of suppliers, to joint-marketing or investments, and so on, allowing them to survive their initial set-up phase and to gradually accumulate the knowledge and capabilities needed to conduct more aggressive and extensive investments in China. On the other hand, to undertake such a project, Taiwanese machine tool firms also cultivated local Chinese networks enabling them to overcome challenges related to the manufacture and sale of products in China.

The growth of the Chinese ties that Taiwanese machine tool firms have built along with their investments in China has implications for their networking with Taiwanese partners. While their entrepreneurial ventures in China have benefited greatly from their Taiwanese networks, the significance of such networks to the current operations of Taiwanese machine tool makers seems to have decreased.

More specifically, after gaining more experience of dealing with Chinese customers, many Taiwanese machine tool firms expressed that they now preferred doing business with the Chinese rather than the Taiwanese. For example, some interviewees complained that Taiwanese buyers would frequently ask for favorable prices or payment conditions, seriously comprising their profit margins. In contrast, Chinese customers not only might place larger orders but rarely bargained for discounts, making them more welcome to Taiwanese machine tool makers.

The relationships between Taiwanese machine tool makers and their Taiwanese suppliers in China also appear to be changing. Although many interviewees emphasized that their current local production networks in China mainly comprised local Taiwanese suppliers, they also pointed out that their cooperation in this remote location have not been that smooth. One typical complaint was that the quality of the parts and processing services provided by their Taiwanese partners has been below expectations. As a result, machine tool firms have to invoke more stringent requirements on their Taiwanese suppliers, such as more frequent quality testing. This situation then increases tensions between these long-term partners, because such strict requirements are rarely implemented in Taiwan's machine tool industry and could be taken as an insult by the affected Taiwanese suppliers. Moreover, as more Taiwanese suppliers have been exposed to China's huge demand for machine tool parts and processing, they might turn to prioritize orders from larger Chinese customers, seriously testing their existing relationships with Taiwanese machine tool makers.

The above instances seem to indicate that the emergence of China as a production site and market for Taiwan's machine tool industry has negatively affected the relations between Taiwanese machine tool makers and their networked Taiwanese partners. However, more evidence is required to substantiate this assertion. Furthermore, it is worth investigating the changing nature and forms of networking among actors in Taiwan's machine tool industry following their aggressive investments in China. Such a study might provide deeper insights into the evolution of industrial networks and organizations in response to external changes.

Notes

1 Typically, the in-depth interviews lasted one to three hours each. In addition to asking interviewees to first describe the history of their investments in China, the interviews addressed questions regarding how interviewees developed and used various networks in their ventures. A variety of secondary data was also used, including governmental statistics, corporate reports, industrial and financial analyses, and business and commercial journals and newspapers.

2 The booming Chinese manufacturing sector has stimulated Chinese demand for imported machine tools. Such demand was driven mainly by the following factors: (1) demand for superior quality and precision technology unavailable in China; (2) expansion of Chinese manufacturing capacity and increased competition among domestic Chinese manufacturers for quality output; (3) influx of foreign-invested manufacturing facilities requiring world-class machinery; and (4) WTO-mandated tariff reductions (USCS 2006).

3 In the CKD arrangement, a machine tool firm dismantles its machine tool products into kit form in Taiwan and ships the kits to its China plant for reassembly, while in the SKD arrangement, some parts are sourced locally in China.
4 Founded in 1990, CICD is a non-profit organization consisting of middle-aged Taiwanese enterprise owners and executives. According to its website, the organization has about 2,100 members. Although the membership of CICD represents just 0.2 percent of the total number of enterprises in Taiwan, the aggregate output of the represented enterprises constitutes over 48 percent of Taiwan's GDP.
5 According to the observations and experiences of some Taiwanese machine tool makers interviewed, many Chinese industrial firms seemed unwilling to buy machine tools produced by Japan and the USA, due to political or historical conflicts between China and these two countries.
6 Another example is that, recognizing that many of their Chinese buyers were from inner China and rarely had the opportunity to visit China's large coastal cities, Taiwanese machine tool makers would include some tourism activities in the business trip itineraries of their Chinese customers.

References

Asanuma, B. 1989. "Manufacturer-Supplier Relationships in Japan and the Concept of Relation-Specific Skill." *Journal of the Japanese and International Economies* 3 (1): 1–30.

Brookfield, J., and R.-J. Liu. 2005. "The Internationalization of a Production Network and the Replication Dilemma: Building Supplier Networks in Mainland China." *Asia Pacific Journal of Management* 22: 355–380.

Carlisle, E., and D. Flynn. 2005. "Small Business Survival in China: Guanxi, Legitimacy, and Social Capital." *Journal of Developmental Entrepreneurship* 10 (1): 79–96.

Chen, L.-C. 2009. "Learning through Informal Local and Global Linkages: The Case of Taiwan's Machine Tool Industry." *Research Policy* 38 (3): 527–535.

Chen, L.-C. 2011. "The Governance and Evolution of Local Production Networks in a Cluster: The Case of Taiwan's Machine Tool Industry." *GeoJournal* 76 (6): 605–622.

Chen, L.-C., and Z.-X. Lin. 2014. "Examining the Role of Geographical Proximity in a Cluster's Transformation Process: The Case of Taiwan's Machine Tool Industry." *European Planning Studies* 22 (1): 1–19.

Cheng, L.-L. 1999. "The Invisible Elbow: Semiperiphery and the Restructuring of International Footwear Market." *Taiwan: A Radical Quarterly in Social Studies* 35: 1–46.

Cousins, P.D., R.B. Handfield, B. Lawson, and K.J. Petersen. 2006. "Creating Supply Chain Relational Capital: The Impact of Formal and Informal Socialization Processes." *Journal of Operations Management* 24 (6): 851–863.

Dyer, J.H., and H. Singh. 1998. "The Relational View: Cooperative Strategy and Sources of Interorganizational Competitive Advantage." *Academy of Management Review* 23 (4): 660–679.

Gardner Publications. 2013. "2013 World Machine Tool Output and Consumption Survey." Accessed July 15, 2013. www.gardnerweb.com/articles/2013-world-machine-tool-output-and-consumption-survey

Gertler, M.S. 2004. *Manufacturing Culture: The Institutional Geography of Industrial Practice*. New York: Oxford University Press.

Hitt, M., H.-U. Lee, and E. Yucel. 2002. "The Importance of Social Capital to the Management of Multinational Enterprises: Relational Networks Among Asian and Western Firms." *Asia Pacific Journal of Management* 19 (2–3): 353–372.

Hoang, H., and B. Antoncic. 2003. "Network-Based Research in Entrepreneurship: A Critical Review." *Journal of Business Venturing* 18 (2): 165–187.

Hsing, Y.-T. 1996. "Blood, Thicker than Water: Interpersonal Relations and Taiwanese Investment in Southern China." *Environment & Planning A* 28: 2241–2261.

Hsing, Y.-T. 1998. *Making Capitalism in China: The Taiwan Connection.* New York: Oxford University Press.

Hsu, S.-C., and D.-S. Chen. Eds. 2011. *Taiwanese Investment in China During the Past Two Decades: Experience, Developments and Prospects.* New Taipei City: Ink Publisher (in Chinese).

ITIS. 2005. *2005 Mechanical Industry Yearbook.* Hsinchu: ITIS (in Chinese).

Ito, S. 2009. "Japanese-Taiwanese Joint Ventures in China." *China Information* 23 (1): 15–44.

Jack, S. L. 2005. "The Role, Use and Activation of Strong and Weak Network Ties: A Qualitative Analysis." *Journal of Management Studies* 42 (6): 1233–1259.

Jarillo, J. C. 1989. "Entrepreneurship and Growth: The Strategic Use of External Resources." *Journal of Business Venturing* 4 (2): 133–147.

Lechner, C., and M. Dowling. 2003. "Firm Networks: External Relationships as Sources for the Growth and Competitiveness of Entrepreneurial Firms." *Entrepreneurship and Regional Development* 15 (1): 1–26.

Lechner, C., M. Dowling, and I. Welpe. 2006. "Firm Networks and Firm Development: The Role of the Relational Mix." *Journal of Business Venturing* 21 (4): 514–540.

Liu, R.-J. 1999. *Networking Division of Labor: Examining the Competitiveness of Taiwan's Machine Tool Industry.* Taipei: Linking.

Liu, R.-J., and J. Brookfield. 2000. "Stars, Rings and Tiers: Organisational Networks and Their Dynamics in Taiwan's Machine Tool Industry." *Long Range Planning* 33 (3): 322–348.

Liu, R.-J., W.-T. Chang, and H.-C. Jien. 2001. *The Machine Tools Subcontracting Networks in Shanghai, Hangzhou and Ningbo, China.* Taichung, Taiwan: Central Taiwan New Century Foundation.

Lorenzoni, G., and A. Lipparini. 1999. "The Leveraging of Interfirm Relationships as a Distinctive Organizational Capability: A Longitudinal Study." *Strategic Management Journal* 20 (4): 317–338.

MIRL. 1995. *1995 Machine Tools Yearbook.* Hsinchu: MIRL (in Chinese).

MOEA. 2007. *2007 Machinery Industry Yearbook.* Taipei: MOEA.

Orru, M., N. W. Biggart, and G. Hamilton. 1997. *The Economic Organization of East Asian Capitalism.* Thousand Oaks: Sage Publications.

Partanen, J., K. Möller, M. Westerlund, R. Rajala, and A. Rajala. 2008. "Social Capital in the Growth of Science-and-technology-based SMEs." *Industrial Marketing Management* 37 (5): 513–522.

Pearce, J. A., and R. B. Robinson Jr. 2000. "Cultivating Guanxi as a Foreign Investor Strategy." *Business Horizons* 43 (1): 31–38.

Porter, M. 2000. "Location, Competition, and Economic Development: Local Cluster in a Global Economy." *Economic Development Quarterly* 14 (1): 15–34.

Sadoi, Y. 2011. "Technology Accumulation and the Division of Labour between China, Taiwan and Japan: Taiwanese Automotive Parts, and Die and Mould Firms in China." *International Journal of Institutions and Economies* 3 (3): 397–414.

Saxenian, A. 1994. *Regional Advantage: Culture and Competition in Silicon Valley and Route 128.* Cambridge: Harvard University Press.

TAMI. 2005. *Sixty Years of Machinery Industry in Taiwan.* Taipei: TAMI (in Chinese).

TAMI. 2012. *2010–2012 Directory of Taiwanese Machinery Firms in China*. Taipei: TAMI (in Chinese).

TAMI. 2013. "2012 Taiwan Machine Tool Production and Sales Statistics." Accessed June 5, 2013. www.tami.org.tw/statistics/week2.htm

Theingi, S. Purchase, and Y. Phungphol. 2008. "Social Capital in Southeast Asian Business Relationships." *Industrial Marketing Management* 37 (5): 523–530.

Ulhøi, J.P. 2005. "The Social Dimensions of Entrepreneurship." *Technovation* 25 (8): 939–946.

USCS. 2006. "2005 Machine Tool Exporters Guide to China." US Department of Commerce.

Wang, C.L. 2007. "Guanxi vs. Relationship Marketing: Exploring Underlying Differences." *Industrial Marketing Management* 36 (1): 81–86.

Wang, J.-H., and C.-K. Lee. 2007. "Global Production Networks and Local Institution Building: The Development of the Information-technology Industry in Suzhou, China." *Environment and Planning A* 39 (8): 1873–1888.

Yang, C. 2009. "Strategic Coupling of Regional Development in Global Production Networks: Redistribution of Taiwanese Personal Computer Investment from the Pearl River Delta to the Yangtze River Delta, China." *Regional Studies* 43 (3): 385–407.

Yang, Y.R., and C.J. Hsia. 2007, "Spatial Clustering and Organizational Dynamics of Transborder Production Networks: A Case Study of Taiwanese Information-technology Companies in the Greater Suzhou Area, China." *Environment and Planning A* 39 (6): 1346–1363.

Yau, H.M., S.Y. Lee, P.M. Chow, Y.M. Sin, and C.B. Tse. 2000, "Relationship Marketing the Chinese Way." *Business Horizons* 43 (1): 16–24.

Yeung, I.Y.M., and R.L. Tung. 1996. "Achieving Business Success in Confucian Societies: The Importance of Guanxi (Connections)." *Organizational Dynamics* 25 (2): 54–65.

Zweig, D. 2002. *Internationalizing China: Domestic Interests and Global Linkages*. Ithaca: Cornell University Press.

10 *Guanxi* and the ancient jade trade

The cross-border antique market in Greater China

Yu-Ying Lee

Introduction[1]

> *Building guanxi is very important, how can you do business without a relationship?*
>
> (Mr. Zhao, antique dealer)

This chapter is to unearth the ways in which social and commercial networks, or *guanxi*, are built and used in trading antiques, especially ancient jade, among businesspeople in China, Hong Kong, Macao, and Taiwan. There is an old Chinese saying, "Buying gold in war time, while collecting antiques in prosperous era." The rapid economic growth in Taiwan and Hong Kong after World War II has nurtured a wealthy upper and middle class that emerged in the 1980s, which has gradually learned to cultivate the traditional taste of collecting precious ancient jade so as to enrich its cultural capital (cf. Bourdieu 1984). This ancient jade fever has not only occurred in Taiwan and Hong Kong but also is happening in China today. The fast-growing economic development of the past thirty years has nurtured a high-income upper and middle class to emerge in China. This class has the similar habitus to collect ancient jade, in a similar fashion to Taiwan and Hong Kong. More precisely, from 2003 onwards, antique consumption in China has become a very popular middle-class hobby. This also generates many TV shows to teach people how to buy and detect real antiques from fake ones. Now, China has become the biggest antique auction market in the world, surpassing that of New York and London, in which ancient jade is one of the main targets.

Where do those vast amounts of ancient jade come from to supply the market? Most of these artifacts are from family heirlooms, and the rest come from ancient tombs of the aristocracy. Chinese officials estimated that about 220,000 tombs were pillaged during 1998–2003 (Passas and Poulx 2011, 61). The main reason was to take antiques from the tombs to the markets for profit. But where did these antiquities go? How were they transported and then traded? Who were the market traders? The destination of this ancient jade first went to Hong Kong and Macao after the Chinese Communist Party established its regime; then they moved on to Taiwan as it became prosperous in the 1980s. Ironically, many more ancient jade has now been brought back to China. An interesting question thus is: How did the cross-border ancient jade trade occur? How could these trades run smoothly, either across and/or within the borders, if they were illegal most of the time due to the pillaging?

I will argue in this chapter that, due to the high uncertainty of the ancient jade trade, *guanxi* thus becomes a proxy for high trust and insurance for the transaction. This chapter aims to depict and analyze the complex cross-border social and commercial *guanxi* among traders in China, Hong Kong, Macao, and Taiwan in trading antiques, especially ancient jade. My focus will be on the role of *guanxi* in the formation of the jade market in Taiwan from 1980 onwards and its relationship with the currently booming antique market in contemporary China. *Guanxi* literally means "relation" or "relationship" as a noun and "relate to" as a verb. *Guanxi,* by definition, refers to "a dyadic, particular, and sentimental tie that has potential of facilitating favor exchange between the parties connected by the tie" (Bian 2006, 312). In a very general sense, *guanxi* resembles Pierre Bourdieu's concept of "social capital" but bears a more complicated sense of relationship between related persons. Specifically, *guanxi* are social ties based mostly on kinship, native birthplace, ethnicity, and acquaintances. Potential business partners may intentionally build or seek to make *guanxi* when no prior basis exists, either by relying on intermediaries or directly establishing a relationship, which is called *la guanxi* (pulling relational streams). In this situation, the process will move on, involving more parties, and stop only when a solution is finally found or the task is abandoned. Hence, *guanxi* is a dynamic process (Fan 2002). *Guanxi* can be consciously constructed, cultivated, and maintained over time (Yang 1994; 2002; Yan 1996; Kipnis 1997; Gold et al. 2002; Bian and Zhang 2014; and also chapter 1 of this book).

I applied a variety of qualitative research techniques to examine the formation of the ancient jade market. These techniques include extensive use of in-depth interviews, observations, and the use of a variety of documentary sources. Five field trips were taken to Shanghai in August 2009 and December 2011, Hangzhou in April 2010, Beijing in September 2011, and Hong Kong in August 2012. I conducted in-depth interviews with individual jade collectors, antique dealers, and jade traders. I also used the snowball method to contact the interviewees. In total, fifty-seven people were interviewed: including twenty-four jade collectors, twenty-five jade dealers, and eight professional jade scholars. I conducted each interview from sixty to ninety minutes, and then every interview was transcribed into written text afterwards.

There are five sections in this chapter. The first one is an introduction. The second section follows a theoretical discussion about *guanxi* and the antique trade. The third section depicts the notion of Chineseness with jade and explains the historical and social context of Taiwan to indicate the conception of Chineseness within the Taiwanese identity. The fourth section elaborates on how *guanxi* facilitates ancient jade business transactions in the Greater China area and is then followed by the conclusion.

Antique trade and guanxi

The antique trade is a special market whose size is not very large and most of the time is not well regulated. Different from industrial goods whose sources can be easily traced back to their original manufacturers, whose value can be predetermined by production and transportation costs, and whose market order can be regulated by the state or by trade associations, the ancient jade trade has a unique and a totally different characteristic. In other words, most ancient jade have no exact sources; their values/prices are difficult to assess and be certain of. Moreover, it is not easy to establish and sustain the order of the antique jade market due to the lack of a formal organization that has ultimate knowledge, authority, and power. With these complex qualities, the question arises as to how the antique jade market is governed?

The nature of the ancient jade trade is not about interfirms and organizational relations that the sociology of the market has traditionally put as a priority in research (Zukin and DiMaggio 1990; Fligstein 1996; Swedberg 2003; Velthuis 2003; Fligstein and Dauter 2007; Morgan 2008; Beckert 2009), but instead, it is about the relationship between traders and trustful sources, about traders and their customers in negotiating prices, and about knowledgeable experts interpreting the value of a piece of ancient jade ware. In this sense, I agree with DiMaggio and Louch's (1998) view that regards the market as "socially embedded" (Granovetter 1985), in which an individual consumer uses social networks in much the same way as an industrial firm does. For avoiding opportunism and reducing risk, they also argue, consumers tend to use interpersonal relations in many expenditure decisions, both in the search process and in the choice of transaction partners (Geertz 1978; Williamson 1983; Yamagishi and Yamagishi 1994; DiMaggio and Louch 1998). Buying or trading ancient jade is the same, due to the fact that this typical trade is full of risks; therefore, building *guanxi* becomes a proxy for reducing uncertainty.

Indeed, there is no standard price for antiques because, in ancient times, each piece of artifact was handmade, and the price varied in terms of materiality, scarcity, aesthetic, and provenance. Thus, each transaction is made in accordance with how much money the buyers are willing to pay and how much the sellers willing to accept. People need to put a lot of effort into obtaining knowledge on the authentication of antiques and their value. Normally, antique dealers become knowledgeable about antiques and authentication that starts from their apprenticeship, by first examining and then selling vast volumes of genuine artifacts and fakes, thus becoming an expert. The antique market is full of information asymmetry. When compared with collectors/consumers, normally, antique dealers have a better understanding on authentication and market price than customers. For the sake of opportunism, deception is common if no trustworthiness has been built. There is a proverb circulating in the traditional Chinese antique market, "No business in three years, one transaction eats three years" (三年不開張，開張吃三年), to describe how one transaction could sustain business for the next three years, as well as how trading antiques can be a lucrative business. In these circumstances, *guanxi* plays a critical role in the antique market either for the trader or the consumer, because a newcomer is vulnerable; thus, it is common practice to be introduced to certain antique shops by friends in the *guanxi* webs. Trust and social ties may reduce the risk of a business transaction.

This trustworthiness can also be found in the diamond trade (Westwood 2000) or the jade stone market (Chang 2004; 2006; 2011), where one or a few family-owned companies dominate the market. In the world diamond markets, for example, a dominant company can control price, quality, and quantity (Spar 2006). The market size and supplied quantity therefore can be controlled. In this trade, powerful family firms monopolize the diamond trade worldwide. Due to its small size and family control, diamond trading is heavily dependent on family ties, which are the basis of trust. Therefore, one cannot afford to be expelled from the family for doing something wrong, because this would lead to this person being distrusted during an economical transaction (Westwood 2000).

However, the ancient jade market is very diverse, with a very dispersive market that involves many different kinds of people in terms of production, source, and consumption. There is no formal organization to consolidate the trade, and neither are there interest groups of dealers to initiate standard prices and quantity in the Chinese antique market. Furthermore, the traditional trading culture of this market implies the element of deception. Consumers always blame themselves for opportunism, and the lack of ability to make a good judgment, that leave the antique dealers free from condemnation. This is different from that of the diamond trade, where family honesty is essential as to keep the trading between families longer lasting (Westwood 2000).

Indeed, in order to reduce the risk and uncertainty, *guanxi* plays a very important role in the trading of ancient jade across borders. For jade traders, they need *guanxi* to acquire business resources and the protection from government officials. For consumers/collectors, they need *guanxi* to access qualified antique dealers and to buy genuine jade wares. I shall elaborate on how the *guanxi* practice works in trading ancient jade in the fourth section. The next section will illustrate how the notion of Chineseness attaches itself to jade and offers a broader view on how and why collectors are enthusiastic about ancient jade wares.

Jade and Chineseness

The charm of jade

Unlike gold or diamonds, which are highly desired by people from all over the world, jade is more closely associated with the Chinese people. Jade has been a valuable artifact throughout Chinese history, with collectors always believing that Chinese culture is equal to jade culture. In Chinese, "jade" (玉) refers to a fine, beautiful stone, with a warm color and rich luster, and in most cases are skillfully and delicately carved. Gold and diamonds have standard prices worldwide, but jade is priceless. It should be noted that jade is considered even more precious than gold to jade lovers, because each piece of carved jade is uniquely sculpted and carries its own characteristics.

Scarcity makes jade valuable, because it comes from a rare mineral material that is not mass produced in factories. Ancient pieces of carved jade are even more precious because they are inscribed with a sign of value throughout history and time (Baudrillard 1996). Furthermore, collectors believe that jade is alive and emits energy. Ancient jade differs from others antiques, which become decrepit through time, as it is sturdy, vibrant, and transformable. Collectors can nurture a specific intimate relationship with a piece of jade ware by "breeding" (*yang yu,* 養玉), which means that ancient jade may change color in accordance with the holder's body heat, and the particle in itself through contact, either by holding it in one's hand or hanging it on one's body. Hence, jade provides not only visual enjoyment but also tactile pleasures for the collectors, as many like to take a piece of jade ware in hand and often scrub it in order to see the color changing in the process of breeding. Under these circumstances, collectors contribute their efforts to their jade collection because a piece of jade ware is reborn in their hands. This practice is fascinating and brings tremendous self-accomplishment to collectors. That's why so many are fond of holding their favorite jade ware when they are sleeping; seldom collectors hold a piece of porcelain or a painting scroll when they go to bed.

Archeological excavation has shown that the Chinese people have revered jade since the Neolithic age when jade wares were made for ritual purposes, as in worshipping gods, because jade was considered the only appropriate medium to communicate with their gods. Jade was hence bestowed with magical powers that can protect one's life and health. The material character of jade is said to be consistent with the impeccable characteristic virtues ascribed to Confucius. According to the Chinese ancient text *Liji* (禮記, *The Book of Rites*), Confucius compared the qualities of jade to a gentleman's five virtues: kindness, wisdom, integrity, courage, and purity. Before the Song Dynasty, jade only belonged to royal families and the aristocracy. Although jade wares have become commercialized since the Song Dynasty, they still belonged to the very rich people that inscribed the noble sign of value to jade.

Simply stated, from the material aspect, jade is a rare mineral and unable to be reproduced, although it may change color over time. From the cultural and spiritual aspects, jade, nevertheless, has been recognized in Chinese culture as a beautiful stone and loaded with symbolic meaning of prestige and eternity. With these cultural and symbolic characteristics, when ancient jade wares can be easily purchased on the market, Taiwanese collectors/consumers are craving to accumulate them.

Taiwan as the keeper of Chinese culture

The Kuomintang (the Chinese nationalist government, KMT) retreated to Taiwan in 1949 after its defeat by the Communist Party in the Chinese Civil War. The Communist Party set up the People's Republic of China (PRC) in Mainland China, while the KMT continued as the Republic of China (ROC) on Taiwan. The ROC government was conscious of identifying itself as the standard-bearer of traditional Chinese culture and the legitimate heir of an orthodoxy that dates back to the ancient emperors Yao, Shun, Yu, Tang, and the great Chinese sage, Confucius.

In 1966, when the fanatic Cultural Revolution (1966–1976) broke out in Mainland China, the ROC government launched the Chinese Cultural Renaissance Movement (中華文化復興運動) in Taiwan to undo the cultural destruction caused by the Communist Party. The government's policy of reviving Chinese culture became especially distinct and received increased impetus, joining with the ongoing modernization of society and the economy.

Taiwan's ideological claim to be the true heir of the Chinese culture has made it a source of ethnic pride for the overseas Chinese and an inspiration for the Chinese people on Mainland China who appreciate the traditions of Chinese culture. Furthermore, the conception of Chinese culture was embedded in historic artifacts; the National Palace Museum in Taipei, a repository for traditional art from Mainland China, is the icon of Chinese culture. During the Cold War, the National Palace Museum worked as an embodiment of Chinese culture that was the sole place to admire Chinese cultural artifacts, not only to Taiwanese, but also to the rest of the world as well. Now, the National Palace Museum is the most popular attraction for tourists from China.

Given these conditions, it is no wonder that the Taiwanese are so closely adhered to the Chinese culture and that Taiwanese can also appreciate the beauty and value of jade. During the Chinese Cultural Revolution, ancient jade, amongst other antiques, was categorized as the "Four Olds" that must be demolished. At the same time, vast amounts of Chinese antiques were trafficked to Hong Kong and Macao and then to other places around the world. Taiwan was the biggest market for consuming Chinese cultural artifacts; naturally, Cantonese traders from Hong Kong and Macao tended to bring Chinese antiques across the Taiwan Strait to feed the demand of the rising middle class.

Guanxi and the trading of ancient jade

Regional trade between Taiwan, Hong Kong, and China

Taiwanese were restricted from traveling abroad when Taiwan was ruled under martial law (1947–1987), when foreign exchange was state controlled and Hong Kong was the nearest free trade market to Taiwan. During 1970–1990, traders from Hong Kong and Macao could travel to Taiwan without restrictions, and these traders were not necessarily Cantonese, as some were Fujianese. They brought lots of Chinese artifacts, legal and illegal, to Taiwan and gradually formed an open-air market in Taipei. This open-air and holiday jade market used to be called Macanese Street (澳門街), since these traders spoke with a Cantonese dialect. In addition, every weekend a group of antique traders from around the island would gather under the bridge of *Guanghua*, which has become the most famous antiques flea market in Taipei since the early 1980s. Traders and buyers came together to trade their antiques, which they had brought extensively from China via Hong Kong and Macao. These open-air sites were designated on a first-come-first-served basis; some of the buyers might buy very good pieces at low prices. In their heyday, some traders would arrive to locate their stalls between 3am to 4am as an early attraction for the eager buyers and customers.

Apart from the open-air market, some local antique dealers also imported substantial amounts of antiques from Hong Kong and Macao. Before 1987, the

Taiwanese antique market was dominated by Cantonese traders, because only they had the sources in Hong Kong, Macao, and Mainland China. Another crucial reason was that Taiwanese were restricted from visiting China before 1988, owing to the political rivalry across the Taiwan Strait. It was only when the Taiwan government allowed its people to visit their relatives in Mainland China in 1988, a vast number of courageous Taiwanese traders started to hunt for antiques there. Previously, Taiwanese traders could only buy merchandise from their associate dealer/supplier in Hong Kong or Macao, and now they wanted to directly search for goods in China in order to avoid Hong Kong's traders manipulating prices and sources.

According to my fieldwork research, most of the jade traders' first journeys to China were led by Cantonese traders who had already built relationships in the antique markets. Nevertheless, some Taiwanese traders could also apply family ties to gain access to China, because they or their parents were mainlanders who came to Taiwan in 1949. Taiwanese traders have linguistic advantages in China because Mandarin was the official language in Taiwan under the KMT regime; therefore, traders were able to quickly and easily build up their own *guanxi* networks.

In the early stage, Guangzhou was the most popular place for Taiwanese jade traders to buy ancient jade because of its location. Gradually, they started to move inland, as well as to remote villages, to search for cheaper and better sources; they also went to open markets, including state-owned cultural relic shops in other major cities. Each trader had their own travel routes and *guanxi* networks in Hong Kong, Macao, Guangzhou, Nanjing, Beijing, Tianjin, Xian, and many other cities.

Some brave traders preferred to travel to China alone, because they regarded *guanxi* as a personal possession and did not want to share their connections with their Taiwanese competitors. Some might choose to travel in a small group with one or two others. According to my interviewees, there were roughly two or three hundred Taiwanese antique jade traders who traveled to China on a daily basis via Hong Kong in the 1990s, as one antique jade dealer, Mr. Lin, said, "I always meet other traders in Hong Kong airport, the old airport was small and it was easy to bump into acquaintances." In the heyday of the jade market, Taiwanese antique jade traders used to travel to Mainland China monthly. Some even went weekly, going on a Monday and coming back on a Friday, so they could provide new merchandise at the weekend jade market in Taipei. These traders might bring small pieces of jade wares in handbags or luggage; sometimes they also transported bigger items by shipping containers.

Ancient jade that travels

Ancient jade cannot travel; it was the traders who traveled. From the aspect of the market, traders always buy goods at low prices and then transport them to the market where they can sell them at higher prices. During 1980–2000, a huge economic discrepancy in terms of living standards existed between Taiwan and China; the rising Taiwanese middle class, which became the social backbone of the emergent jade market, were able to take advantage of the low commodity prices in Mainland China.

Mr. Wen was an insurance agent before he became an antique dealer in the late 1980s; he described his first experience of encountering a piece of ancient bronze in China as follows:

> It was about in the year of 1987, when I first visited my mother's hometown at a village in Hunan province, I saw an old bronze vase dumped in dirt. No one seemed to pay attention to it. I felt exhilarated when I hold it in my hand because such a thing was only shown in history textbooks. I only paid little money for buying it, because the villagers were poor and they were willing to sell anything for cash.

Mr. Wen explained that he had adored Chinese artifacts since his childhood; he used to contemplate beautiful Chinese artifacts on a calendar published by the National Palace Museum. He also loved to visit the National Palace Museum for a whole day, longing to admire those delicate collections. Therefore, he was overjoyed that he could have the chance to own something equivalent to the museum's collection. After the first encounter with ancient bronze, Mr. Wen became an antique dealer who eagerly searched for Chinese antiques from Mainland China. He traveled almost the length of the country in order to obtain as many antique artifacts as possible. In the 1990s, Taiwan's economy was far better than China's, so it was very easy to buy and sell. Mr. Wen stated:

> Upon arriving at the airport of Taipei, there were already some passionate collectors/buyers waiting for me, they grabbed whatever they saw and eagerly wanted to buy without bargain. I usually sold out all goods within a week then I got enough cash and went to China again to get more antiques.

Actually, there were hundreds of antique traders traveling back and forth across the Taiwan Strait, and Mr. Wen was only one of them. Under these circumstances, a vast amount of ancient Chinese jade was brought to Taiwan. The jade collectors whom I interviewed shared similar experiences on the heyday of ancient jade consumption. Mr. Hong, a jade collector, exaggeratedly said, "There were so many people went to jade market with buckets at hands to grab jades!" Note he used the word "grab" to emphasize the passionate emotion of collectors/consumers, and the word "bucket" to overstate the vast amount of purchasing during that time. Another collector, Mr. Zai, stated:

> In the heydays of jade market, everyone went crazy. Usually the market opened at 9 o'clock but we arrived there at 8 o'clock to wait. Some people think that 8 o'clock is not early enough, so they decide to go to jade trader's home one night before the businesses opening day. Some even went to the airport to meet jade traders in order to obtain first hand jades immediately. Anyway, everyone tried to figure out a tactic to grab jades before the others. It was a mad time indeed.

According to Mr. Wen and collector Mr. Zai, consumers who have close relationships with the traders would have the privilege of seeing goods firsthand and then choosing whatever they wanted. Usually these customers were from the inner circle of the *guanxi* web with traders in terms of a long-term business relationship; they did not haggle and were willing to pay a high price. Thus, jade traders were delighted to offer better quality jade to them. It was normal in a jade market that traders offered a different level of goods to different customers in accordance with their monetary proficiency, appreciation of jade, and, most crucially, being closer or further away in their *guanxi* networks. Normally, each trader has their own *guanxi* networks to support their trading.

As for the price, actually, most jade traders really did not know the "real" price for a piece of carved jade; they would add 10–30 percent on the price they paid in the Chinese market. Because the price of ancient jade in China was low in the 1980s and 1990s, so the price in Taiwan's jade market was low as well. Sometimes, jade traders even lowered the price before they were about to leave on a new business trip, because they needed cash as capital to acquire more jade wares from China. As jade trader, Ms. Judy, recalled, "We sell ancient jades as cheap as vegetables." Before the 1980s, customers went to antique shops to buy ancient jade, which was rare and expensive. But in the 1990s, jade traders sold inexpensive ancient jade in the open-air markets, and these jade traders truly changed the ways of selling and buying jade in Taiwan.

However, that kind of prosperous ancient jade trading did not last for very long, as the trade had been declining since 2000 onwards. There are at least two reasons that can explain the slowdown of the ancient jade market in Taiwan. First of all, the price of jade wares continued to rise in the Chinese market, so there was no cheap and beautiful jade ware for public collection anymore. As Ms. Judy recalled:

> In early stage, I can buy top level of jade wares for only RMB¥3,000–RMB¥5,000, then it rises to RMB¥10,000 for buying similar goods, and last I have to pay RMB¥30,000. You can see the huge change in price.

Second, the rapid economic growth in China has brought about a wealthy middle class who have enough spare money for leisure consumption. Under these circumstances, rich Chinese not only collect antiques to express their social prestige but also travel to buy Chinese cultural artifacts overseas and bring them back to China to show patriotism and national pride.

From 2000 onwards, a number of Taiwanese jade traders started to set up businesses in China to serve the booming antique market. They moved ancient jade back to China. which they had transported to Taiwan less than ten years ago. Owing to the price of ancient jade. which has jumped to a high level in China, there was no reason to sell ancient jade in Taiwan's market. On April 11, 2011, the Taiwanese government announced a new policy that allowed individual Chinese tourists to visit Taiwan. A new tendency is to buy ancient jade and take it back to China from Taiwan, so Chinese antique dealers have joined this business by purchasing goods from Taiwan's antique shops, open-air jade markets, and auction houses. Taiwan has been a hot market that has consumed ancient jade from China for more than twenty years; now it has transformed to become a place to supply ancient jade back to China.

Trading ancient jade and guanxi *network*

The jade market is a highly segmented one, which means that consumers/collectors are divided by different social networks and economical capital. Top-tier collectors buy antiques from auction houses and antique shops, while middle-class buyers hunt treasure in the open-air jade markets and antique shops. Some wealthy collectors may hire agents as advisors, allowing them to stay at home waiting for the agents to provide collectable items to them. It is only the richest that have a strong *guanxi* network with antique dealers who have close networks with Hong Kong and Macao traders, who in turn can share the source of "new" antiques that were recently excavated from tombs in China. Members in this kind of circle always keep a low profile, and messages are only exchanged within their network, with outsiders hardly having any access.

According to some Chinese news reports, there is a comprehensive "production chain" on smuggling antiquities that can transport antiques from a tomb to another country within three days.[2] It is very difficult for outsiders to know how it really works. According to related research and my conversations with interviewees, the local army and police officers always become involved in illicit antiques transportation, particularly in cross-border trading.[3] A jade dealer, Mr. Xu, told me how his *guanxi* facilitated transporting antiques. He strategically makes an effort to build relationships *(la guanxi)* with a high-ranking customs officer in the airport and they became "good friends." Later on, the government official always helps him to transport ancient jade out of China. Mr. Xu did not need to carry any ancient jade on his person when passing through the custom's security check; his friend would make arrangements to put his cargo box inside the flight cabinet exactly above his seat. This favor exchange only highlights how one customs officer plays a role in the ancient jade trade. One can imagine that there are various intricate social networks underpinning antique markets in China, Hong Kong, and Taiwan.

Another key mediator in the ancient jade "production chain" is the middleman, who can judge the value of antiques and is able to access the buyers so as to distribute these goods for the tomb robbers. These men are called *mazai* (馬仔) and are experts on antiques and have a strong network with antique dealers. The *Mazai* supplies goods to antique dealers in Hong Kong and Macao, and from there, illicit antiques they become legalized commodities to be sold to consumers/collectors. This *guanxi* trading route is similar to the trade of jade stones from Burma to Thailand (Chang 2004). Many top-tier Taiwanese antique dealers imported such newly excavated antiques from Hong Kong antique shops. Usually, these antiques would not go to open-air markets because the price is very high. Once antique dealers acquire illicit antiquities, they usually know which collectors desire these types of artifacts and are willing to pay the price.

Antique dealers always contact target consumers by cellphone and then send them pictures to examine and make decisions. This illicit source is only shared within trusted networks, not only for the sake of security, but also for the price as well.

According to a top antique dealer, Mr. Chen, who always waits for the precious artifacts to be brought to him by a middleman rather than seeking the antiques himself in the market:

> We top level antique dealers seldom go to China to buy antiques. Actually the goods will come to us, because we are willing to pay high price. Sometimes we cannot obtain the wanted object first hand, nevertheless after one or two transactions, it comes to me eventually.

Another example is Mr. Wang who owns some precious ancient jade. Many pieces in his collection came from Hong Kong and Macao antique dealers, whose sources delivered them from tombs in Mainland China transported by the *Mazai*. According to his account, the source was the most crucial means to judge the quality of ancient jade. Mr. Wang stated:

> Actually those antique dealers do not necessarily know where the sources are but *Mazai* does. As a middleman between legal antique shop and illicit tomb digger, *Mazai* knows the price and how to tell genuine ancient jade from counterfeit. However, it is not because *Mazai* is diligent and doing research hard. *Mazai* only concerns whether the supplier belongs to the group of tomb digger, so that he believes the objects are genuine.

Mr. Wang said that each *Mazai* had their personal channels to obtain illicit antiques. The *Mazai* depends on only his most trusted supplier and dares not collect any objects from strangers. Thus, one can see the *guanxi* network exercises a pivotal role in trading ancient jade where trust is the basic principle to make every transaction possible. This exists not only between traders but also between dealers and customers.

Cultivating guanxi *to secure business*

For consumers, buying ancient jade is high-risk consumption because most consumers lack any knowledge of ancient jade and are therefore more likely to accept suggestions from a jade dealer whom they met in a *guanxi* network. In the jade market, the dealer usually acts as a mentor who distributes knowledge on how to appreciate jade wares. Normally, customers like to chat with a jade dealer whilst drinking tea, discussing, and producing knowledge together on evaluating jade wares. This means that they share the same level/taste on evaluating the quality and aesthetic of a piece of jade ware. But group members hardly ever have the chance to communicate with outsiders, because they are already convinced by the jade dealer not to believe other dealers. Each group carries a knowledgeable difference about jade and hardly ever makes exchanges. Veteran antique dealer, Mr. Chen observed:

> In the early stage, a group of collectors gathered around a dealer and they became friends and met quite often. Their knowledge on jade was made by conversations during meetings and became a consensus within the group. But those beliefs were only valid within circle and could hardly apply beyond the group, such as price and conception on authentication. Sometimes a group of collectors were willing to pay high price on a piece of jade ware but the other groups of collector just didn't even want to give a look. It was really a highly segmented market.

Rarity, and being one-of-a-kind, make ancient jade transactions a distinctive type of consumption. There is no space for consumers/collectors to shop around and compare prices. Actually, there is no identical jade ware unless it is counterfeit jade. When consumers/collectors encounter a piece of exquisite jade ware at first sight, they tend to buy it, or it may not be seen again, as there is no room for second thoughts. Consumers/collectors tend to be convinced by jade dealers to immediately commit to a transaction for fear of losing an ideal piece of artifact. Thus, there is power asymmetry between the dealer and the buyer unless the buyer has enough knowledge to distinguish genuine goods from replicas. Occasionally, jade dealers may fabricate a story on excavating ancient jade ware and, therefore, would strategically advise consumers/collectors to secretly keep the purchased jade, the so-called "national treasure." Customers are told not to tell others or the trader will be punished for trading in illicit ancient artifacts. After a period of time, when consumers/collectors want to sell the so-called "national treasure" for profit, they would then realize that their precious collection is counterfeit. All collectors whom I interviewed have experiences of buying counterfeits. One collector Mr. Yan says:

> My master is the first jade dealer I met; he taught me knowledge on how to appreciate ancient jade. I brought lots of ancient jade from him because I trusted him. My master even swore to me: if the object is counterfeit, I will ground it into powder and swallowed it.

However, when Mr. Yan had the chance to access other dealers and gained more knowledge on ancient jade, he realized that his master had sold fakes to him. In this circumstance, trust had been abused in their *guanxi* network. Nevertheless, Mr. Yan did not go back to argue with his master and gives the reason as follows:

> I regard the money as paying tuition fee. Maybe he does believe the goods sold to me are genuine. After all those ancient jades are what he has and the only goods he can offer.

Hence, veteran collectors like to advise novices to use their eyes rather than their ears to buy jade. In the antique trading market, it is the norm to blame oneself for opportunism and the lack of knowledge, rather than accusing the dealer of being dishonest in public. Collectors/consumers dare not allow others to know that they have brought the wrong collectables for self-esteem's sake. Since the jade market is segregated, some sellers are inclined to behave opportunistically, as there are always newcomers, so the trading continues relentlessly.

Luck is also crucial in the jade market. In order not to be cheated, normally, the consumer/collector is inclined to apply their personal relationship to gain access to vendors or antique shops. Novices are always introduced by their social ties to access jade dealers. However, this kind of trust does not necessarily secure the quality of jade as I mentioned above. Every collector has their *guanxi* network that directs them to a different jade dealer, which however, does not guarantee the quality of the jade. Actually, the dealers can only offer what they have and try to make a sale. Not every dealer has a good eye and knowledge regarding ancient jade, but they can always tell interesting stories to charm their customers. It is common practice that jade dealers have insufficient knowledge about ancient jade, as they gradually learn from other dealers, or even from diligent customers who have studied hard on their collections. As Ms. Judy says:

> I have the talent to choose carved jades according to my sense of beauty. I do not know the provenance of jades and the history behind ancient jades, because I am lazy in studying. I just buy and sell those jades which look nice to me. Actually I was taught by my customers on the detailed information about each piece of jade, I learnt a lot from my customers.

Ms. Judy is not exceptional. Many jade dealers may not have any ancient jade knowledge in the beginning, but they gradually extend it during their learning process. A jade dealer confessed to me that he finally accumulated enough knowledge to discern ancient jade wares after five years of trading. This indicates that there are so many unqualified jade traders in the market, as *guanxi* directs one to certain networks but does not guarantee the quality of purchase. Hence, the term "paying a tuition fee" is a common self-mocking maxim among jade collectors.

Conclusion

This chapter has shown how *guanxi* networks underpin the ancient jade trade in Taiwan, Hong Kong, and China. I highlighted that jade culture has been embedded in Chinese society and that the Chinese appreciate ancient jade for spiritual and material reasons. In the course of the Cultural Revolution, while the Chinese government allowed the Red Guard to destroy traditional art works and antiquities, many in the Taiwanese middle class zealously collected them via Hong Kong. Before martial law was lifted in Taiwan, trading ancient jade was mainly dominated by traders from Hong Kong and Macao; however, after 1987, many Taiwanese traders went directly to China to buy antiques and build their own social networks. There are various sources that fed the needs of Taiwan and Hong Kong in China: existing commodities, counterfeits, and illicit tomb objects.

Therefore, unlike the diamond (Westwood 2000) and jade stone market (Chang 2006; 2011), which might be dominated by one or a few companies, the ancient jade market is very dispersive in terms of production (source) and consumption. Besides, ancient jade traders/dealers or antique shops are considered small-scale businesses, so that there is no organization or formal regulation that can govern the market. Furthermore, since illicit ancient jade are secretly transported, neither traders nor consumers want to be regulated by law. It is trust and personal relationships underpinning jade trading. Above all, the *guanxi* network is the most influential.

From the aspect of the consumer/collector, buying ancient jade ware is high-risk consumption. The degree of risk is directly related to the quality of the goods and information asymmetry between the buyer and the seller. Fortunate collectors meet honest antique dealers and friends who introduce them to buy genuine ancient jade. Unsuccessful collectors accumulate less important jade or replicas. Each collector tries their luck to access a good antique dealer in accordance with their economic and social capital.

In sum, this chapter has shown the paradox of *guanxi* in trading ancient jade. The ancient jade market is a high-trust and a high-risk market. In order to reduce risk, *guanxi* facilitates each transaction, but *guanxi* may also lead to an adverse ending. There are some other research that suggests that by sharing social ties, it reduces the risk of poor purchases of goods and services (Williamson 1983; Yamagishi and Yamagishi 1994; DiMaggio and Louch 1998). However, the same norm cannot be applied to the antique jade market. Even with personal connections and relationships, it still does not guarantee honest transactions. The antique market lacks the mechanism of sanctions and/or legal punishments. Unlike the diamond market, which is regulated by family ethic, or the financial market, which is governed by state law, the antique market is a small and dispersive trading field where sellers and buyers are friends, and each transaction is made by free choice. Collectors/consumers take the initiative to make a purchase, so they have to take responsibility for their decision. Once they know that they have made a wrong purchase, they always regard that as a lesson. The only thing collectors/consumers can do is to stop visiting the dealer again in private, but the public still wouldn't know all the facts. There are always newcomers in the *guanxi* network and the market, so the trade will always continue to move forward.

Notes

1 Funding for this research derives from Taiwan's National Science Council (NSC 98–2412-H-035–029, 99–2412-H-155–055). The author is grateful to those interviewees who contributed valuable information on jade market and knowledge on appreciation of ancient jade.

2 There are many reports on websites revealing the inside story of tomb digging and its production chain. I list two for reference: Zhu Wenyi, "The Secret of Digging Tomb—Smuggling Cultural Relics and Curses of Ancient Tomb." Accessed November 25, 2014. http://history.people.com.cn/n/2012/0824/c200623–18826439–1.html,

and "The Industrial Chain of Pillaging Tomb." Accessed November 28, 2014. www. licai.com/yuedu/201409/61426.html.
3 Wu Shu, a Chinese journalist who spent seven years investigating Chinese antique market. He published three related books on antique collection and the market, which includes detail reports on illicit antiques. Most of his reports can be found in his blog, http://mengmiancike.blog.sohu.com/.

References

Baudrillard, Jean. 1996. *The System of Objects*, translated by James Benedict. New York: Verso.

Beckert, Jens. 2009. "The Social Order of Markets." *Theory and Society* 38: 245–269.

Bian, Yanjie. 2006. "*Guanxi.*" In *International Encyclopedia of Economic Sociology*, edited by J. Beckert and M. Zafirovski, 312–314. London: Routledge.

Bian, Yanjie, and Lei Zhang. 2014. "Corporate Social Capital in Chinese *Guanxi* Culture." *Research in the Sociology of Organizations* 40: 421–443.

Bourdieu, Pierre. 1984. *Distinction: A Social Critique of the Judgment of Taste*. London: Routledge and Kegan Paul.

Chang Wen-Chin. 2004. "*Guanxi* and Regulation in Network: The Yunnanese Jade Trade between Burma and Thailand, 1962–1988." *Journal of Southeast Asian Studies* 35 (3): 479–501.

Chang Wen-Chin. 2006. "The Trading Culture of Jade Stones among the Yunnanese in Burma and Thailand, 1962–1988." *Journal of Chinese Overseas* 2 (2): 269–293.

Chang Wen-Chin. 2011. "From a Shiji Episode to the Forbidden Jade Trade during the Socialist Regime in Burma." In *Chinese Circulations: Capital, Commodities, and Networks in Southeast Asia,* edited by Eric Tagliacozzo and Wen-Chin Chang, 455–479. Durham: Duke University Press.

DiMaggio, Paul, and Hugh Louch. 1998. "Socially Embedded Consumer Transactions: For What Kinds of Purchases Do People Most Often Use Networks?" *American Sociological Review* 63 (5): 619–637.

Fan, Y. 2002. "Questioning Guanxi: Definition, Classification and Implications." *International Business Review* 11 (5): 543–561.

Fligstein, Neil. 1996. "Markets as Politics: A Political-cultural Approach to Market Institutions." *American Sociological Review* 61: 656–673.

Fligstein, Neil, and Luke Dauter. 2007. "The Sociology of Markets." *Annual Review of Sociology* 33: 105–128.

Geertz, Clifford. 1978. "The Bazaar Economy: Information and Search in Peasant Marketing." *The American Economic Review* 68 (2): 28–32.

Gold, Thomas, Doug Guthrie, and David Wank. 2002. *Social Connections in China: Institutions, Culture, and the Changing Nature of Guanxi*. Cambridge, UK; New York: Cambridge University Press.

Granovetter, M. 1985. "Economic Action and Social Structure: The Problem of Embeddedness." *American Journal of Sociology* 91: 481–510.

Kipnis, Andrew B. 1997. *Producing Guanxi: Sentiment, Self, and Subculture in a North China Village*. Durham: Duke University Press.

Morgan, Glenn. 2008. "Market Formation and Governance in International Financial Markets: The Case of OTC Derivatives." *Human Relations* 61 (5): 637–660.

Passas, Nikos, and Blythe Bowman Proulx. 2011. "Overview of Crimes and Antiquities." In *Crime in the Art and Antiquities World: Illegal Trafficking in Cultural Property*, edited by S. Manacorda and D. Chappell, 51–67. New York, NY: Springer Science+Business Media, LLC.

Spar, Debora L. 2006. "Continuity and Change in the International Diamond Market." *Journal of Economic Perspectives* 20 (3): 195–208.

Swedberg, R. 2003. *Principles of Economic Sociology*. New Jersey: Princeton University Press.

Velthuis, Olav. 2003. "Symbolic Meanings of Prices: Constructing the Value of Contemporary Art in Amsterdam and New York Galleries." *Theory and Society* 32: 181–215.

Westwood, Sallie 2000. "A Real Romance': Gender, Ethnicity, Trust and Risk in the Indian Diamond Trade." *Ethnic and Racial Studies* 23 (5): 857–870.

Williamson, Oliver E. 1983. "Credible Commitments: Using Hostages to Support Exchange." *The American Economic Review* 73 (4): 519–540.

Yamagishi, Toshio, and Midori Yamagishi. 1994. "Trust and Commitment in the United States and Japan." *Motivation and Emotion* 18: 129–166.

Yan, Yunxiang. 1996. *The Flow of Gifts: Reciprocity and Social Networks in a Chinese Village*. Stanford, CA: Stanford University Press.

Yang, Mayfair Mei-hui. 1994. *Gifts, Favors, and Banquets: The Art of Social Relationships in China*. Ithaca, NY: Cornell University Press.

Zukin, S., and P. DiMaggio. 1990. *Structure of Capital: The Social Organization of the Economy*. Cambridge: Cambridge University Press.

11 Transnational entrepreneurship and social capital

Rebuilding a Taiwanese temple to Mazu in Kunshan, China

Shiuh-shen Chien and Chiu-wan Liu

Introduction

The development of postsocialist China has been partly facilitated by overseas investment (Pan 2003), including investment from Taiwanese firms. Despite long-term political hostility across the Taiwan Strait, the two sides have undergone a significant economic integration since China opened up its economy in the 1980s. Today, between two and three million Taiwanese are thought to live full-time in China, with a particular concentration in the Yangtze River Delta (Wang and Lee 2007; Yang and Hsia 2007; Wei et al. 2009).

The existing literature on Taiwanese entrepreneurship in China focuses on three different aspects: (1) political lobbying by the business community (Shigeto 2014), (2) changing economic structures and industrial upgrading (Deng 2014), and (3) social and cultural interactions between overseas Taiwanese and local Chinese (Shen 2014). This chapter focuses specifically on the third social and cultural dimension and asks whether Taiwanese religious traditions can be relocated to China. Migration research suggests that migrants are generally keen to establish religious spaces like temples or churches to build and reinforce their specific cultural identity and spiritual well-being (Chou 1991; Min 2002; Vertovec 2008). However, in China, the government officially promotes atheism and tightly controls religious expression (Yang 2004; Abramson 2011), suggesting it would be difficult, if not impossible, for newcomers to establish temples or religious centers in China.

We examine a case in which Taiwanese investors, local officials in Kunshan (a city in Jiangsu province), and officials in Beijing cooperated in the establishment of a temple dedicated to Mazu, the Chinese goddess of the sea who is particularly revered in Taiwan and along the southeastern China coast, but not in Jiangsu (Yeh et al. 2009). Specifically, the Kunshan Mazu Temple was allowed to be built and operated in the relatively authentic Taiwanese style, using Taiwanese temple architectural elements and incorporating incense and percussion instruments in religious rituals. This signals a departure from previous practice in China and deserves to be better understood.

We argue the development of the Mazu temple in Kunshan should be regarded as a form of interaction between Taiwanese transnational entrepreneurs leveraging their social networks to establish and reinforce their cultural identity and local officials competing against each other for political promotion. Over the past few decades, many Taiwanese entrepreneurs have arrived in Kunshan to establish factories or other businesses. While some commute regularly between Kunshan and Taiwan, others have opted to stay in Kunshan as long-term residents. As part of their acculturation in China, these migrants have sought to establish cultural institutions that reflect their Taiwanese origins, including authentic Taiwanese temples. Local officials in Kunshan are under pressure to attract external investment and boost their local economic output (Li and Zhou 2005; Chien and Gordon 2008; Chien 2010) and also seek to establish the region as a pioneer in forging close ties between China and Taiwan and were thus willing to entertain such ideas. Since 2003, the authors have observed the development and transformation of Kunshan first hand, conducting hundreds of interviews with Taiwanese and local actors. The arguments presented in this chapter are based on these first-hand interviews, along with official documents, annual reports, and news reports.

The rest of the chapter is divided into four main sections. The first section reviews the history of Mazu worship in Taiwan and China. The following section describes the development of Kunshan in the context of Taiwanese investment in postsocialist China. The third section describes the process of establishing the Kunshan Mazu Temple, the measures taken to allow for official approval of the project, and the actual construction including the incorporation of Taiwanese style with local Chinese features. The final section discusses how Taiwanese investment in China drove the construction process.

Globalization of Mazu and China

Mazu: from China to Taiwan and overseas

Chinese migrants have dispersed around the world over the past few centuries, and the worship of Mazu has followed them as they sought to preserve their cultural identity. Legend has it that Lin Moniang, the original name of Mazu, was born in a Fujian fishing village in the tenth century (around the Song Dynasty). She is credited with rescuing members of her family from being drowned in a typhoon and has since been widely worshipped as the patron saint of fishermen and sailors, in particular, and of Chinese living overseas. Mazu's popularity increased through the establishment of ties to Buddhism and Taoism through the propagation of a legend that Mazu was the daughter or a direct manifestation of Guanyin, a key figure in Buddhism and Taoism.

As more Chinese migrated through the Asian Pacific region, worship of Mazu spread from Fujian to locations around the world through the process a process known as *bunrei* or *wakemitama* (*fenling*, 分靈 in Chinese) by which relics and icons from existing temples can be re-enshrined elsewhere to consecrate a new temple. Today, Mazu temples are found in Taiwan, Hong Kong, Malaysia, Singapore, Australia, the United States, and throughout China's coastal provinces and cities including Guangdong, Tianjin, and Qingdao (Yeh et al. 2009). Taiwan is largely populated by the descendants of migrants who came from Fujian and neighboring provinces of China over four hundred years ago. These migrants established Mazu temples in Taiwan partly to express appreciation for their safe journey across the Taiwan Strait and to ensure the continuity of their cultural identification with China. These new temples were consecrated using new Mazu statues taken from existing temples in China, and these statues were regularly returned to their original temple as part of the *bunrei* pilgrimage process (*yezu-jinxiang*, 謁祖進香) (Yeh et al. 2009). However, these exchanges were stopped by Cold War restrictions on travel between Taiwan and China.

Today, Taiwan has hundreds of Mazu temples, and it is estimated that 75 percent of Taiwanese express at least a degree of faith in Mazu's divinity (Yeh et al. 2009), making Mazu the most widely worshipped goddess in Taiwan. This has translated into significant political influence for Mazu temples (Katz 2003), and certain Mazu temples are regular campaign stops for politicians seeking support and votes from devotees.

In addition, Mazu has also played a role in cross-Strait politics. In September 1987, the Meizhou Mazu Temple, arguably the world's oldest Mazu temple, invited pilgrims from Mazu temples from all over the world to visit to mark the 1,000-year anniversary of the goddesses' death. Leaders of the Dajia Mazu Temple in Taiwan took advantage of recent political opening in Taiwan (martial law had only been listed two months previously) to organize a pilgrimage group traveling to China via Japan without any ex-ante official permission, marking the first such pilgrimage to China since 1949 (Katz 2003). This set a significant precedent for cross-Strait interaction and Taiwan dropped the ban on cross-Strait ties a few years later.

Taiwan and China since 1978

Before 1978, China kept itself isolated from the rest of the world, forbidding most overseas trade and inward investment. These restrictions were only gradually lifted after the death of Mao. Established infrastructure and institutions for transferring capital and knowledge from outside the country accelerated the industrialization of postsocialist China (Huang 2001), and initial investment was dominated by overseas Chinese from Hong Kong and Taiwan who played a key role in developing China's export-oriented industrialization.

Taiwanese investment in China occurred in at least three distinct waves (Wang 2014). In the mid-1980s, Taiwanese investments were mainly focused in labor-intensive manufacturing (especially shoes and clothing) in Fujian and Guangdong, the first two provinces opened to foreign direct investment (FDI). In 1992, Deng Xiaoping famously toured southern China to promote further economic liberalization. Subsequently, more Taiwanese high-tech-based information and technology (IT) and computer firms moved to China, mainly in the Yangtze River Delta area. These efforts were spearheaded by high-level Taiwanese managers along with mid-level engineers and their families (Hsu 2006). With China's accession to the WTO in the mid-2000s, Taiwanese investment expanded into China's interior and to the service industries (Deng 2014), attracting younger Taiwanese professionals specializing in service industries like wholesale, finance and insurance, advertising, marketing, law, education, architecture, and so on. While many of these young Taiwanese work for local or foreign firms, many have also established their own companies (Tseng 2014).

This transformation of Taiwanese forms of investment was accompanied by certain social changes. First, Taiwanese in China tended to adopt one of two lifestyles. One group was characterized as isolated expatriates. These Taiwanese tended to live in factory dormitories with limited access to local society in China. These people come to China to work only, leaving their families behind in Taiwan, with the understanding that they "live" in Taiwan. This arrangement was facilitated by the establishment of regular direct flights across the Taiwan Strait.[1]

Another type of Taiwanese settled in China to manage their business affairs, and many married local Chinese and raised families in China. Beginning in the 1990s, Taiwan's economy stagnated, in marked contrast with the rapid expansion of market opportunities in China, incentivizing more Taiwanese to relocate permanently or semi-permanently to China. In the context of Kunshan, the expansion of the local community of long-term Taiwanese residents was a key motivation to begin construction of the Mazu temple.

Another key issue is the distinct cultural identity of the Taiwanese in China. In terms of political identity, some still regard themselves exclusively as Taiwanese, but others increasingly identify themselves as Chinese. Some hold dual citizenship and thus are able to access government insurance schemes in China without having to relinquish Taiwanese citizenship (Tseng and Wu 2011). Despite having distinct political identities, Taiwanese in China still maintain a strong cultural connections with Taiwan by reading Taiwanese newspapers, watching Taiwanese television shows, eating Taiwanese food, singing Taiwanese songs, shopping for Taiwanese products (Deng 2009), and even building Taiwanese temples. Maintaining these cultural ties to Taiwan allows Taiwanese people to avoid social and cultural alienation in China.

Understanding China as host country for migrants in search of a cultural identity

Long-term migrants frequently seek various means to establish and maintain a distinct cultural identity in their host countries. Many migrants do this by establishing religious spaces like temples and churches (Leonard 2006; Stepick 2006). The architectural designs and interior decorations of these spaces provide direct visual representations and embodied experiences that are reminiscent of the migrants' home country (Min 2002). The rituals conducted within these building also contribute heavily to the construction and maintenance of cultural identities (Stepick 2006). Religious activities organized in churches and temples enable migrants to present a specific lifestyle, which facilitates the establishment of mutual understanding between local communities and overseas migrants (Vertovec 2008). These religious spaces also act both as platforms for the development of social capital, allowing newcomers to find jobs and accommodation, and as bridges to connect newcomers with established social networks (Guest 2006).

While previous studies have highlighted the importance of religious spaces for migrants, the impact of local politics on the process by which migrants establish and maintain their cultural identity has received less attention. In addition, most previous studies of migrants focused on advanced liberalized countries, and few have thought to examine issues related to migrants in China, where religious practices are tightly controlled and atheism is officially encouraged (Yang 2004). We argue that the process by which migrants build new temples in China requires a certain degree of trust based on social capital established between the migrants on the one hand and local and central officials of both the host and home countries.

Second, local officials are not elected locally but are assigned to their posts by upper-level administrators. Therefore, theoretically, local officials have incentives to make an effort to address the needs assigned from the top as doing so has direct bearing on their career prospects. China regards Taiwan as a "renegade province," and prior to 2008, interaction between the two sides was highly restricted (more details below). This provided local officials with an incentive to promote cross-Strait rapprochement through local initiatives (Tung 2003). The following discussion of the establishment of the Kunshan Mazu Temple is presented in light of two propositions.

Postsocialist Kunshan – "Little Taiwan"

According to official statistics, about one-third of Taiwanese investments in China have been allocated in Jiangsu, while roughly 50 percent has been placed in the Yangtze River Delta. These investments have been crucial to the transformation of many Jiangsu cities from rural backwaters to key nodes in globalized high-tech industries. Kunshan is an excellent example, emerging over three decades from agricultural backwardness to an economically strong and diverse county-level city in the mid-2000s.

Previous studies have noted that the transformation of Kunshan is primarily attributed to three factors: (1) geographical proximity to Shanghai, (2) highly entrepreneurial local leaders, and (3) Taiwanese investment (Wei 2002; Chien 2007; Chien and Zhao 2008). Kunshan's geographical proximity to Shanghai serves to attract investors who need to be near Shanghai but lack sufficient capital to afford the high land prices there. Kunshan leaders are also well known for their willingness to try new methods and approaches, seeking ex-post endorsement from above, rather than prior approval. The economic development resulting from these initiatives help local leaders in terms of their annual performance reviews, upon which their future career development is based, and Kunshan leaders have been regularly promoted to higher positions.

Taiwanese investment contributes to Kunshan in three ways. Taiwanese investors have played a key role in boosting local GDP and fiscal revenue, and Taiwanese involvement in the local economy is summed up in a local catchphrase "5, 6, 7, 8, 9," which indicates that, in Kunshan, Taiwanese companies account for 50 percent of fiscal revenue, 60 percent of tax revenue, 70 percent of business sales, 80 percent of investment, and 90 percent of trade.

In addition, Taiwanese service industry entrepreneurs in Kunshan have established services including Taiwanese cable television, karaoke, restaurants, and boutiques, along with K-12 schools taught using Taiwan-published textbooks. These developments have resulted in Kunshan taking on the nickname "Little Taiwan," and this welcoming social atmosphere is a key factor in the city's enduring and expanding appeal to additional incoming Taiwanese entrepreneurs and professionals.

Even more importantly, the Taiwanese introduced many innovative ideas that helped Kunshan leaders continuously upgrade local institutional infrastructure. The Taiwanese Businesspersons Association in Kunshan (TBA Kunshan), the first county-level Taiwanese business association recognized by the National Council due to its nationwide importance for Taiwanese investment in China, played a key role in lobbying local officials to address specific business challenges. The TBA Kunshan office is located adjacent to the Taiwan Affairs Office of Kunshan City Government in Kunshan City Hall, giving an indication of the organization's institutional clout. In the early 2000s, TBA Kunshan officials were invited to attend the Chinese People's Political Consultative Conference of Kunshan (Chien and Zhao 2008), a rare honor.

In the early 1990s, TBA Kunshan promoted the adoption of a land leasing system and successfully pushed Kunshan to become the first county in China to implement policies that separated land use rights from land ownership. Starting in the late 1990s, the organization encouraged the development of an export processing zone (EPZ), enabling Kunshan to set many national precedents for EPZ policy-making and management and producing an EPZ operational handbook at the request of the General Customs Bureau of China. In the 2000s, Kunshan became the first county-level administration to establish an intellectual property rights (IPR) court, and Kunshan today enjoys a superior reputation for aggressive protection of IPR.[2] This interaction between Taiwanese investors and local officials, and the resulting policy initiatives, are widely seen as having played a crucial role in Kunshan's rapid and stable development, and this contribution has been recognized in various ways, such as the naming of two roads in Kunshan after localities in Taiwan, such as Xinzhu Road and Nanzi Road.

However, as an increasing number of Taiwanese entrepreneurs and workers relocated to Kunshan, they faced increasing needs to maintain a distinct cultural identity, and suggestions surfaced to build a Taiwanese-style temple in the city. The construction of the Kunshan Mazu Temple was proposed by President Lin Rong-de (林榮德) of Champion Tile Co Ltd. first and then President Tsai Qi-rui (蔡其瑞) of the Pou Chen Group. Tsai had first launched his business in Lukang (鹿港), Taiwan, in the 1950s and then relocated to Kunshan in the 1990s. Tsai was brought up near the Lukang Mazu Temple and donated US$2 million to repair the temple when it suffered severe earthquake damage. After years of living in Kunshan, Tsai proposed to *bunrei* an icon from the Lukang Mazu Temple to Kunshan and personally donated US$2 million to initiate the construction of a Mazu temple in Kunshan.

Bunrei Mazu from Taiwan back to China

Prior to the proposal to construct the temple, Kunshan locals were not very famil-iar with Mazu culture. But the project of Kunshan Mazu Temple was surprisingly approved to be built under the name of Huiju (慧聚). To date, the Kunshan Mazu Temple is the only large-scale Mazu temple in China with a Mazu statue that was *bunrei*-ed directly from Taiwan as the principle icon.[3] As of this writing in 2014, the main hall areas of Kunshan Mazu Temple had been completed.

Authentic Taiwanese styles

After receiving official approval to initiate construction, the temple faced some local obstacles, partly due to the sensitivity of religious issues in China and partly because local officials were unsure of how to go about approving building codes and reviewing design papers. To simplify the process, local officials suggested inviting local architects and artisans (the so-called *xiangshan* group 香山幫)[4] to build the Kunshan Mazu Temple and to *bunrei* a Mazu statue from Meizhou in Fujian Province, rather than from Taiwan.

Adopting these two suggestions would have critically compromised the Taiwan-ese authenticity of the Kunshan Mazu Temple. A temple built by local architects and artisans would have been built in the Suzhou or Yangtze River Delta vernacular, which is quite different from Taiwanese temple styles. In addition, though Mazu originally came from Meizhou, Taiwanese in Kunshan associated their attachment to Mazu with their ties to Taiwan. As described below, negotiations resolved these differences and finally the Kunshan Mazu Temple was built in a Taiwanese style and with a Mazu statue *bunrei*-ed from the Lukang Mazu Temple in 2010.

In terms of architectural designs, the engravings, ornamentation, roof, and win-dows in Kunshan Mazu Temple are modelled after temples in Taiwan like the Lukang Longshan Temple, the Lukang Mazu Temple, and the Wanhua Longshan Temple with a basic layout including three main palaces, several halls, bell and drum towers, and an enclosed gallery. Instead of using modern concrete materials, the Kunshan Mazu Temple used stone or wood mainly imported from outside of Jiangsu. Skilled artisans were brought in from Fujian to build the Taiwanese-style temple. Beams (樑), columns (柱), joists (檁 or 桁), lintels (楣), and brackets (斗拱) were assem-bled with a *pak-kua* well (八卦藻井) on top of the building, along with traditional engraved walls and windows (石窗透雕) and colorful *chien nien* (剪黏) statues on the roof.[5] The temple roof is decorated with a complex arrangement of ceramic human and animal figures. Wall paintings incorporate images from Taiwan including Taipei 101, the Queen's Head rock formation at Yehliu Geopark, and the Chiang Kai-shek Memorial Hall. Other paintings illustrate several Taiwan legends about Mazu.

Local Chinese features

The Kunshan Mazu Temple also incorporates certain aspects of local Kunshan and Suzhou history. For example, the official name of the Kunshan Mazu Temple is Kunshan Huiju Tianhou Temple. *Tianhou* is the Chinese goddess of Heaven, but the inclusion of the term *Huiju* is an innovation to cope with the political constraints imposed by the CCP's religious controls that make it very difficult for the construction of a new temple to be approved. *Huiju* is the original name of a Kunshan temple dating from the sixth century (around the Nan Dynasty), which was damaged in World War II, but then completely demolished during the Cultural Revolution in the 1970s.

By adopting the name *Huiju*, the Kunshan Mazu Temple project has been positioned as a restoration of the old Huiju Temple. Under current laws, restoring an existing temple is much more straightforward to arrange than to build a new temple. However, this is a fairly thin ruse as the site of the original Huiju Temple is far removed from the location of the new Kunshan Mazu Temple in the Kunshan export processing zone (EPZ).

The Kunshan Mazu Temple is much larger than any Mazu temple in Taiwan and is on a scale more akin to temples found in China. The original proposal was to build a temple the same size as the Lukang Mazu Temple. But this proposal was rejected by local officials as too small. The current complex, now called the Kunshan Mazu Temple Park covers an area four times larger than the original plan, featuring large-scale statuary. In addition to the main temple area, the complex includes a service center, a library, traditional Taiwanese-style commercial and dining streets, and an underground car park, making it the world's largest Mazu temple.

The extended size of the complex allows for the integration of Taiwanese and local Chinese cultural traditions. For example, the northeast corner of the complex features a pagoda, which is typical of temple complexes in the Yangtze River Delta but is rarely seen in Taiwan. The pagoda is named for the Huiju Temple, which was originally built in a pagoda style, thus reinforcing the fiction that the new temple is the rebuilt Huiju Temple.

The veranda of the new pagoda is furnished with plaques commemorating the old Huiju Temple and providing visitors with important information on that historic structure. The complex's gardens feature Suzhou-style bridges and paths lined with ornamental stones taken from Tai Lake to illustrate the harmony of Taiwan and Suzhou architectures. In addition, the walls and windows of the temple feature engravings depicting Chinese legends and myths, poetry of renowned Chinese poets He-jing Lin (林和靖), Dun-yi Chou (周敦頤), and Yuan-ming Tao (陶淵明).

Cross-strait social networking

The political sensitivity of religious and cross-Strait issues made the construction of a new temple a particular challenge, especially one adopting a vernacular style clearly identified with Taiwan. Interviews with key participants revealed that Kunshan officials and members of the TBA Kunshan had established mutual trust on a basis of their past interaction. For example, three former mayors and party secretaries of Kunshan – Cao Xin-ping (曹新平), Zhang Guo-hua (張國華) and Guan Ai-guo (管愛國) – frequently interacted with TBA Kunshan members in their official capacities and had all visited Taiwan. During their Taiwan trips, Cao, Zhang, and Guan paid a visit to the Lukang Mazu Temple at the request of Lin and Tsai to understand the spiritual importance of Mazu to Taiwanese people and to assess the economic potential of the Mazu temple as a cultural and tourism attraction. The relationships established during these meetings and visits laid a solid foundation for the Kunshan Mazu project.

Also, some TBA Kunshan members and Kunshan officials leveraged their social connections to elevate the construction of the temple from a purely local matter to the provincial and national level, seeking to mobilize the support of higher-level officials. The temple building process included certain important religious rituals, such as the erection of the building's central beam (*shanliang*, 上樑), the installation of religious icons (*anzuo,* 安座), the pilgrimage of Mazu, and so on, each of which was attended by key political figures from both China and Taiwan.

In Taiwan, the Kuomintang (KMT) Party is widely seen as more favorable to closer ties between Taiwan and China and thus commands widespread support from the Taiwanese expatriate community in China (Wu 2005; Keng and Schubert 2010), including key members of the TBA Kunshan. For example, Lin of Champion Tile has served on the KMT Central Standing Committee since 2010. Over the years, key KMT figures have regularly visited Kunshan, including Lian Zhan (連戰), former vice president of Taiwan (1996–2000) and honorary KMT chairman (since 2005); Lin Feng-zheng (林豐正), former minister of domestic affairs (1996–1998), former minister of communication and transportation (1999–2000), and former secretary general of KMT (2000–2005); and Jiang Bing-kun (江丙坤), former director of the Council for Economic Planning and Development (1996–2000), vice speaker of Legislative Yuan (2002–2005), and president of the Straits Exchange Foundation of Taiwan (SEF 2008–2012).

TBA Kunshan officials arranged for Jiang Bing-kun to attend the *bunrei* ceremony in Lukang in 2010 in his capacity as president of the SEF, while Zhan Chun-bo (詹春柏) attended the erection of the central beam of the new temple in 2011 in his capacity as KMT vice president. Lin Zhong-sen (林中森), president of the SEF since 2012, has also visited the Kunshan Mazu Temple three times since being appointed president of the SEF. In 2014, Hong Xiu-chu (洪秀柱), Vice Speaker of the Legislative Yuan since 2012 led the delegation to escort the Mazu icon back to Taiwan from Kunshan (*hui luanhujia*, 回鑾護駕).

Kunshan officials and TBA Kunshan leaders also successfully mobilized certain important figures in the central government in Beijing. For example, Chen Yun-lin (陳雲林), then director of Association for Relations Across the Taiwan Straits (ARATS, 海協會) accepted an invitation to attend the central beam erection in 2010. Though he was unable to attend the ceremony due to illness, he sent his vice director on his behalf. Zhang Zhi-jun (張志軍), the director of the Taiwan Office of the National Council of China (since 2013), donated Mazu-themed lacquerware to the Kunshan Mazu Temple on the behalf of the central government in Beijing.[6] Zhang had planned to join the delegation to escort the Mazu icon back to the Lukang Mazu Temple in 2014 but sent a deputy in his stead when Taiwanese protesters blocked him from entering the temple (see Table 11.1).

Table 11.1 Featured religious activities held by the Kunshan Mazu Temple in 2010–2014

Date	Religious Activities	VIPs in Attendance
September 15, 2010	Bunrei Ceremony in Lugang Mazu Temple	Jiang Ping-kun (江丙坤), former president of Straits Exchange Foundation of Taiwan (SEF) (2008–2012); Zhuo Bo-yuan (卓伯源), Zhanghua County commissioner (2005–2014); Tsai Qi-jian (蔡其建), Tsai Qi-rui (蔡其瑞), Pou Chen Group; Sun De-cong (孫德聰), chairman of Taiwanese Businesspersons Associations in Kunshan (2009–2011)
September 19, 2010	Installation of icons (*anzuo*, 安座)	Jiang Ping-kun (江丙坤); Li Ya-fei (李亞飛), deputy president of the Association for Relations Across the Taiwan Straits (ARATS) (2009–)
August 7, 2011	Erection of the central beam (*shangliang*, 上樑) for the main hall (*tianwandian*, 天王殿)	Zhan Chun-bo (詹春柏), KMT deputy chairman (2007–2014); Chen Yun-lin (陳雲林), then director of ARATS (1996–2013) (cancelled due to illness)
September 17, 2013	Lantern lighting (*diandeng*, 點燈) for the 2013 Cross-Strait Mid-Autumn Festival	Lin Zhong-sen (林中森), president of SEFT (2012–); Chen De-ming (陳德銘), president of ARATS (2013–)
June 26, 2014	Return of the Mazu icon to the Lugang Mazu Temple	Zhang Zhi-jun (張志軍), director of Taiwan Office of the National Council of China (2013–) (Cancelled due to unexpected protectors blocking the way he entered the temple)
June 28, 2014	Mazu's royal return to Kunshan	Hong Xiu-zhu (洪秀柱), vice speaker of the Legislative Yuan (2012–); Guan Ai-guo (管愛國), secretary of the Kunshan City Party Committee (2011–2014)

Upgrading Kunshan's cultural significance through the authentic *bunrei* from Taiwan

The construction of the Kunshan Mazu Temple echoes the case of a new church built in the Shanghai Zhangjiang High-Tech Park by a Taiwanese entrepreneur (Richard Chang, 張汝京) who helped to establish the region's first high-level semi-conductor factory (Tong 2012). In this section, we further discuss Taiwanese migrants and Kunshan officials in building the Kunshan Mazu Temple.

Reproduction of Mazu life in Kunshan

In addition to the actual temple complex (hardware), the Kunshan Mazu Temple is a cultural and social artifact (software). Unlike in China, where different religious traditions maintain distinct temples, in Taiwan, Mazu temples usually accommodate the gods and deities of Confucianism, Taoism, and Buddhism. Thus, the Kunshan Mazu Temple had to apply for a special permit to combine iconography of these three traditions, including the Laughing Buddha and Avalokiteśvara from Buddhism and Mazu from Taoism. Collectively, these icons provide blessings for the departed, peace, pregnancy, marriage, and academic success. Also, the Kunshan Cross-Strait Mazu Cultural Exchange Association (hereafter, the Kunshan Mazu Association) was established to manage the temple's daily operations, led by a retired vice mayor of Kunshan with four vice directors, including the chief of the Kunshan Bureau of Religious Affairs and the director of the TBA Kunshan. The inclusion of outsiders in temple management committees in China is very rare and can be seen as further evidence of unusual privileges extended to Taiwanese migrants in Kunshan.

Prior to the construction of the Kunshan Mazu Temple, Taiwanese Mazu devotees in Kunshan could only pay their respects when they returned to Taiwan. Today, the new temple not only allows worshippers to pray in their adopted home but also provides replicas of important Mazu icons, which devotees then *bunrei* to shrines in their homes and factories in Kunshan for daily worship.

In addition, the Kunshan Mazu Association was commissioned to organize religious services on the first and fifteenth of each month of the lunar calendar along with the two most important festivals associated with Mazu commemorating the day of her birth (23rd day of the 3rd month in the lunar calendar) and the day of her ascension to heaven (9th day of the 9th month in the lunar calendar). Many Taiwanese migrants in the Kunshan area are actively involved in these ceremonies, including ritual offerings, music, and dance, and hundreds of children participated in Taiwanese coming of age rituals (*cheng nian li* 成年禮), thus establishing the Kunshan Mazu Temple as a cultural and spiritual epicenter of the Taiwanese community in Kunshan.

Upgrading Kunshan in the cross-strait Mazu economy

The construction of the Kunshan Mazu Temple was significant, not only in helping transnational entrepreneurs establish their cultural identity, but also in playing a role in the means by which local Chinese officials competing amongst themselves for professional recognition and promotion. In postsocialist China, local governments are encouraged to behave entrepreneurially in mobilizing resources to fulfill policy directives and quotas. Local officials are incentivized to introduce new projects, negotiate with investors, and strategically allocate resources. These efforts are frequently reported in the mass media and in academic reports.

Over the past decade, land and labor costs in China's coastal regions have increased steadily, encouraging businesses to expand into China's interior regions, a trend that is officially encouraged by government incentives. The support from Kunshan leaders for the construction of the Kunshan Mazu Temple can be placed in this context, as officials sought to encourage Taiwanese entrepreneurs to sink local roots that would dissuade them from moving their businesses and families from the area. Thus Kunshan leaders cleverly used the symbolic resonance of Mazu for Taiwanese migrants to improve and maintain their economic performance. This provided Kunshan leaders with the incentive to wholeheartedly support the construction of a large-scale temple, built in a relatively authentic Taiwanese style and dedicated specifically to a deity that resonated strongly with a migrant group rather than with the local population. As a result, Kunshan is expected to become a key pilgrimage site for Mazu devotees around the world, creating further economic opportunities from cultural and tourism industries, allowing Kunshan to diversify its economy away from exclusively manufacturing.

Janus-faced Chinese local state

However, the successful construction of the Kunshan Mazu Temple should not be taken as an indication that local authorities are losing their authoritarian habits. Without open and institutionalized checks and balances, the social capital and trust established through personal interactions between Taiwanese entrepreneurs and local officials remains vulnerable to disruption by the higher political concerns of local leaders. Facing a severe shortage of land for conversion to industrial or residential use, local leaders in Kunshan have tightened standards for new development projects, forcing incumbent labor-intensive and relatively low value-added operations to relocate and make way for carefully selected and strategically important investment projects (Chien and Wu 2011). For example, local officials refused to extend favorable tax incentives for Compaq Electrics, the leading notebook computer producer at the time, compelling the company to abandon its facilities in Kunshan.[7]

The flip side of this authoritarian selection and management of inward investment is that local officials have greater latitude in improving the institutional environment for favored investors. We argue that the construction of the Kunshan Mazu Temple needs to be understood in the context of this "carrot and stick" approach to local governance.

Conclusion

Since 1978, China's economic development has attracted many Taiwanese entrepreneurs, many of whom reside full-time in China and thus actively seek ways to establish and maintain their distinct cultural identity. This chapter examines how and under what circumstances the construction and consecration of a relatively authentic Taiwanese Mazu temple in Kunshan took place, an undertaking that entailed overcoming considerable political and social obstacles. The completion of the temple, however, has allowed Kunshan to emerge as an important cultural center for the Taiwanese population in China.

Taiwanese entrepreneurs and local Kunshan leaders leveraged their social networks to elevate the political significance of the temple's construction to the provincial and national level, involving significant political figures from Taiwan and China in supporting the project through to completion. In the process, local leaders not only earned political recognition for their efforts, but also successfully diversified the local economy from manufacturing into culture and tourism.

Certain theoretical and policy implications can be drawn from the process of building the Kunshan Mazu Temple. This is the first example of a large-scale Mazu temple in China consecrated through *burnei* from Taiwan to China, and it will be interesting to see whether the temple emerges as a center of political and cultural activism for Taiwanese expatriates to influence trends and events back in Taiwan. Such a development could have implications from similar activism on the part of US-based migrants from Fujian mobilizing their religious community to engage in social projects in their hometowns in China. This chapter also contributes to a better understanding of the impact of local politics and entrepreneur migrants on the development and maintenance of migrant cultural identities. However, as China continues to open up to the world as both an important manufacturing center and market for global exports, further research is needed on how officially atheist China can accommodate more diverse and dynamic cultural identities brought by entrepreneurs and economic migrants from around the world.

Notes

1 Prior to 2008, travelers between Taiwan and China were required to transfer in a third country (e.g., Hong Kong or Macao) and travel between Taipei and Shanghai typically took between six and eight hours. Since 2008, direct flights between Taipei and Shanghai have reduced travel time to less than two hours.

2 Prior to this, the IPR court of first instance was located in Nanjing, the provincial capital of Jiangsu, and the IPR court of cassation was in Beijing, making it very difficult for high-tech companies to pursue IPR. Following reform, an IPR court of first instance was established in Kunshan, with an IPR court of cassation in Suzhou.

3 While other temples in China feature a Mazu icon *bunrei*-ed from Taiwan, none of these feature Mazu as the main deity.

4 The Xiangshan Group (named after a hill in Suzhou) is a school of architects and artisans who specialize in traditional Suzhou-style buildings. The Xingashan Group can be traced back Kuai Xiang (蒯祥), a key architect of Beijing's Forbidden City dating to the Ming Dynasty (fifteenth century)

5 For example, the Pak-Kua well incorporates a rich carved spider web pattern. The well also features a bats motif, (the Chinese word for bat is a homonym for "good fortune"). To protect the complex from fire, the roof features a water dragon (*Chiwan*, 螭吻) motif, along with golden dragons, a phoenix, fish, and statues of legendary generals

6 Lacquerware techniques date to the Shang Dynasty (fifteenth to ninth centuries BC). Today, lacquerware is recognized as an essential cultural heritage in China.

7 Many labor-intensive Taiwanese firms established in Kunshan in the 1980s and 1990s are still in operation today. In 2014, Zhongrong, a Taiwanese firm producing metal processing and materials, was forced to shut down after an explosion at its Kunshan factory caused hundreds of serious injuries and several deaths.

References

Abramson, Daniel Benjamin. 2011. "Places for the Gods: Urban Planning as Orthopraxy and Heteropraxy in China." *Environment and Planning D: Society and Space* 29 (1): 67–88.

Chien, Shiuh-Shen. 2007. "Institutional Innovation, Asymmetric Decentralization, and Local Economic Development-Case of post-Mao Kunshan, China." *Environment and Planning C: Government and Policy* 25 (2): 269–290.

Chien, Shiuh-Shen. 2010. "Economic Freedom and Political Control in Post-Mao China – A Perspective of Upward Accountability and Asymmetric Decentralization." *Asian Journal of Political Science* 18 (1): 69–89.

Chien, Shiuh-Shen, and Fulong Wu. 2011. "Transformation of China's Urban Entrepreneurialism: Case Study of the City of Kunshan." *Cross Current: East Asian History and Culture Review Inaugural Issue of Cross-Currents E-Journal* (No. 1). http://cross-currents.berkeley.edu/e-journal/inaugural-issue/transformation-chinas-urban-entrepreneurialism-case-study-city-kunshan

Chien, Shiuh-Shen, and Ian Gordon. 2008. "Territorial Competition in China and the West." *Regional Studies* 42 (1): 31–49.

Chien, Shiuh-Shen, and Litao Zhao. 2008. "Kunshan Model: Learning from Taiwanese Investors." *Built Environment* 34 (4): 427–443.

Chou, Shi-Deh Chang. 1991. "Religion and Chinese Life in the United States." *Etudes Migrations* 28 (103): 455–464.

Deng, Jian-Bang. 2009. "Making a Living on the Move: Transnational Lives of Taiwanese Managers in the Shanghai Area (in Chinese)." *Taiwanese Sociology* (18): 139–179.

Deng, Jian-Bang. 2014. "Marginal Mobilities: Taiwanese Manufacturing Companies' Migration to Inner China." In *Border Crossing in Greater China: Production, Community and Identity*, edited by Jenn-Hwan Wang, 133–148. New York: Routledge.

Guest, Kenneth J. 2006. "Religion and Transnational Migration in the New Chinatown." In *Immigrant Faiths: Transforming Religious Life in America*, edited by Karen I. Leonard, Alex Stepick, Manuel Vasquez, and Jennifer Holdaway, 145–163. Oxford, UK: AltaMira Press.

Hsu, Jinn-yuh. 2006. "The Dynamic Firm-Territory Nexus of Taiwanese Information Industry Investments in China." *Growth and Change* 37 (2): 230–254.

Huang, Yasheng. 2001. "Economic Fragmentation and FDI in China." Working Paper Number 374, Harvard Business School, Boston.

Katz, Paul R. 2003. "Religion and the State in Post-war Taiwan." *The China Quarterly* 174: 395–412.

Keng, Shu, and Gunter Schubert. 2010. "Agents of Unification? the Political Role of Taiwanese Businessmen in the Process of Cross-Strait Integration." *Asian Survey* 50 (2): 287–310.

Leonard, Karen. 2006. "Introduction." In *Immigrant Faiths: Transforming Religious Life in America*, edited by Karen I. Leonard, Alex Stepick, Manuel Vasquez, and Jennifer Holdaway, 1–10. London: AltaMira Press.

Li, Hong, and Li-An Zhou. 2005. "Political Turnover and Economic Performance: The Incentive Roles of Personnel Control in China." *Journal of Public Economics* 89 (9–10): 1743–1762.

Min, Pyong Gap. 2002. "Immigrants Religion and Ethnicity: A Comparison of Indian Hindu and Korean Protestant Immigrants in New York." *Social Science Research Council Fellows Conference on Immigration Religion and Civic Life*, University of Texas at Arlington.

Pan, Yigang. 2003. "The Inflow of Foreign Direct Investment to China: The Impact of Country-specific Factors." *Journal of Business Research* 56 (10): 829–833.

Shen, Hsiu-Hua. 2014. "Cross-Strait Economic Exchanges by Night: Pleasure, Work and Power in Chinese Karaoke Hostess Bars." In *Border Crossing in Greater China: Production, Community and Identity*, edited by Jenn-hwan Wang, 149–172. New York: Routledge.

Shigeto, Sonoda. 2014. "Establishing Guanxi in the Chinese Market: Comparative Analysis of Japanese, Korean and Taiwanese Expatriates in Mainland China." In *Border Crossing in Greater China: Production, Community and Identity*, edited by Jenn-hwan Wang, 77–90. New York: Routledge.

Stepick, Alex. 2006. "God is Apparently Not Dead: The Obvious, the Emergent, and the Still Unknown in Immigration and Religion." In *Immigrant Faiths: Transforming Religious Life in America*, edited by Karen Leonard, 11–38. UK: AltaMira Press.

Tong, Joy Kooi-Chin. 2012. *Overseas Chinese Christian Entrepreneurs in Modern China: A Case Study of the Influence of Christian Ethics on Business Life*. New York: Anthem Press.

Tseng, Yen-Fen. 2014. "How Do Identities Matters? Taiwanese Cultural Workers in China." In *Border Crossing in Greater China: Production, Community and Identity*, edited by Jenn-hwan Wang, 189–201. New York: Routledge.

Tseng, Yen-Fen, and Jieh-min Wu. 2011. "Reconfiguring Citizenship and Nationality: Dual Citizenship of Taiwanese Migrants in China." *Citizenship Studies* 15 (2): 265–282.

Tung, Chen-Yuan. 2003. "Cross-Strait Economic Relations: China's Leverage and Taiwan's Vulnerability." *Asian Survey* 39 (3): 137–175.

Vertovec, Steven. 2008. "Religion and Diaspora." In *New Approaches to the Study of Religion, Volume 2: Textual, Comparative, Sociological, and Cognitive Approaches*, edited by Peter Antes, Armin W. Geertz, and Randi R. Warne, 275–303. Berlin, DEU: Walter de Gruyter.

Wang, Jenn-Hwan. 2014. "Introduction: Cross-Borders in Greater China- a Multi-dimensional Perspective." In *Border Crossing in Greater China: Production, Community and Identity*, edited by Jenn-Hwan Wang, 1–14. New York: Routledge.

Wang, Jenn-Hwan, and Chuan-Kai Lee. 2007. "Global Production Networks and Local Institution Building: The Development of the Information-Technology Industry in Suzhou, China." *Environment and Planning A* 39 (8): 1873–1888.

Wei, Yehua Dennis. 2002. "Beyond the Susan Model: Trajectory and Underlying Factors of Development in Kunshan, China." *Environment and Planning A* 34: 1725–1747.

Wei, Yehua Dennis, Yuqi Lu, and Wen Chen. 2009. "Globalizing Regional Development in Sunan, China: Does Suzhou Industrial Park Fit a Neo-Marshallian District Model?" *Regional Studies* 43 (3): 409–427.

Wu, Y-S. 2005. "Taiwan's Domestic Politics and Cross-Strait Relations." *The China Journal* 53 (Jan): 35–60.

Yang, Fenggang. 2004. "Between Secularist Ideology and Desecularizing Reality: The Birth and Growth of Religious Research in Communist China." *Sociology of Religion* 65 (2): 101–119.

Yang, You-ren, and Chu-Joe Hsia. 2007. "Spatial Clustering and Organizational Dynamics of Transborder Production Networks: A Case Study of Taiwanese Information-technology Companies in the Greater Suzhou Area, China." *Environment and Planning A* 39: 1346–1363.

Yeh, Shih Shuo, Chris Ryan, and Ge Liu. 2009. "Taoism, Temples and Tourists: The Case of Mazu Pilgrimage Tourism." *Tourism Management* 30 (4): 581–588.

12 The Epoch Foundation

The creation of a social innovation network

Chao-Tung Wen and Chen-Ya Wang

Introduction

June 2010 marked the twentieth anniversary of the Epoch Foundation. The foundation held a series of commemorative events, inviting the president of the Massachusetts Institute of Technology (MIT), the dean of the MIT Sloan School of Management, and ten top scientists to Taiwan to discuss their vision for 2020, exploring global issues, the impact of science and technology, the power of social culture, and the future role of business with Taiwanese elites from various fields. These experts also gave suggestions for Taiwan's scientific, technological, and industrial development. The significance of this event and the previous night's twenty-year anniversary dinner event is a reflection of two decades of hard work: The Epoch Foundation has not only become one of the primary platforms for Taiwanese businesses to initiate exchanges with MIT, but more importantly, these networks, rather than declining over time, have grown even more robust. Thus, utilizing extensive firsthand experience, interview, and document analysis, this study explores how this nonprofit organization (NPO) began, how was it built, and how has it utilized strengths to expand and play an instrumental role bridging Taiwan to global technology and industry trends.

Research background

The year 1990 marked a period of immense global change. Beginning in 1989, the Tiananmen Incident occurred in China; the Communist Party in Eastern Europe collapsed, as did the Soviet Union; and the Cold War ended. A new world order was forming, rebuilding power structures in the process. MIT was also affected by the ending of the Cold War as research funding for high-energy physics from the US Department of Defense was reduced, and the university was forced to turn to external sources in its search for funding. Meanwhile, Taiwan's economy was taking off, as the average national income reached US$10,000, and companies such as ASUS and BenQ were founded, while the Taiwan Semiconductor Manufacturing Company (TSMC) celebrated its fourth anniversary. Taiwan's burgeoning business community recognized the inevitable trend towards globalization, foreseeing the potential for the development of Chinese-based economies outside of the world's two other great economies, the North American Free Trade Area (NAFTA) and the European Community. With hopes for Taiwan's future development in mind, business leaders sought to bring together businesses from throughout the private sector to jointly pursue development in Taiwan.

It was during this time that Mr. Paul Hsu had a chance meeting with Lester Thurow, then dean of the MIT Sloan School of Management. With similar views on global economic integration and recognition of the key role that Asian-Pacific and Chinese economies would play in global economic development, the pair launched a project that provided twenty Taiwanese companies with US$500,000 each in aid, totaling US$10 million. In December 1990 a Strategic Development Alliance was established, forming a long-term partnership with MIT via an endowment fund designated to Chair Professor Donald Lessard, who is currently still active in this relationship.

In March 1991, the alliance was renamed, marking the official establishment of the Epoch Foundation. The foundation's initial mission was to integrate businesses into the private sector; to utilize talent and funding from academic institutions, domestic and international alike; to conduct research on Taiwan's economic issues; and to promote relevant research on Chinese-based economies in order to aid Taiwan's economic development and promote global cooperation with other Chinese economies. In recent years, the foundation has sharpened its focus, concentrating on facilitating Taiwanese industrial development and promoting the economic prosperity of the Asia-Pacific region. Over the past twenty years, the Epoch Foundation has expanded its scope in three major directions: liaison services for top-notch institutes, future trends of industrial development, and innovation and entrepreneurship education.

Research questions

Although major universities in the US have extensive alumni networks, the kind of comprehensive interaction and cooperation that the Epoch Foundation has with MIT is particularly notable. This study employs a "social capital theory" research framework to attempt to answer the following questions:

1) As an organization able to accumulate social capital and mobilize social network resources, how did the Epoch Foundation grow into its current form in terms of social capital formation, building, and gain? What are the innovative characteristics of this network, and why has it been able to forge in-depth interactions and cooperation with the world's top universities and institutions?

2) What kind of value do relevant parties gain from these network relationships? What contributions do these network relationships offer to Taiwanese industry and society, such as through the conversion of social capital to economic capital?

In traditional social network research, relationship capital is relatively static and stable, regardless whether accessed chronologically or horizontally. An in-depth discussion of the formation, development, and techniques employed in the maintenance of these relationships will illustrate the development of the foundation's social network.

The theories of social capital and research approach

Reviewing the literature from more than two decades of vigorous social capital theory development, we find that there are several approaches for studying social capital, including an element approach (examining the content, categories, and levels of social capital); a consequence approach; and a process approach, in addition to theoretical expansion (cross-disciplinary research). The literature review in this section focuses on the element and process approaches.

The element approach

Research on social capital originated in terms of sociology, describing the basis for trust, cooperation, norms, and gathering in communities, which after a period of time results in the development of strong and effective networks of personal relationships (Jacobs 1979). Putnam (1995) also indicated that social capital is formed through elements such as networks, trust, and norms. Thus, the production of social capital emerges through mutual interpersonal understanding and awareness. The accumulation of feelings such as gratitude, respect, and friendship of group members towards each other influences the production of a sustained and mutual sense of duty and responsibility (Bourdieu 1986). Coleman (1988) blends elements of Loury (1987) and Granovetter (1985) in a theory that holds individual production of social capital via social interaction creates both social structures and personal resources, and thus social capital exists in networked trust relationships, offering a sense of recognition and belonging and providing benefits to both the individual and society.

In recent years, the concept of social capital has expanded to explain social phenomena such as internal and external family relations (Coleman 1988), relationships internal and external to the firm (Burt 1992), the intersection of organizations and the market, and livelihoods in modern society. The focus of applied social capital seems to be on the transfer of human capital into firm-level economic performance, regional social welfare (Cohen and Fields 1999), and even the rise and fall of nations. Studies (e.g., Tsai and Ghoshal 1998) have indicated that, similar to human and physical capital, social capital is a resource with benefits for production and a range of outcomes, including personal career achievements or commercial operations within a company.

Based on previous literature, it can be seen that the definition of social capital has been extremely divided, a situation we argue is due to both the conceptual breadth the construct covers as well as its application to various levels of analysis. For example, Bourdieu (1985) analyzes the social sphere to study relationships between and within different social classes. Coleman, on the other hand, centered attention on the individual in explorations of trust, norms, and networks in relationships and the benefits of their various forms. Fukuyama (1995) discussed the impact of trust systems on economic development by analyzing nations and ethnicities, arguing that if members of an organization have a high level of trust, the costs of management decrease. Despite different levels of analysis, a majority of scholars agree that social networks and embedded resources are core related concepts.

Nahapiet and Ghoshal (1998), adopting the organizational level of analysis, hold that social capital is the sum of actual or potential resources constructed through networks of relationships between individuals or social groups. Further, these resources, accumulated through interpersonal interactions, can be utilized within organizational networks, such that an organization can learn to share resources between departments. This process requires organizations to establish mutual linking relationships between departments based on the social context in order to facilitate the exchange and integration of resources (Tsai 2000). If this concept is extended further to include relationships between manufacturers in strategic alliances, then the interpersonal relationships amongst manufacturers within the alliance should influence its effectiveness.

Nahapiet and Ghoshal (1998) divide social capital into three categories: structural, relational, and cognitive capital. In terms of the structure of social capital, the qualities and relationships of the entire social system are viewed as a single entity, which illustrates a comprehensive framework of linkages between members of an organization. In addition, descriptions of the types of links between members, measures of interaction density, connectivity, and hierarchy are used to demonstrate the presence of network relationships or network structures. The relational facet of social capital primarily describes types of interpersonal relationships developed and accumulated during interpersonal interactions (Granovetter 1985). Emphasized here are the specific influences of various elements of interpersonal relationships, such as respect, friendship, and reciprocal behaviors. Finally the cognitive element of social capital refers to resources internal to the group that are related to the interpretation, discussion, and formation of value systems based on specific actions. From this perspective, we understand that resources that fall under social or relational capital do not belong to an individual but are available to each member of the group, and that their interaction influences group member behavior.

The process approach

Alternatively, the process approach primarily examines a comprehensive picture of how social capital emerges from scratch, a process that includes how it is built, formed, gained, created, and maintained, as well as its transfer. This research has primarily discussed the topic of succession in family businesses, with less about how social capital is transferred among and within non-profit organizations, which we consider an important gap in the social capital literature.

According to Chung-Hwa Ku's analysis (2004), the relationship between social capital and nonprofit organizations can be divided into three levels: "First, nonprofit organizations contribute greatly to the 'generation' and 'transformation' of social capital; second, nonprofits work as an important channel for the 'circulation' and 'utilization' of social capital; and third, nonprofits are sites of social capital 'gathering' and 'accumulation.'" In truth, many social interactions place greater emphasis on organization and systemization than economic behavior. A foundation of trust allows for the circulation and sharing of public goods. These circulated public goods will be further transformed into social capital. This type of social capital has a continuously accumulative effect on mutual trust and cooperation, thereby generating added value.

In the late 1950s, Harvard University's Professor George Homans (1958) first introduced the concept of social exchange theory. The core concept of this theory is that, besides a specific goal that can be achieved after a social activity or exchange, there is also social surplus value. Social surplus value is both a social product and a potential resource, providing an incentive for further engagement in the social process. This type of surplus value can facilitate social capital accumulation.

The accumulation or increase of social capital can also be accomplished through the generation of new resources (Astone et al. 1999; Portes 1998; Astone et al. 1999). Social capital consists three elements: activities, interaction, and emotion. Activities refer to social participation; interaction involves evaluation conducted through social linkages or networks; and emotion refers to the level of trust in a relationship. These three elements parallel Granovetter's (1973) definition of strong and weak ties, namely, with relation to amount of time (interaction), emotional strength and level of intimacy (emotion), and reciprocal services (activities). If these elements are able to produce new resources, they can transform the production capacity of social capital.

The concept proposed in Koch and Lockwood's *Superconnect* (2010) is much akin to the one discussed in Burt's *Structural Holes: The Social Structure of Competition* (1992). Burt holds that strong linkages represent a high level of interactivity between actors. Some relatively routine interactions can easily become closed systems; thus, strong intraorganizational linkages are not effective channels for innovation. However, weak linkages have a greater ability to transmit non-repetitive information between different groups, providing opportunities for network members to further correct former points of view and bringing people together from other networks to reduce social structure limitations and achieve structural benefits.

Adler and Kwon (2002) proposed that social capital can be divided into bridging ties and bonding ties. Bonding ties are strong ties within a group that foster cohesiveness and the pursuit of common goals. Bridging ties are individuals or organizations that obtain resources and benefits through direct or indirect linkages with others. Using a business as an example, bridging ties can aid in the establishment of social capital and networks (Peng and Luo 2000).

The structure of the dynamic development of social capital

Lin (2001) consolidated research on the elements of social capital and proposed that social capital is an individual "investment in social relationship networks" (Hsung 2001). Moreover, a major factor behind social relationship network formation is whether an individual is able to invest resources into building a

Table 12.1 Primary research framework: categories of social capital formation

	Internal	*External*
Individual	Assets or resources acquired through individually accessible relationships	Assets or resources acquired through boundary-crossing social relationships
Organizational	Assets or resources acquired through relationships in organizational structures	Assets or resources acquired through boundary-crossing network links

Source: Payne et al. 2011

relationship. These resources are acquired via social behaviors such as instrumental or expressive actions.

After the abovementioned literature review of the previous chapter, we have adopted Payne et al.'s (2011) 2 by 2 matrix to categorize social capital development as the foundation of the exploratory framework for this case study. The matrix (Table 12.1) divided categories into 1) internal individual social capital (assets or resources acquired through individually accessible relationships), 2) internal organizational social capital (assets or resources acquired through boundary-crossing social relationships), 3) external individual social capital (assets or resources acquired through relationships in organizational structures), and 4) external organizational social capital (assets or resources acquired through boundary-crossing network links).

Data collection

Both authors of this study have participated in various Epoch Foundation activities over an extended period of time, involving significant interaction with primary leaders and executives. This has provided many firsthand channels for data collection, as well as access to interviews. It was thus possible to triangulate data and achieve as objective and realistic description as possible. Besides participant observation, a wide selection of both internal and external secondary data was gathered. In terms of primary data, in order to obtain perspectives from direct and indirect stakeholders, we interviewed the board chairperson, executive director, several donators, MIT professors, many network participants, and beneficiaries. The following is an example of an experience participating in Epoch Foundation activities in 1996.

In 1996, the first author traveled with Epoch Foundation members to MIT for a weeklong visit. During this visit, I observed the latest laboratory R&D achievements, attended symposia, and had face-to-face conversations with noted faculty. At the time, MIT's labs were in the process of developing somersaulting robots and 3D technologies. However, I was most struck by the fact that, because most visiting members were from finance backgrounds, communication challenges often emerged while MIT was showcasing latest technologies or R&D

innovations. This situation highlights the fact that the spread of technology must be accompanied by appropriate translators or intermediaries. The Epoch Foundation now has members in both the technology and finance fields to meet this need.

That year, visiting members were fortunate to have the opportunity to speak face-to-face with Tim Berners-Lee, the inventor of the Internet, and Michael Dertouzos, director of the MIT Laboratory for Computer Science (LCS) and host of MIT's Project Oxygen. In 1997, Dertouzos visited Taiwan and proposed the Taiwan Information Marketplace (TIM) to the government, arguing that in response to the rise of the Internet, Taiwan should move beyond hardware production and grasp business opportunities in content and software.

Opportunities emerged from this point, leading to the Asia Entrepreneurship Development Center (AEDC) initiative in 2000, the development of which I participated in over four years. Although this ultimately failed, it laid a foundation for the later successful Young Entrepreneurs of the Future (YEF) program. Over more than a decade of YEF operations, I have served as a lecturer and offered perspectives from industry, encouraging students to participate in activities, and overseen more than ten students as they visited MIT to study, among them the second author. After returning to Taiwan, these community and network relationships became strong sources of support for further learning or career opportunities.

In the following sections, this study will examine how the Epoch Foundation fostered social capital from scratch, as well as explore the foundation's trajectory. Further, we ask what are the special characteristics of the foundation's process of forming and building social capital, and what gains have been realized on its path from creation to stability and maintenance? Finally, how are these closely related elements mutually reinforcing?

However, an analysis of static social capital is probably not sufficient to explain the development trajectory of the Epoch Foundation. Thus, this study adds the concept of "social exchange" to describe the changes from social exchange theory to the foundation's dynamic social capital and clarify how it has corresponded to the different categories of social capital over the last two decades through development and operations. Moreover, this study examines how the Epoch Foundation has utilized circulation-producing interactions with other capital to create value, accumulate resources, transfer resources, and strengthen linkages (Figure 12.1).

The Epoch Foundation case

Creation of the Epoch Foundation

Apart from the contributions of the foundation's twenty domestic member businesses, CEO Paul Hsu played a definitive role in the establishment of the Epoch Foundation. Mr. Hsu pursued advanced studies in top-tier educational institutions in Taiwan and abroad, including the National Taiwan University School of Law, Tufts University Fletcher School of Law and Diplomacy, and New York University School of Law. Beginning in 1970 and while still in the US, Mr. Hsu began to participate in large-scale cooperative business events with Taiwanese economic

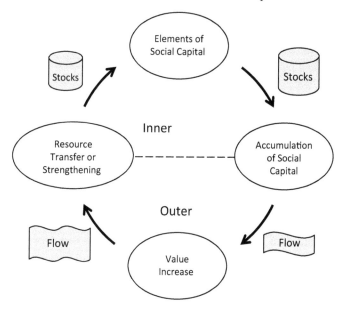

Figure 12.1 Static and dynamic changes in the Epoch Foundation's social capital

and financial officials. Mr. Hsu is recognized as one of Taiwan's multinational economic and commercial affairs experts. He actively participates in government affairs and is well known in academic circles abroad due to his time studying in the US. His expertise and international background, as well as his good relations with both government and industry, have enabled Mr. Hsu to see eye-to-eye with Professor Sloan on economic development and achieve the support of the business sector, factors key to his successful founding of the Epoch Foundation.

Another key player in the Epoch Foundation is Deputy Executive Director Josephine Chao, who joined the foundation in 1998. Before joining, Ms. Chao worked for over ten years in the communications, sales, and public relations fields. She has also held consultancy positions for the government, corporations, and welfare organizations. Thus, she has government and industry network connections. After joining the Epoch Foundation, Ms. Chao immediately took on the responsibility of connecting with top-tier educational institutions such as MIT, MIT-Sloan School, University of California, Berkeley (UC Berkeley), and International Institute for Management Development (IMD) Business School in Switzerland, as well as engaging in cooperative business projects.

Services offered to member enterprises (1990–present)

Under the cooperative agreement between the Epoch Foundation and MIT, the foundation could draw 5 percent interest from the funds donated to MIT to promote related events. At the same time, the foundation also receives annual dues from member companies in order to provide companies with the individualized aid they need. Take the Epoch Industrial Liaison Program (Epoch-ILP) as an example. Epoch-ILP illustrates the types of assistance brought to foundation members through the establishment of networks. The MIT Industrial Liaison Program was founded in 1948 against the backdrop of the Second World War. The US government contracted MIT to undertake extensive technological research projects, granting companies corporate commercialization rights to the fruits of this research. Later on, these projects became a platform for cooperation between MIT, industries, and enterprises. The Epoch Foundation has used Epoch-ILP as a communication channel to spur industry-university cooperation and understand the latest R&D trends from abroad. Every year Epoch-ILP brings various cutting-edge technologies, resources for product development, and innovative ideas in technology and management to Taiwan in order to allow members to grasp the latest directions in R&D and market trends. Energy, economic trends, nano-technology, and even education have all been hot-button issues in recent years. Member businesses may travel to MIT every two years to tour the campus and engage in advanced studies. Besides observing MIT's research labs and their most recent R&D achievements, members also have the opportunity to attend lectures by noted scholars and managers on topics such as international political and economic affairs and the latest schools of thought in management studies. As of 2011, over 400 member company representatives had visited MIT to engage in advanced studies or observations. Furthermore, every other year, MIT organizes groups of professors to come to Taiwan for roughly one week. Besides engaging in open exchange forums, these professors also visit each donating member company, offering valuable advice.

When businesses join Epoch-ILP, not only can they take advantage of full use of MIT's research resources by establishing communication channels with the university, they also have opportunities to meet important researchers in specialized fields and recruit MIT talent. In addition, ILP also provides updates on MIT's latest conferences and courses to member companies and regularly distributes important technology and management periodicals. In order to keep abreast of the latest information, the Epoch Foundation publishes a quarterly report including three sections: technology focus, Epoch trends, and a bulletin of the next quarter's events. The technology focus section features recently commercialized products and technologies from across the globe, while Epoch trends reports on Epoch events from the previous quarter to allow readers to rapidly form international linkages.

Thus, as discussed above, knowledge and technology exchange between 1991 and 2000 primarily relied on conferences and seminars, yet Epoch member companies were able to reap benefits from these exchanges, which evolved in scope over the years. With the changing times, the Epoch Foundation has acknowledged the rise of computer technology. Thus, besides joining the Epoch-ILP and Epoch-Sloan projects in 1993, in 1998, the foundation established Epoch-IT with the MIT Laboratory for Computer Science and Artificial Intelligence Lab. This program allows Taiwanese firms to send personnel directly to either lab to participate in technological research.

Table 12.2 Timetable of the Epoch Foundation's member company service projects

Year	Partner	Project	Annual Fees
1993	MIT	Epoch-ILP	US$70,000
1993	MIT	Epoch-Sloan	US$500,000 (founding member, one-off payment)
1998	MIT	Epoch-IT	US$30,000
2007	UC Berkeley	Epoch-UC Berkeley	By project
2008	Stanford	Stanford-Taiwan Biomedical Fellow Program	Project closed

The Epoch Foundation's many cooperative projects with MIT also enabled the foundation to cooperate further with other well-known universities. For example, UC Berkeley's College of Engineering began to cooperate with the Epoch Foundation in 2007. The current goal is to maintain exchanges with Asian industries to provide education, transportation, environmental, and health and medical technology solutions. In addition, in order to foster the innovative capacity of technology personnel, starting in 2009, the UC Berkeley College of Engineering and the Epoch Foundation created and implemented training courses for high-level technology personnel. These courses are designed to cultivate leadership, innovation, and productization abilities integrated with the global economy.

Educational innovations of the foundation (1998–present)

After linking Taiwan's businesses with MIT, the Epoch Foundation has continued to put out feelers for collaborations with other top universities abroad. In addition, the foundation has learned that, once current member companies have gradually grown and strengthened, they may no longer require the Epoch's network platform and group ethos. Thus, the Epoch Foundation has further extended the value of social capital to encompass talent education and future business incubation programs.

The first of these was the 1998 Epoch Internship Program. In order to provide students with early exposure to the work environment and foster team communication and competitive capacities, the Epoch Foundation organizes yearlong internships and training aimed at local university and master's students. The work includes data collection and analysis, event planning and implementation, and specialized training for those entering the workplace for the first time. Outstanding interns also receive priority when enterprises seek foundation recommendations.

Beginning in 2000, Paul Hsu and several other business leaders raised US$250,000 in seed money in order to expand the service level and network platform of the Epoch Foundation and entered into negotiations with MIT to establish the Asian Entrepreneurship Development Center (AEDC), another US$2 million project. Hsu went back and forth between Taiwan's five largest universities

(National Taiwan University, National Chengchi University, National Tsing Hua University, National Chiao Tung University, and National Sun Yat-sen University) and various government institutions, and in four years, the project was revised seven times. During this time, ten professors from these five universities were able to take part in MIT's Entrepreneurial Development Program (EDP) courses thanks to a seed fund. This experience directly influenced a number of professors to invest in entrepreneurship education. This project was supported by the Ministry of Economic Affairs' Small and Medium Enterprise Administration and Industrial Development Bureau. However, because Taiwan's participating universities and MIT were unable to reach a consensus, the project was eventually shelved.

Despite the project's failure, Mr. Hsu and Ms. Chao believed personnel education is the foundation for national economic development. In order to foster international vision and competitiveness among the youth, funds originally allotted for AEDC became today's YEF project. In 2003, the Epoch Foundation raised funding to hold the event. In particular, in 2012, YEF began to provide financial aid (the Star Project) for qualified students who have potential but are unable to exclusively focus on training courses due to financial considerations. The project also provides transportation fees for participating students coming from southern Taiwan. Among the 211 students in the 2012 academic year, 8 percent came from underprivileged backgrounds; at the same time, 18 percent of the students came from the vocational education system. In 2014, the YEF project even reached out to international students from countries such as China, Malaysia, and the Netherlands. This outreach creates a rich multicultural environment for the YEF project.

The Epoch Foundation invites entrepreneurs and professionals to serve as mentors to guide YEF alumni, actively cultivating an international vision, global competitiveness, and innovative talent possessing entrepreneurial spirit in order to contribute to Taiwan's competitiveness. The YEF program encourages cross-university linkages through a series of fast-paced learning processes, in which participants strengthen their teamwork, innovation, entrepreneurship, implementation, and international networking skills. There are nearly ten months of successive events including: an individual online application, team building, a boot camp, a garage party, business statement evaluations, business plan evaluations, an elevator pitch competition, entrepreneurship workshops, and an English oral assessment. After the English oral assessment is completed, YEF selects fifteen to twenty finalists to visit major innovation hubs all over the world. In past years, finalists have traveled to the world's top R&D centers such as Silicon Valley and Boston in the US, Beijing and Shenzhen in China, and Toronto and Waterloo in Canada. During these visits, finalists also engaged in creative exchanges with world-renowned universities, innovative entrepreneurship organizations, and entrepreneurs. The program finishes after a November Wrap-Up Presentation. Besides being popular among students, over the last ten years, YEF has also resonated with universities. Starting in 2010, National Taiwan University, National Chengchi University, and National Tsing Hwa University invited YEF to become the three schools' only accredited extra-university entrepreneurship training program. In 2011, National Chiao Tung University, National Taiwan University of

Science and Technology, and Fu Jen Catholic University followed suit. National Cheng Kung University also joined YEF in 2013. The project has further included ten additional higher education institutes, including National Sun Yat-sen University, National Central University, and Tamkang University.

This entrepreneurship competition gives Taiwanese youth the opportunity to travel to and learn from the world's top academic institutions and new businesses. Many students' lives have been changed from these learning experiences, encouraging them to start their own businesses.

In addition to talent education, the Epoch Foundation has programs to develop and incubate future star companies. These programs include the Taiwan Healthcare Biotech Industry Excellence Awards, which began in 2007 at the urging of industry and academic leaders concerned with Taiwan's life sciences technologies. In 2010, the event was expanded to today's Taiwan Healthcare and Agricultural Biotech Industries Innovation Excellence Awards, with the aim of promoting life science industry development and the cultivation of future flagship healthcare and agricultural biotech industries. Dr. Chi-Huey Wong, president of Academia Sinica, acted as convener for the project, inviting experts and specialists with rich industry experience and penetrating insight into global trends in the biotech industry to serve as judges. In recent years, the vice president of Taiwan has been invited to speak at the award ceremony. Of the sixty-five prize-winning companies (including gold, silver, bronze, and promising enterprise award winners) between 2007 and 2013, twenty-two have been publicly listed on local stock exchange markets, while the remainder have applied for listing. This demonstrates the power of these companies.

The Epoch Foundation's projects include entrepreneurial training for China returnees and the Garage+ incubation center. Also, in light of competition from globalization, the foundation offers policy recommendations via special essays written by Mr. Hsu, conferences, and findings of expert researchers. Not only are the trends and economic situations of Taiwan's businesses discussed, the development trends of Taiwanese businesses in the international market are also examined in the hopes of outlining a development blueprint for the future of Taiwanese businesses.

The offered talent-training programs and future industry businesses of the Epoch Foundation are shown in Tables 12.3 and 12.4.

Table 12.3 Timetable of the Epoch Foundation's personnel training projects

Year	1998	2000	2003	2007	2009	2011
Partner	Epoch	MIT & Taiwanese universities	Taiwanese industries & universities	Taiwanese industries	WXSTC	SIPAC
Project	Internship program	AEDC (Cancelled)	YEF	Talent search	Wuxi 530	Entrepreneurs of Suzhou

Table 12.4 Timetable of the Epoch Foundation's future business incubation projects

Year	2001	2007	2011	2012
Partner	Epoch	Taiwanese industries and universities	Chatham House	The CID Group
Project	Policy recommendations	Taiwan Healthcare and Agricultural Biotech Industries Innovation and Excellence Awards	Financial centers in Greater China	Garage+

Case analysis of Epoch Foundation social capital

Analysis of the process of social capital accumulation

This collaboration between the Epoch Foundation and MIT afforded Taiwan the opportunity to maintain a sustained link with one of the world's premier academic institutions during a time of immense change. Of course, this originated with Paul Hsu's personal background and relationship network.

First, Hsu has a legal background and is a venture capital expert. His father, Po-yuen Hsu, was former head of the Ministry of Finance and CEO of the Central Bank of the Republic of China, while his mother, Han-bo Lu, was a famous leader in the women's rights movement. Thus, Hsu had many opportunities to interact with political and business figures. Furthermore, beginning in 1970 as he pursued his studies abroad, Hsu had many opportunities to coordinate with financial and economic officials participating in large-scale international business talks. While working at Lee and Li Attorneys-at-Law, he participated in a project to introduce businesses into the market that included Bank of America, McDonald's, and Merrill Lynch. Thus, Hsu possessed a degree of personal social capital.

Based on Taiwan's business leaders' trust in Paul Hsu, the Epoch Foundation gained recognition, allowing the foundation to put its capacity to connect with external networks on display. As a result, even more family enterprises and start-ups were willing to continue membership or join. By 2012, besides the twenty enterprises originally affiliated with the foundation, companies and institutes including Quanta Computer, Wistron, Academia Sinica, Adimmune Corporation, Taiwan Fixed Network, and MediaTek became members.

Though past social capital discourse has primarily focused on unidirectional "giving" relationships, Hsu has taken his personal network and extended it to the Epoch Foundation, affording members a sense of cohesiveness and common goals via intrafoundation ties. Moreover, the continuous establishment of activities, interaction, and even emotion between MIT and Taiwanese businesses through annual programs has allowed both sides to acquire resources and reap benefits. For instance, Quanta Computer has set up an R&D facility near the MIT campus (Quanta Research Cambridge), which hires mostly MIT graduates to develop new technologies that are both innovative and adhere to Quanta Computer's future

Table 12.5 Presidents and directors at MIT and the Sloan School of Business

Year	MIT		Epoch Foundation
	President	Dean of the Sloan School	CEO/Vice CEO
1987	Paul E. Gray	Lester Thurow, collaboration founder; has visited Taiwan many times	Paul Hsu, collaboration founder
1990	Charles Vest (15th), came to Taiwan for the Epoch Foundation's		
1993	10th anniversary	Glen L. Urban	
1998		Richard L. Schmalensee, came to Taiwan for the Epoch Foundation's 10th anniversary	Paul Hsu and Josephine Chao
2004	Susan Hockfield (16th), came to Taiwan for the Epoch Foundation's 20th anniversary		
2007		David C. Schmittlein, came to Taiwan in 2009 to deliver a speech	
2012	L. Rafael Reif (17th), came to Taiwan in November; the Epoch Foundation arranged for him to meet President Ma		

trajectory. From this, it can be seen that the Epoch Foundation transforms social capital from static linkages to a dynamic resource that is constructed, gradually strengthened, and expanded.

From this, we can see that, because the Epoch Foundation's social capital is continuously accumulated from Mr. Hsu to the organization itself, and because of MIT and related institution's satisfaction with the foundation's performance in collaborative projects (such as MIT-LP and MIT-Sloan), the Epoch Foundation and MIT have been able to maintain good relations in spite of personnel changes on both sides (Table 12.5) and extend the relationship with MIT to Taiwanese businesses. This is also a possible model for transfer and inheritance of social capital networks.

Increasing social capital and structural hole analysis

The accumulation of the Epoch Foundation's social capital depends on the inter-action between the foundation and network organizations. Through these analyses, we learn that, if the foundation can create new resources, the volume of the social capital energy will change. Of course, the foundation might play the role of a structural hole, allowing for the connection between two organizations or individuals in the network, which otherwise might not emerge. Through foundation assistance, two previously unconnected agents are linked together, increasing their social capital.

Although, as earlier stated, there were inevitably some failed collaboration projects (such as the AEDC project), we discovered that the trust garnered by Mr. Paul Hsu from Taiwanese businesses, core work with Taiwanese industrial sectors, and Hsu's connection with Professor Thurow, dean of MIT Sloan School of Management, have all created a strong platform for mutual communication, which has resulted in an advantageous structural hole linking Taiwanese business to world leading universities.

The interaction between the foundation and member businesses are specifically discussed by a professional team, and each project gets undivided attention. Due to the variety of activities, the number of member businesses has consistently risen. Further, these businesses are going global. As the foundation is proactive in pushing existent borders, frequent contact exists between the government, academic world, venture capital institutes, startups, and industry. Therefore, social capital stock increases with frequent interactions, connections, emotional contact, and beneficial activities. In turn, the gradually accumulated social capital is fed back into the value of each network platform member.

One of the most outstanding collaboration projects with world leading universities is the Epoch-oxygen Program with MIT-LCS and MIT-AI. The project was part of Epoch-IT and related R&D was sponsored by and conducted with six companies, including Acer Group, Delta Electronics Inc. from Taiwan, and four other global top companies – HP, Philips, NTT, and Nokia. The Epoch-Information Technology Program aims to produce humanized and futuristic computers. Each member company will be offered research funding of US$1 million and opportunities to do extensive work with MIT.

The content of the research includes portable items that can listen to human directions, mobile Internet products, and customized information reception access. They will also develop systems and software to support these products. Members will be able to visit each other and collaborate on technology. When Acer Group joined the platform, it benefited its sub-divisions, such as Acer, BenQ Corporation, Acer-Net Group, i-D SoftCapital Group, Ali Corporation, and Ambit.

In 2000, Quanta Computer Chairman Barry Lam, who has sustained a positive relationship with Epoch members, witnessed the coming of the IT age and joined the Epoch membership through the service of Epoch-ILP. In 2004, Quanta Computer and CSAIL established the T-Party Project for long-term future collaboration; the project was implemented in 2005. Because of a mutually satisfying working relationship, the five-year project was extended for another five years: In the first five years, the project focused on human-centered programming, while the last five years was dedicated to cloud computing. Furthermore, Quanta Computer established Quanta Research Cambridge (QRC) right next to the MIT campus in Boston; QRC hires directly from the excellent talent pool in Boston and develops innovative technology that suits Quanta's future development.

Similarly, in 2004, due to foundation connections, the Yuen Foong Group, having recognized that RFID (radio frequency identification) would become a mainstream industry, began to actively participate in an international RFID forum and initiated standardization processes. When the MIT Auto-ID Center established

EPCglobal in 2003, Yuen Foong Group had access to the latest RFID Electronic Product Code (EPC) standard, thereby controlling the leadership of RFID in the pan-Chinese market.

Talent network expansion

Apart from Professor Paul Hsu's leadership and contact with Taiwanese businesses, talent nurturing projects are crucial parts of social capital accumulation. The Epoch Foundation first initiated the Internship Flagship Project (IFP) in 1998, and since the initiation of the YEF project in 2003, the foundation has trained more than 2,000 college students and graduate students; these young entrepreneurs form a multi-disciplinary yet closely knit, well-educated, and diverse community of human capital. Possessing an invaluable talent network and recognizing a great need for top talent among Taiwanese businesses, the foundation established the Search for Talent human resources bank in 2007. The HR bank serves as an official channel to recommend potential and suitable young graduates to businesses. The Search for Talent network holds gatherings every two months, during which predecessors share work experiences, industry specialists share life stories, and/or charity campaigns are held. Any company can work with the network in the form of a business donation; in turn, the network conducts talent recruitment or offers year-round head-hunting campaigns. It works as a win-win platform.

Foundation member companies seem to understand its potential as a human resources network. Take Quanta Computer for example. The chairman, Barry Lam, came up with three C slogans (Cloud Computing, Connectivity, Client Device) for future development. In order to achieve projected targets, Quanta examined if they had sufficient human resources and the right talent. Following discussions with the foundation, Quanta proposed a management associates (MA) project, hoping the foundation could both promote the project and provide human resource support. The project was launched in 2010 and recruits twice a year. In comparison to other MA projects, Quanta Computer includes a training and mentoring program. The senior product managers give MAs work guidance through mentoring. This mentoring program is similar to the YEF project.

Apart from the IT industry, both Fubon Bank and Procter & Gamble (P&G) use Search for Talent in their MA projects. Cacafly, a company founded by YEF graduate Chiu Chi-hong, is another example. With foundation assistance, Cacafly has moved through its early stage into the growing stage. This is the time when a company needs exceptional talent, and thus Cacafly collaborated with the foundation to launch an MA project that can attract more recruits. When startups can recruit via the foundation's platform, it allows young participants opportunities to broaden horizons and join top companies. The foundation has created a positive cycle of new value through accumulated social capital.

In May 2012, the Epoch Foundation and Greater China Venture Capital Fund (CID) launched the incubator project Garage+, which originated from a hub concept, with the foundation serving as a key piece of the network relationship jigsaw puzzle. In one of the 2014 board meetings, the Giashin Zhaofu Culture Foundation decided to donate Giashin Building space for use by Garage+. This space is now a new venue for the foundation to serve startup entrepreneurs. This Garage+ project is the best evidence of the dynamic channeling produced by linking the Epoch Foundation's accumulated social capital to external links. Figure 12.2 shows the route of accumulation and added value of the Epoch Foundation's social capital. The solid line indicates the route of accumulation of social capital while the dotted line indicates the increased impact generated from social capital.

Through the linkage in the figure we understand that the foundation's social capital has maximized benefits by exchanging resources within the network. Apart from the aforementioned YEF and Garage+ projects, the foundation board decided to launch the Taiwan Medical-Biological-Agricultural Competition to recruit talent during a development meeting. This competition demonstrates the dynamic way the energy of social capital can be transferred once enough has been accumulated.

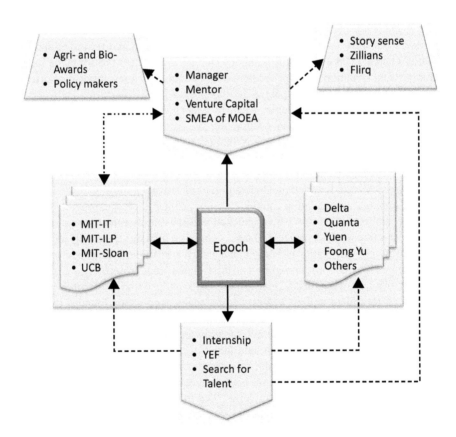

Figure 12.2 Flowchart of the accumulation and increase of the Epoch Foundation's social capital

Source: Epoch Foundation

Research findings and conclusion

Research findings 1: the creation and construction of social capital

The reason the Epoch Foundation has been able to establish a network platform of this scale lies in the foundation itself, its member companies, and its partner universities who, through the process of mutual understanding, trust, and collaboration, have engendered a sense of duty and responsibility towards other members and institutions. Furthermore, the foundation transforms the application of social capital from its human capital focus to a phenomenon that drives economic performance and increases social responsibility among enterprises, making social capital a brand-new resource that is beneficial to production. The benefit is available to all, from students and newly established enterprises to large-scale enterprises. Thus, we can see that social capital, not only has a macro-level group influence, but also micro-level individual impact.

Research findings 2: value gained by the parties involved and contributions to Taiwan

We illustrated earlier the value gained by companies such as Quanta Computer, Yeong Foong Group, and the Acer Group from the foundation's network. However, we must ask ourselves what that value is and what it means for a project to be successful. Take, for instance, Quanta and Delta Electronics Inc., which are pioneers of cloud computing in Taiwan. If they had not joined the Epoch-MIT projects, perhaps both companies would not have so quickly discovered this opportunity or recognized it as a trend.

While other business members – such as MediaTek, Foxconn, Wistron Corporation – work with MIT on other projects, they stay within the platform offered by the Epoch Foundation. For Quanta, the foundation serves as an official window to the external world, allowing Quanta to officially participate in MIT's projects. Even if the companies establish direct working relationships with MIT laboratories, the foundation can still introduce project content, thus channeling this social capital. This is the added value brought about by the connection of social capital: The value isn't just material (new products resulting from technique transfers, patents, or work partners) but immaterial gains, such as the capacity for innovation, horizon expansion, network reliance, and influences on company culture.

Of course, the degree to which each business member participates in campaigns varies and the frequency of resource use differs, and these differences create difficulties for the foundation. The foundation has to adjust to each company's participation situation. For example, because most of the financial institutes here serve local clients, they are more reserved towards new technology. Big data and the security industry are crucial for the finance sector, yet in general, domestic financial institutions do not eagerly apply new developments. At the same time, the IT industry is passionate about new technologies because it serves globally.

Research findings 3: the social network formed the Epoch Foundation

Twenty years ago, the Epoch Foundation's role was to serve as a bridge, providing multi-point, multi-line networking to afford people linkages and opportunities, facilitating interpersonal interactions from point-to-point and line-to-line until an extensive network was formed. It is precisely because of its diverse resources and the capacity of distributing its resources that the foundation's social capital accumulated rapidly and generated new social value. In the process of accumulation, resources tend to be transferred to other agents, in turn becoming more valuable. Therefore, the social network formed this way has shifted from two- to three-dimensional. As Figure 12.3 shows, this three-dimensional aspect of the social network is one of the most unique and innovative aspects of the Epoch Foundation.

Most importantly, during this match-making process, the Epoch Foundation did not interfere with competition on the business side. On the university side, the foundation actively recommended excellent students to MIT. These actions resulted in even firmer trust in the foundation from businesses and universities and increased relationship stability. As the Epoch Foundation's reputation spread, it attracted more new blood into its network, including schools, businesses, and groups with an interest in entrepreneurship, gradually increasing its influence. This is the new and constant energy injected by the Epoch Foundation into Taiwanese industries and society. According to the findings presented here, social

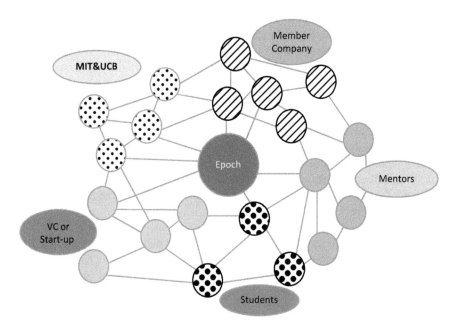

Figure 12.3 Diagram of the three-dimensional social network of the Epoch Foundation

capital possesses two properties simultaneously: 1) increased stocks and two-way channeling and 2) maximization of value through a dynamic circulation system.

Conclusion – the initiation and transformation of social capital and the value created

Grasping the significance of the Tiananmen Incident and the realization by the US of the increased value of relationships with Chinese societies, Mr. Hsu created the Epoch Foundation with Lester Thurow, establishing a relationship with MIT. Although Taiwan's technological capacities were a far cry from the first-class engineering technology at MIT, inroads were made linking important labs through the School of Management, leading to the gradual build-up of relationships between Taiwanese companies and leading universities. During this time, Taiwanese industry also progressed to a level where they could collaborate with MIT. Thus Taiwan became a partner in jointly proposed research topics with MIT and began to send outstanding students to MIT for study, deepening the relationship.

At the beginning, the platform of the Epoch Foundation was founded on social capital built through Paul Hsu's personal network. Next, because of the interaction between first-rate, technology- and science-led institutes such as MIT, the foundation offered new competitive edges to many members in the growing IT industry. Not only do member businesses gain an understanding of the latest technologies, but they may also take advantage of MIT's resources in order to understand industry trends. Member companies such as Quanta, YFY Paper (E Ink Holdings), and Delta Electronics have technological exchanges with MIT, and many member companies have engaged in technology transfers or collaborations with the university. For example, the fact that Quanta Company has an office right next to MIT's campus offers a foothold for the Taiwanese IT industry in the global market. Still the Epoch Foundation expects itself to offer more comprehensive assistance to Taiwanese industries.

Next, the Epoch Foundation regards educating the young as the foundation for national development. Therefore, the foundation has integrated available resources and has devoted itself to nurturing talent. Since 1998, the foundation has cultivated over 2,000 young people; these talented individuals have returned to society to work for Taiwanese industries and in academia. Of course, some graduates have opted to start their own businesses. In order to maximize the value of resources, the foundation further established its incubation project, hoping to assist potential startups to survive fierce market competition. Given the holistic development of the foundation's three focus areas (top-notch institute liaison service, future trends of industrial development, innovation and entrepreneurship education), the individuals and organizations within its network can interact, enabling a positive cycle.

From the Epoch Foundation's experiences, we can see an innovative NPO that contributes to enterprises and society as a whole. The Epoch Foundation not only generates and transforms social capital but functions as a channel of social capital circulation and application. What is most important is that the foundation has become a carrier for centralizing and accumulating social capital. To answer the

Table 12.6 Value created by the Epoch Foundation

Building a platform	Establishing an international image for Taiwanese enterprises and assisting these enterprises in linking and interacting with the world's top universities, e.g., MIT and UC Berkeley.
Subverting the traditional cooperation model	Japan's Hitachi and America's Google both individually initiated alliances with MIT; however, Taiwan's enterprises followed a group model for collaboration with MIT. This made knowledge and technology exchanges between both parties more extensive and comprehensive.
Training system	Epoch's financial planning, management, and marketing training are not only renowned throughout Taiwan, but in recent years, the foundation has received invitations from Chinese authorities to carry out education and training programs in Wuxi and Suzhou entrepreneurial centers.
Competing for government bids	Actively competing for government bids through business-university alliances.
Talent education	The YEF project has already received accreditation from National Taiwan University, National Chengchi University, National Taiwan University of Science and Technology, National Tsing Hwa University, National Chiao Tung University, and Fu Jen Catholic University, making it Taiwan's premier education event. Many YEF alumni have broadened their horizons through the program's international visits, traveling to foreign academic institutions to pursue advanced studies while maintaining ties with other alumni and forming a pervasive talent network.
New enterprise development	The Epoch Foundation's management model turns the traditional understanding of enterprises on its head. Although profitable, enterprises establish social value through creating side value. Besides member services, the value of social capital is extended to talent education and the incubation programs. The business world, academia, and students all have a platform through the Epoch Foundation. Moreover, the foundation offers opportunities for international linkages to broaden horizons and create even greater value.

proposition at the beginning of this study, we can conclude that the Epoch Foundation does not merely possess the capacity to form social networks and accumulate or increase the stock of social capital but that its social capital is characteristic of dynamic transfer and circulation.

References

Adler, P.S., and S.W. Kwon. 2002. "Social Capital: Prospects for New Concept." *The Academy of Management Review* 27 (1): 17–40.

Astone, N.M., C.A. Nathanson, R. Shoen, and Y.J. Kim. 1999. "Family Demography, Social Theory, and Investment in Social Capital." *Population and Development Review* 25 (1): 1–31.

Bourdieu, P. 1985. "The Social Space and Genesis of Groups." *Theory and Society* 14 (6): 723–744.

Bourdieu, P. 1986. *The Forms of Social Capital: Handbook of Theory and Research for the Sociology of Education.* Westport, CT: Greenwood Press.

Burt, R. S. 1992. *Structure.* New York: Research Center in Structural Analysis, Columbia University.

Cohen, S. S., and G. Fields 1999. "Social Capital and Capital Gains in Silicon Valley." *California Management Review* 41 (2): 108–130.

Coleman, J. S. 1988. "Social Capital in Creation of Human Capital." *American Journal of Sociology* 94: S95–S120.

Fukuyama, F. 1995. *Trust: The Social Virtues and the Creation of Prosperity.* New York: Free Press.

Granovetter, M. S. 1973. "The Strength of Weak Ties." *American Journal of Sociology* 78 (6): 1360–1380.

Granovetter, M. S. 1985. "Economic Action and Social Structure: The Problem of Embeddedness." *American Journal of Sociology* 91 (3): 481–510.

Homans, G. C. 1958. "Social Behavior as Exchange." *American Journal of Sociology* 63 (6): 597–606. Emile Durkheim-Georg Simmel

Hsung, Ray-May. 2001. "Gender, Personal Networks and Social Capital." In *Survey Research in Chinese Societies: Methods and Findings,* edited by Yanjie Bian, Jow-ching Tu, and Alvin Y. So, 179–215. Hong Kong: Oxford University.

Jacobs, B. J. 1979. "A Preliminary Model of Particularistic Ties in China Political Alliances: Kan-ching and Kuan-his in a Rural Taiwanese Township." *China Quarterly* 78: 237–273.

Koch, R., and G. Lockwood. 2010. *Superconnect.* New York: China Times Publishing Co.

Ku, Chung-Hwa. 2004. *The Research Concept of Social Capital and NPO.*

Lin, N. 2001. *Social Capital: A Theory of Social Structure and Action.* Cambridge, UK: Cambridge University Press.

Loury, G. 1987. "Why Should We Care about Group Inequality?" *Social Philosophy and Policy* 5: 249–271.

Nahapiet, J., and S. Ghoshal. 1998. "Social Capital, Intellectual Capital, and the Organizational Advantage." *Academy of Management Review* 23: 242–266.

Payne, G. T., C. B. Moore, S. E. Griffis, and C. W. Autry. 2011. "Multilevel Challenges and Opportunities in Social Capital Research." *Journal of Management* 37 (2): 491–520.

Peng, M. W., and Y. Luo. 2000. "Managerial Ties and Firm Performance in a Transition Economy: The Nature of a Micro-Macro Link." *The Academy of Management Journal* 43 (3): 486–501.

Portes, A. 1998. "Social Capital: Its Origins and Applications in Modern Sociology." *Annual Review of Sociology* 24: 1–24.

Putnam, R. D. 1995. "Turning In, Turning Out: The Strange Disappearance of Social Capital in America." *Political Science and Politics* 28 (4): 664–683.

Tsai, W. 2000. "Social Capital, Strategic Relatedness and the Formation of Intraorganizational Linkages." *Strategic Management Journal* 21: 925–940.

Tsai, W., and S. Ghoshal. 1998. "Social Capital and Value Creation: The Role of Intrafirm Networks." *Academy of Management Journal* 41 (4): 464–476.

Index

For Product Safety Concerns and Information please contact our EU
representative GPSR@taylorandfrancis.com
Taylor & Francis Verlag GmbH, Kaufingerstraße 24, 80331 München, Germany

www.ingramcontent.com/pod-product-compliance
Ingram Content Group UK Ltd.
Pitfield, Milton Keynes, MK11 3LW, UK
UKHW021617240425
457818UK00018B/610